To Patricia Aburdene

John Naisbitt is a social forecaster, speaker, and adviser to many of America's leading corporations. As publisher of the quarterly *Trend Report*, John Naisbitt has become the country's top authority on America's deeply rooted social, economic, political, and techological movements and has counseled and advised AT&T, United Technologies, Control Data, Atlantic Richfield, IBM, General Electric, and the White House.

He is chairman of the Naisbitt Group, a Washington, DC-based research and consulting firm.

John Naisbitt

Megatrends

Ten New Directions Transforming Our Lives

Futura
Macdonald & Co
London & Sydney

A Futura Book

First published in Great Britain in 1984 by
Macdonald & Co (Publishers) Ltd
London & Sydney

This Futura edition published in 1984
Reprinted 1984

This edition published by arrangement with Warner Books, Inc.,
New York

ISBN 0 7088 2508 7

Reproduced, printed and bound in Great Britain by
Hazell Watson & Viney Limited,
Member of the BPCC Group,
Aylesbury, Bucks

Futura Publications
A Division of
Macdonald & Co (Publishers) Ltd
Maxwell House
74 Worship Street
London EC2A 2EN
A BPCC plc Company

Foreword by Kevin Pakenham

"The power to become habituated to his surroundings is a marked characteristic of mankind" (J. M. Keynes). This book steps back from those surroundings and confronts us with the decisive shift occurring in the world's major power as it transforms from an industrial to an information society. John Naisbitt is supremely well qualified to observe this with his personal experience of the highest levels of American business and government as well as his Group's profound studies of American society. He follows in the tradition of Herman Khan and Alvin Toffler with the practical approach to management of Peter Drucker, an American way of thought that continues to prove a power-house of ideas. The book's relevance to non-American readers is direct and immediate.

In this history of the future the critical trends in the USA are drawn out and the non-American reader will have no difficulty in recognizing the parallels. Some of the trends can reasonably be said to have been experienced first in Britain: the decline of industrial activity to be replaced by efficient service companies whose means of production is knowledge and whose product information is a new entrepreneurship and a spirit of self-help with less confidence in the central authorities to get it right, whether from government or business.

Social and economic trends are more than the sum of their parts. It is necessary to go beyond mere itemizing and develop a larger vision of how they interlock or conflict. As this book unfolds it is the cumulative sense of a society on the brink of a new order that forcefully impresses.

This new order is founded on profound technological developments. Beginning with the communication technology of satellites and carried forward with increasing power by the miniaturization of computers no moving part will be left unaffected, no office or home will be the same; and with these are coming changes in work attitudes, business organization and social interaction. It is not a matter of whether but when and how.

The British are great adapters and pragmatists, reluctant to confront change, but would rather adjust as the occasion demands. Change in America by contrast is thoroughly discussed and almost epitomizes the national ethic. In the words of the management consultant: "If you are not part of the solution, you are part of the problem". Thus major trends in America are usually more apparent and more easily dissected as they cut their swathe into the future. But the same broad forces are at work in most of Western society. The forms they take may reflect the national character but we cannot fail to feel them, for good or ill. Like John Naisbitt I strongly believe it will be for good – and this book, by confronting us with those forces, will help to make it so.

Contents

Acknowledgments

While I have taken a number of years to synthesize the ideas in this book, they would never have gotten between two covers without the help of friends and associates. Among the first to be acknowledged are my colleagues, past and present, at The Naisbitt Group who daily monitor events in every corner of this society, especially my close associate and friend Jeffrey Hallett, president of our group, who ran our company during the year that I was preoccupied with this book and whose counsel and guidance have been invaluable. To my colleagues of The Foresight Group in Sweden, Gustaf Delin, Sven Atterhed, and Lennart Boksjö, I am indebted for helping me think through many of the basic ideas in the book, both in a U.S. and Swedish context. David MacMichael, with whom I have had many discussions and who read and commented on the entire manuscript, has given much wise counsel and historical perspective. I am also indebted to a number of people who read various parts of the manuscript for their valuable comments and contributions: Marilyn Ferguson, Elsa Porter and Hink Porter, Debbie Cameron, Carolyn Long, Lynn Pounian, Joan Tapper, Stephen Arbeit, Susan Davis, and Wilford Lewis. I also owe a large debt to my clients who have helped shape many of the ideas expressed in this book. Esperance Moscatelli is to be especially thanked for her virtually faultless typing and retyping of the manuscript. My researcher, Gavin Clabaugh, has brought to bear throughout the project a calm, thoughtful, persistent, and gifted approach to finding what we needed and making the necessary connections among the ideas. I must also acknowledge the important work of my son, Jim Naisbitt, who did much of the early research on this book, until he went off to law school. I am grateful to my literary agent, Raphael Sagalyn, who got me organized more than once and has been unfailing in his warm support of this work. Thanks are due also to my Warner Books editor, Nansey Neiman, a real professional with a steady hand, a warm heart, and a wonderfully sunny spirit. And lastly, and most importantly, this book is dedicated to my beautiful wife, Patricia Aburdene, without whom this book would never have been written. She has been my collaborator in every phase of its development from conception through its numerous drafts. The final responsibility for what is in the book is mine, but we shared in its creation.

Introduction

As a society, we have been moving from the old to the new. And we are still in motion. Caught between eras, we experience turbulence. Yet, amid the sometimes painful and uncertain present, the restructuring of America proceeds unrelentingly.

This book is about a new American society that is not yet fully evolved. Nevertheless, the restructuring of America is already changing our inner and outer lives. Each of this book's ten chapters examines one of these critical restructurings: (1) Although we continue to think we live in an industrial society, we have in fact changed to an economy based on the creation and distribution of information. (2) We are moving in the dual directions of high tech/high touch, matching each new technology with a compensatory human response. (3) No longer do we have the luxury of operating within an isolated, self-sufficient, national economic system; we now must acknowledge that we are part of a global economy. We have begun to let go of the idea that the United States is and must remain the world's industrial leader as we move on to other tasks. (4) We are restructuring from a society run by short-term considerations and rewards in favor of dealing with things in much longer-term time frames. (5) In cities and states, in small organizations and subdivisions, we have

1

rediscovered the ability to act innovatively and to achieve results—from the bottom up. (6) We are shifting from institutional help to more self-reliance in all aspects of our lives. (7) We are discovering that the framework of representative democracy has become obsolete in an era of instantaneously shared information. (8) We are giving up our dependence on hierarchical structures in favor of informal networks. This will be especially important to the business community. (9) More Americans are living in the South and West, leaving behind the old industrial cities of the North. (10) From a narrow either/or society with a limited range of personal choices, we are exploding into a free-wheeling multiple-option society.

These larger patterns are not always clear. Helped by the news media, especially television, we seem to be a society of events, just moving from one incident—sometimes, even crisis—to the next, rarely pausing (or caring) to notice the process going on underneath. Yet only by understanding the larger patterns, or restructurings, do the individual events begin to make sense.

This book focuses on the megatrends or broad outlines that will define the new society. No one can predict the shape of that new world. Attempts to describe it in detail are the stuff of science fiction and futuristic guessing games that often prove inaccurate and annoying.

The most reliable way to anticipate the future is by understanding the present.

That is the premise of this book.

For the past twelve years, I have been working with major American corporations to try to understand what is really happening in the United States by monitoring local events and behavior, because collectively what is going on locally is what is going on in America.

Despite the conceits of New York and Washington, almost nothing starts there.

In the course of my work, I have been overwhelmingly impressed with the extent to which America is a bottom-up society, that is, where new trends and ideas begin in cities and local communities—for example, Tampa, Hartford, San Diego, Seattle, and Denver, not New York City or Washington, D.C. My colleagues and I have studied this great country by reading its local newspapers. We have discovered that trends are generated from the bottom up, fads from the top down. The findings in this book are based on an analysis of more than 2 million local articles about local events in the cities and towns of this country during a twelve-year period.

Out of such highly localized data bases, I have watched the general outlines of a new society slowly emerge.

Trends are bottom-up, fads top-down.

Content Analysis

We learn about this society through a method called *content analysis,* which has its roots in World War II. During that war, intelligence experts sought to find a method for obtaining the kinds of information on enemy nations that public opinion polls would have normally provided. Under the leadership of Paul Lazarsfeld and Harold Lasswell, later to become well-known communication theorists, it was decided that we would do an analysis of the content of the German newspapers, which we could get—although some days after publication. The strain on Germany's people, industry, and economy began to show up in its newspapers, even though information about the country's supplies, production, transportation, and food situation remained secret. Over time, it was possible to piece together what was going on in Germany and to figure out whether conditions were improving or deteriorating by carefully tracking local stories about factory openings, closings, and production targets, about train arrivals, departures, and delays, and so on. For example, the local papers listed the names of area soldiers killed in action. We were able to get a good idea of German military casualties by adding up these local listings. Impressed by what we learned, we then began to analyze the changing content of Japanese newspapers.

Although this method of monitoring public behavior and events continues to be the choice of the intelligence community—the United States annually spends millions of dollars doing newspaper content analysis in various parts of the world—it has rarely been applied commercially. In fact, The Naisbitt Group is the first, and presently the only, organization to utilize this approach in analyzing our society.

Why are we so confident that content analysis is an effective way to monitor social change? Simply stated, because the *news hole* in a newspaper is a closed system. For economic reasons, the amount of space devoted to news in a newspaper does not change significantly over time. So, when something new is introduced, something else or a combination of things must be omitted. You cannot add unless you subtract. It is the principle of forced choice in a closed system.

The news-reporting process is forced choice in a closed system.

In this forced-choice situation, societies add new preoccupations and forget old ones. In keeping track of the ones that are added and the ones that are given up, we are in a sense measuring the changing *share of the market* that competing societal concerns command.

Societies, like individuals, can handle only so many concerns at one time.

Evidently, societies are like human beings. A person can keep only so many problems and concerns in his or her head or heart at any one time. If new problems or concerns are introduced, some existing ones are given up. All of this is reflected in the collective news hole that becomes a mechanical representation of society sorting out its priorities.

Over the years, we have watched a variety of social issues emerge, gain, and then lose market share. About a dozen years ago, for example, the closed system started to fill up with new concerns about the environment. There was extensive reaction to the Santa Barbara oil spills. Students in California buried automobiles. Earth Day was followed by Earth Day II. The amount of space devoted to the environment accelerated dramatically.

What issue—or combination of issues—was reduced in the closed system to accommodate the intrusion of environmental concerns? It was not a combination of things, but one thing. As the column inches of environmental news increased, news about civil rights decreased—on a one-to-one, line-by-line basis. One yielded as the other gained. By 1973 the system showed a cross-over and the environment became, for the first time, a more important preoccupation than civil rights.

During the past decade, we also witnessed a declining interest in our category Drug Use and Abuse. If all the local news space devoted to drug use and abuse during the year 1970 were equated to 100, the amount of space devoted to that subject during the year 1979 dropped to 8, although it has risen since.

During the 1960s almost all of the space devoted to what could be described as concerns about discrimination was filled with concerns about racism. Then, beginning in 1969, that space began to be shared with material about sexism, until by 1975 half of the space was filled with material about sexism and the other half with material about racism. Starting in 1977 both subjects began to yield to concerns about ageism until two-thirds of the discrimination space was filled with material about ageism, with racism and sexism splitting the remaining one-third. At that point, almost overnight, the Congress outlawed mandatory retirement in the public sector and extended it from sixty-five to seventy years in the private sector. Congress acted at the crest. Concern about age discrimination has since been declining.

This process of forced choice in a closed system is a very trustworthy process for the purposes of our studies; none of the people engaged by it (the reporters and editors) know it is occurring. As anyone who has worked on a newspaper knows, the dominant consideration is to get the paper out on time. There is a certain amount of choice over which stories will appear in the paper, but not much.

The methodology we have developed is also free from the effects of biased reporting because it is only the event or behavior itself that we are interested in.

A sports analogy is useful here. If I read that the Chicago Cubs beat the Los Angeles Dodgers 7 to 3, I have close to 100-percent confidence that that occurred. If I read in the box score that Steve Henderson went 2 for 5, I have a high degree of confidence that that occurred. But if the sports reporter tells me in the fourth paragraph that Steve Garvey's bone-headed play in the sixth inning blew the whole game, he is introducing a judgment call that may or may not be true. In our work, what we are essentially doing is looking at the local box scores of the society: The zoning board changed a rule by a vote of 6 to 3; twenty people sat in at the governor's office; a transit bond issue was passed; a state referendum passed, cutting property taxes in half.

The Bellwether States

Most of the social invention in America occurs in just five states.

Our group collects information about what's going on locally across the country and then looks for patterns. The results can be fascinating. For example, we have learned that there are five states in which most social invention occurs in this country. The other forty-five are in effect followers.

Not surprisingly, California is the key indicator state; Florida is second, although not too far behind; the other three trendsetter states are Washington, Colorado, and Connecticut.

When we trace back new trends or positions on issues eventually adopted by most of the fifty states, we find that these five states are again and again the places where new trends began. It's difficult to say why, other than to observe that all five are characterized by a rich mix of people. And the richness of the mix always results in creativity, experimentation, and change.

California, of course, is famous as a trend setter. The whole granola ethic started there: the vitamin and nutrition craze leading to the invention of the salad bar, most of the human potential groups, and the physical-fitness trend—which is not fad, by the way, but an important and enduring change in lifestyles. Proposition 13 in California was really a subset of a larger trend toward citizen-initiated referenda. Now that trend has spread across the nation, with people leapfrogging the political apparatus to make quality-of-life decisions themselves at the ballot box.

Colorado initiated "sunset laws" that closed down new agencies unless legislatures explicitly renewed them. Along with Florida and California (both of which acted within a two-month period in 1970), Colorado passed laws limiting growth—of population, highways, shopping centers, housing units. That sudden occurrence in three trend-setting states encouraged us to predict a national trend. In fact, those seemingly unrelated events did mature into the important and pervasive trend toward managed growth.

Connecticut, and later Washington, was the first state to elect a woman governor in her own right. With Florida, Connecticut was a leader in requiring minimum competency standards for high school graduates. This is part of the accountability trend moving across the whole country; teacher standards are the next step.

Now Connecticut is setting the trend in the workplace. It passed the nation's first workers' right-to-know law, requiring manufacturers who use suspected carcinogens to identify the ingredients and give new employees information on hazardous substances they will come in contact with; New York has already followed with a similar statute.

The Connecticut Supreme Court, in a precedent-setting decision, ruled that whistle blowers can't be fired. The court said employees without a specific contract can't be dismissed for complaining about a company practice that violates state law or creates a public hazard.

Connecticut was the first to eliminate monthly minimum utility charges for poverty-level customers, and other states are now looking into it.

Washington's largest city, Seattle, was the first place in the nation to outlaw mandatory retirement laws, a trend that has since spread across the nation.

Florida, of course, started the boom in condominiums, and it is pioneering time-shared vacations, under which homes in high-priced vacation areas are purchased under divided ownership; Florida was also the first state to adopt guidelines governing time sharing. "Sunshine laws"—requiring public agencies to hold open meetings—also began in Florida and have since spread to almost every state.

In fact, Florida is becoming increasingly important as a bellwether state and may soon surpass California. The reason is demographics. In 1980 Florida had the nation's oldest population and Floridians experienced growing tension between the state's older and younger residents. This conflict is especially noteworthy, because by about the year 1995 the entire U.S. population will reflect the same age-youth ratio that Florida has now, ac-

7

cording to Census Bureau projections. By carefully watching what is happening now in Florida, we stand to learn a wealth of information about the problems and opportunities the whole nation will face in the future.

Trend Reports

Our findings are published quarterly in a national *Trend Report* and in four regional reports: the *California Trend Report,* the *Rocky Mountain Trend Report,* the *Florida Trend Report,* and the *Midwest Trend Report.* Three times each year we hold seminars for our clients. At the seminars we discuss the emerging trends and their impact on business and on our lives. Among our longtime clients, from whom we have learned a great deal, are United Technologies, Sears, Ogilvy & Mather, Atlantic Richfield, Edison Electric Institute, Security Pacific National Bank, General Electric, General Motors, Merrill Lynch, and AT&T.

The *Trend Report* staff continually monitors 6,000 local newspapers each month. Daily exposure to the ebb and flow of local action in cities and towns across the United States enables staff analysts to pinpoint, trace, and evaluate the important issues and trends.

After a dozen years of carefully monitoring local events in this way, I have slowly developed what to me is a clear sense of the directions in which we are restructuring America.

I do not mean to suggest that every idea and every bit of information contained in this book come out of the pages of the *Trend Report,* although a good deal of it does. I have read thousands of other newspaper, magazine, and journal articles, and where I have drawn upon these sources rather than the *Trend Report,* I have noted it in the back of the book. What the *Trend Report* research provides me is a framework into which I mentally sort all of the other information I come across, either in my own reading or in speaking to groups and individuals across the country.

This is a book of synthesis in an age of analysis. Its purpose is to provide an overview. To do that, it is necessary to generalize, although I have tried to give many concrete examples to support my ideas and have provided the key examples that persuaded me personally to shift my world view.

Nevertheless, I risk displeasing the experts and subject specialists who can argue that to take the leap of describing the world in terms of ten shifting categories is too simplistic. In their way, they are probably right. Yet, I think it is worth the risk.

In a world where events and ideas are analyzed to the point of lifelessness, where complexity grows by quantum leaps, where the information din is so high we must shriek to be heard above it, we are hungry for structure.

With a simple framework we can begin to make sense of the world. And we can change that framework as the world itself changes.

Trends, like horses, are easier to ride in the direction they are already going.

The ten megatrends discussed in this book will affect your life and your business. Trends tell you the direction the country is moving in. The decisions are up to you. But trends, like horses, are easier to ride in the direction they are already going. When you make a decision that is compatible with the overarching trend, the trend helps you along. You may decide to buck the trend, but it is still helpful to know it is there.

This book describes the environment in which to consider the decisions of life: what to study; the right job path; where to live; where to invest money; whether to start a business, join a union, or run for public office.

My purpose is to offer readers a new context within which to sort out and assess today's events.

1

From an Industrial Society to an Information Society

This book is about ten major transformations taking place right now in our society. None is more subtle, yet more explosive, I think, than this first, the megashift from an industrial to an information society.

I say this because of my experience in talking about this megatrend with people all across America. It always surprises me that so many people passionately resist the notion of an economy built on information and, despite a wealth of evidence, deny that the industrial era is over. I think this depth of feeling represents our collective unwillingness to say good-bye to a magnificent era.

I am not, of course, the first to speak about the information society. It is not a new idea. In fact, it is no longer an idea—it is a reality.

The information society had its beginnings in 1956 and 1957, two years in the decade that embodied American industrial power.

The year 1956 was one of prosperity, productivity, and industrial growth for Americans. Eisenhower was reelected president. Japan, still recovering from the devastation of World War II, was admitted to the United Nations. Transatlantic cable telephone service was inaugurated. And William H. Whyte published *The Organization Man*—the quintessential description of business management in industrial America.

Outwardly, the United States appeared to be a thriving industrial economy, yet a little-noticed symbolic milestone heralded the end of an era: In 1956, for the first time in American history, white-collar workers in technical, managerial, and clerical positions outnumbered blue-collar workers. Industrial America was giving way to a new society, where, for the first time in history, most of us worked with information rather than producing goods.

The following year—1957—marked the beginning of the globalization of the information revolution: The Russians launched Sputnik, the missing technological catalyst in a growing information society. The real importance of Sputnik is *not* that it began the space age, but that it introduced the era of global satellite communications.

Similarly, we misinterpreted the successful launch and spectacular return of the space shuttle Columbia in 1981. For our lifetime, it was far more important to the information society than to any future age of space exploration.

Satellites have turned the earth inward, upon itself.

Today's shuttle can orbit a 65,000-pound payload, 355 times the size of Sputnik and many, many times more sophisticated. In the past, the complex parts of a satellite system had to be in the ground station. But the new shuttle can launch larger satellites that incorporate ground station functions—and ground stations will now fit on the rooftops of houses.

The space shuttle has a lot more to do with the globalized information economy than it will ever have to do—in our lifetimes—with space exploration.

I do not want to minimize the importance of Sputnik and Columbia in opening up the heavens to us. But what has not been stressed enough is the way the satellites transformed the earth into what Marshall McLuhan called a global village. Instead of turning us outward toward space, the satellite era turned the globe inward upon itself. (McLuhan saw television as the instrument that would bring about the global village; we now know it is the communication satellite.)

Today's information technology—from computers to cable television—did not bring about the new information society. It was already well under way by the late 1950s. Today's sophisticated technology only hastens our plunge into the information society that is already here.

The problem is that our thinking, our attitudes, and consequently our decision making have not caught up with the reality of things. Like the nine other basic shifts discussed in this book, the level of change involved is so fundamental yet so subtle that we tend not to see it, or if we see it, we dismiss it as overly simplistic, and then we ignore it.

Yet, we do so at great risk to our companies, our individual careers, our economy as a whole. It makes no sense, for instance, to reindustrialize an economy that is based not on industry, but on the production and distribution of information. Without an appreciation of the larger shifts that are restructuring our society, we act on assumptions that are out of date. Out of touch with the present, we are doomed to fail in the unfolding future.

But we have to release this deathgrip on the past and deal with the future. We must understand this new information society and the changes it brings. We need to reconceptualize our national and global objectives to fit the new economics of information.

The years 1956 and 1957 were a turning point, the end of the industrial era. Confused, unwilling to give up the past, even our best thinkers were at a loss to describe the coming epoch. Harvard sociologist Daniel Bell termed it the *post-industrial society* and the name stuck. We always name eras and movements "post" or "neo" when we don't know what to call them.

It is now clear that the post-industrial society is the information society, and that is what I call it throughout this book. (In any case, Daniel Bell was one of the earliest, and perhaps the best, thinker on the subject, and much of what I have to say builds on his work.)

Bell's post-industrial society was misunderstood. Again and again, scholars told us the post-industrial economy would be based on services. At first glance, the notion seems logical, since we traditionally think in economic terms of either goods or services. With most of us no longer manufacturing goods, the assumption is that we are providing services.

But a careful look at the so-called service occupations tells a different story. The overwhelming majority of service workers are actually engaged in the creation, processing, and distribution of information. The so-called service sector minus the information or knowledge workers has remained a fairly steady 11 or 12 percent since 1950. The character of service jobs has changed—virtually no domestics today, and thousands of fast-food workers, for example—but the numbers have remained quite steady; about one-tenth of the U.S. workforce can usually be found in the traditional service sector.

The real increase has been in information occupations. In 1950, only about 17 percent of us worked in information jobs. Now more than 60 percent of us work with information as programmers, teachers, clerks, secretaries, accountants, stock brokers, managers, insurance people, bureaucrats, lawyers, bankers, and technicians. And many more workers hold information jobs within manufacturing companies. Most Americans spend their time creating, processing, or distributing information. For example, workers in banking, the stock market, and insurance all hold information jobs. David L. Birch of MIT reports that only 13 percent of our labor force is engaged in manufacturing operations today.

It is important to acknowledge the kind of work we do because we are what we do, and what we do shapes society.

Farmer, laborer, clerk: That's a brief history of the United States.

The occupational history of the United States tells a lot about us. For example, in 1979, the number-one occupation in the United States, numerically, became clerk, succeeding laborer, succeeding farmer. Farmer, laborer, clerk—that is a brief history of the United States. Farmers, who as recently as the turn of the century constituted more than one-third of the total labor force, now are about 3 percent of the workforce. In fact, today there are more people employed full-time in our universities than in agriculture.

The second largest classification after clerk is professional, completely in tune with the new information society, where knowledge is the critical ingredient. The demand for professional workers has gained substantially since 1960, even more dramatically than the rising need for clerical workers.

Professional workers are almost all information workers—lawyers, teachers, engineers, computer programmers, systems analysts, doctors, architects, accountants, librarians, newspaper reporters, social workers, nurses, and clergy. Of course, everyone needs some kind of knowledge to do a job. Industrial workers, machinists, welders, jig makers, for example, are very knowledgeable about the tasks they perform. The difference is that for professional and clerical workers, the creation, processing, and distribution of information *is* the job.

In 1960 the approximately 7.5 million professional workers were the fifth largest job category and employed about 11 percent of the workforce. By 1979 that group had doubled to 15 million workers and made up some 16 percent of the overall workforce.

The New Wealth—Know-how

In an industrial society, the strategic resource is capital; a hundred years ago, a lot of people may have known how to build a steel plant, but not very many could get the money to build one. Consequently, access to the system was limited. But in our new society, as Daniel Bell first pointed out, the *strategic* resource is information. Not the only resource, but the most important. With information as the strategic resource, access to the economic system is much easier.

The creation of the now well-known Intel Corporation is a good example of this. Intel was formed in 1968 when Robert Noyce and Gordon Moore split off from their former employer, Fairchild Semiconductor. Intel was started with $2.5 million in venture capital, but it was the brainpower behind the financial resource that led to the technological breakthroughs that brought the firm annual sales of $850 million by 1980. Noyce is credited with being the coinventor of the integrated circuit and Intel with developing the microprocessor.

Noyce, the firm's founder, is well aware of which resource is the strategic one:

"Unlike steel, autos, and some others, this industry has never been an oligopoly," he said about the field of semiconductors. "It has always been a *brain-intensive* industry, rather than a capital-intensive one." (Italics added.)

That is the most important reason for the current entrepreneurial explosion in the United States, the huge growth in new small businesses. In 1950 we were creating new businesses at the rate of 93,000 per year. Today, we are creating new companies in this country at the rate of about 600,000 a year.

The transition times between economies are the times when entrepreneurship blooms. We are now in such a period.

The entrepreneurs who are creating new businesses are also creating jobs for the rest of us. During a seven-year period ending in 1976, we added 9 million new workers to the labor force—a lot of people! How many of those were jobs in the *Fortune* 1,000 largest industrial concerns? Zero. But 6 million were jobs in small businesses, most of which had been in existence for four years or less. (The remaining 3 million went to work for state and local, but not federal, government—a significant part of political decentralization dealt with in Chapter 5.)

We now mass-produce information the way we used to mass-produce cars.

In the information society, we have systematized the production of knowledge and amplified our brainpower. To use an industrial metaphor, we now mass-produce knowledge and this knowledge is the driving force of our economy.

The new source of power is not money in the hands of a few but information in the hands of many.

Unlike other forces in the universe, however, knowledge is not subject to the law of conservation: It can be created, it can be destroyed, and most importantly it is synergetic—that is, the whole is usually greater than the sum of the parts. Notes Peter

Drucker, "The productivity of knowledge has already become the key to productivity, competitive strength, and economic achievement. Knowledge has already become the primary industry, the industry that supplies the economy the essential and central resources of production."

We need to create a knowledge theory of value to replace Marx's obsolete labor theory of value.

In an information economy, then, value is increased, not by labor, but by knowledge. Marx's "labor theory of value," born at the beginning of the industrial economy, must be replaced with a new *knowledge theory of value*. In an information society, value is increased by knowledge, a different kind of labor than Marx had in mind. We have just to look at one of our major exports to realize the value of knowledge. In a day of shrinking U.S. markets abroad, American companies have little trouble selling their know-how, their expertise, their management skills.

Nevertheless, the notion that knowledge can create economic value is generally absent from most economic analysis, though there is some evidence that it is now beginning to be taken into account. An economist with the U.S. Department of Commerce, Edward Denison, did a study to pinpoint which factors contributed most to economic growth during the period 1948 to 1973. Denison concluded that about two-thirds of the economic growth came about because of the increased size and education of the workforce and the greater pool of knowledge available to workers.

MIT's David Birch has demonstrated that of the 19 million new jobs created in the United States during the 1970s—more than ever before in our history—only 5 percent were in manufacturing and only 11 percent in the goods-producing sector as a whole. Almost 90 percent, then—17 million new jobs—were not in the goods-producing sector. As Birch says, "We are working ourselves out of the manufacturing business and into the thinking business." Birch's figures are particularly trustworthy because they are built bottom-up through computer analysis of millions of companies rather than top-down by simply (and conventionally) looking at the gross, macroemployment figures.

17

Other Shifts: Time and the Game of Life

The restructuring of America from an industrial to an information society will easily be as profound as the shift from an agricultural society to an industrial society.

But there is one important difference. While the shift from an agricultural to an industrial society took 100 years, the present restructuring from an industrial to an information society took only two decades. Change is occurring so rapidly that there is no time to react; instead we must anticipate the future. With the new information society, then, there is a change in time orientation as well.

In our agricultural period, the time orientation was to the past. Farmers learned from the past how to plant, how to harvest, and how to store. The time orientation in an industrial society is *now*. Get it out, get it done, *ad hoc*, the bottom line, and all that.

We must learn from the future in precisely the ways we have learned from the past.

In our new information society, the time orientation is to the future. This is one of the reasons we are so interested in it. We must now learn from the present how to anticipate the future. When we can do that, we will understand that a trend is not destiny; we will be able to learn from the future the way we have been learning from the past.

This change in time orientation accounts for the growing popular and professional interest in the future during the 1970s. For example, the number of universities offering some type of futures-oriented degree has increased from 2 in 1969 to over 45 in 1978. Membership in the World Future Society grew from 200 in 1967 to well over 49,000 in 1979, and the number of popular and professional periodicals devoted to understanding or studying the future has dramatically increased from 12 in 1965 to over 122 in 1978.

It is quite possible for a single country to be in various states of agricultural, industrial, and information societies simultaneously. Yet, the object of life is different in all three, as Daniel Bell has said. During our agricultural period, the game was man

18

against nature. An industrial society pits man against fabricated nature. In an information society—for the first time in civilization—the game is people interacting with other people. This increases personal transactions geometrically, that is, all forms of interactive communication: telephone calls, checks written, memos, messages, letters, and more. This is one basic reason why we are bound to continue to be a litigious-intensive society: Some of the greatly increasing personal transactions will undoubtedly go sour, resulting in more lawsuits. The bad news is that there is no end to lawyers and lawyering.

Lawyers are like beavers: They get in the mainstream and damn it up.

The *Chicago Sun-Times* reported that between 1970 and 1978 the lawyer population increased 14 percent, while the general population increased by only 6 percent. Still, law schools remain as popular as ever. In 1980, there were more than 125,000 students enrolled in A.B.A.-approved U.S. law schools.

The Five Key Points

The five most important things to remember about the shift from an industrial to an information society are:

- The information society is an economic reality, not an intellectual abstraction.
- Innovations in communications and computer technology will accelerate the pace of change by collapsing the *information float*.
- New information technologies will at first be applied to old industrial tasks, then, gradually, give birth to new activities, processes, and products.
- In this literacy-intensive society, when we need basic reading and writing skills more than ever before, our education system is turning out an increasingly inferior product.
- The technology of the new information age is not absolute. It will succeed or fail according to the principle of high tech/ high touch.

19

The Information Economy Is Real

If we are to speak of an information economy, we must be able to measure it in concrete terms. How much of the nation's wealth is actually produced in the information sector? How many of us earn a living in information jobs?

Without answers to these questions, most of us will probably choose to pledge continued allegiance to the economic reality we have experienced firsthand, the industrial era, where we produced "real" goods with "real" price tags. We will dismiss the information economy as ephemeral paperwork existing only as an adjunct to goods-producing sectors.

Documenting the information economy is difficult, to be sure. Pinpointing the economics of the creation, production, and distribution of information requires quantifying and codification of highly detailed minutiae.

Fortunately, these questions have been asked and extensively answered in a landmark study by information specialist Dr. Marc Porat. Under the sponsorship of the U.S. Department of Commerce, Porat painstakingly dissected the nation's economy and established criteria for labeling a job or part of a job and its income as part of the information sector or the goods-producing sector, or something other.

"Stating precisely who is an information worker and who is not is a risky proposition," writes Porat. However, his study documents his conclusions extensively enough to convince the information economy's skeptics.

Porat sorted through some 440 occupations in 201 industries, identified the information jobs, and compiled their contribution to the GNP. Questionable jobs were excluded so that the study's conclusions err on the conservative side.

Porat's study is incredibly detailed. He begins with the obvious sorting-out and tallying-up of the economic value of easily identifiable information jobs such as clerks, librarians, systems analysts, calling this first group the *Primary Information Sector*. According to Porat's calculations for the year 1967, 25.1 percent of the U.S. GNP was produced in the Primary Information Sector, that is, the part of the economy that produces, processes, and distributes information goods and services. Included here are computer manufacturing, telecommunications, printing, mass media, advertising, accounting, and education, as well as risk-management industries, including parts of the finance and insurance businesses.

But Porat's study goes on to deal with the more difficult questions that have overwhelmed other researchers. How does one categorize those individuals holding information jobs with manufacturers and other noninformation firms? To answer this question required "tearing firms apart in an accounting sense into information and non-information parts."

Porat creates a new information grouping called the *Secondary Information Sector.* It quantifies the economic contribution of information workers employed in noninformation firms.

These workers produce information goods and services for internal consumption within goods-producing and other companies. In effect their information products are sold on a fictitious account to the goods-producing side of the company. The Secondary Information Sector generated an additional 21.1 percent of the GNP.

Porat's study concludes, then, that the information economy accounted for some 46 percent of the GNP and more than 53 percent of income earned. This was in 1967.

Porat is unwilling to estimate how much the information economy has grown since, except to say it has increased, "by leaps and bounds."

Porat's study leaves little room for doubt. David Birch's more recent finding that only 5 percent of the almost 20 million new jobs created in the 1970s were in manufacturing (almost 90 percent were in information, knowledge, or service jobs) further substantiates the fact that we are now a nation of information workers. For example, while the total labor force grew only 18 percent between 1970 and 1978, the number of administrators and managers grew more than three times that rate—58 percent. Health administrators grew at an astounding 118 percent; public officials were up 76 percent; bankers, 83 percent; systems analysts, 84 percent. In contrast, engineers grew by less than 3 percent.

New York City, once a leading light of industrial America, has lost half the manufacturing jobs it had in 1947. The city lost 40,000 manufacturing jobs in the years between 1977 and 1980 alone. In contrast, New York is experiencing a boom in information jobs. The Regional Planning Association estimates that more than half of New York's gross city product is now generated by people who work in information. In recent years, legal services have replaced apparel as New York City's leading export.

Several states are attempting to replicate the industry-to-information shift that seems to have occurred naturally in New York City. The key strategy is to offer more incentives to high-tech information companies:

- California's Governor Jerry Brown wants the state to offer direct subsidies to high-tech information companies.
- In 1980 North Carolina invested millions in a new microelectronics research center. General Electric Company promptly decided to build a new plant nearby.
- The Minnesota legislature is considering financing the expansion of the University of Minnesota's microelectronics facility in order to attract more high-tech information firms.
- Ohio has established a $5-million fund to make direct loans to high-technology companies.

The cities, states, and companies that plan for the new information age will be in a key position to reap its rewards. And those rewards will be ample.

Today's information companies have emerged as some of the nation's largest. AT&T grossed $58 billion in 1981, far surpassing the GNP of many nations. Other information companies include IBM, ITT, Xerox, RCA, all the banks and insurance companies, the broadcasters, publishers, and computer companies. Almost all of the people in these companies and industries spend their time processing information in one way or another and generating value that is purchased in domestic and global markets.

Collapsing the Information Float

The pace of change will accelerate even more as communications technology collapses the information float. The life channel of the information age is communication. In simple terms, communication requires a sender, a receiver, and a communication channel. The introduction of increasingly sophisticated information technology has revolutionized that simple process. The net effect is a faster flow of information through the information channel, bringing sender and receiver closer together, or collapsing the information float—the amount of time information spends in the communication channel. If I mail a letter to you, it takes three or four days for you to receive it. If I send you a letter electronically, it will take a couple of seconds. That is collapsing the information float. If you respond to my electronic letter within an hour, we have negotiated our business in an hour rather than a week, accelerating life and commerce. Any changes that are occurring will occur much faster because of this foreshortening of the information float.

When President Lincoln was shot, the word was communicated by telegraph to most parts of the United States, but because we had no links to England, it was five days before London heard of the event. When President Reagan was shot, journalist Henry Fairlie, working at his typewriter within a block of the shooting, got word of it by telephone from his editor at the *Spectator* in London, who had seen a rerun of the assassination attempt on television shortly after it occurred.

One way to think about the foreshortening of the information float is to think about when the world changed from trading goods and services to standardized currencies. Just imagine how that speeded up transactions. Now, with the use of electrons to send money around the world at the speed of light, we have almost completely collapsed the money information float. The shift from money to electronics is as basic as when we went from barter to money.

To the benefit of both sender and receiver, the new technology has opened up new information channels with wider range and greater sophistication. It has shortened the distance between sender and receiver and increased the velocity of the information flow. But most importantly, it has collapsed the information float.

With the coming of the information society, we have for the first time an economy based on a key resource that is not only renewable but self-generating.

Now, more than 100 years after the creation of the first data communication devices, we stand at the threshold of a mammoth communication revolution. The combined technologies of the telephone, computer, and television have merged into an integrated information and communication system that transmits data and permits instantaneous interactions between persons and computers. As our transportation network carried the products of industrialization in the past, so too will this emerging communications network carry the new products of the information society. This new integrated communication system will fuel the information society the way energy—electricity, oil, nuclear—kept the industrial society humming and the way natural power—wind, water, and brute force—sustained agricultural society.

We have for the first time an economy based on a key resource that is not only renewable, but self-generating. Running out of it is not a problem, but drowning in it is. For example:

- Between 6,000 and 7,000 scientific articles are written each day.
- Scientific and technical information now increases 13 percent per year, which means it doubles every 5.5 years.
- But the rate will soon jump to perhaps 40 percent per year because of new, more powerful information systems and an increasing population of scientists. That means that data will double every twenty months.
- By 1985 the volume of information will be somewhere between four and seven times what it was only a few years earlier.

We are drowning in information but starved for knowledge.

This level of information is clearly impossible to handle by present means. Uncontrolled and unorganized information is no longer a resource in an information society. Instead, it becomes the enemy of the information worker. Scientists who are overwhelmed with technical data complain of information pollution and charge that it takes less time to do an experiment than to find out whether or not it has already been done.

Information technology brings order to the chaos of information pollution and therefore gives value to data that would otherwise be useless. If users—through information utilities— can locate the information they need, they will pay for it. The emphasis of the whole information society shifts, then, from supply to *selection*.

This principle is the driving force behind the new electronic publishers who provide on-line data bases, communication channels for sorting through and selecting. These new businesses are selling a medium, not information as such.

The on-line information selection business has already become a $1.5-billion-a-year enterprise; approximately 80 percent of the business gives users direct access to sources (source data bases), while the other 20 percent (bibliographic data bases) tells the user where to find what is sought. Just listing some of the resources is instructive. For example, available through Lockheed's Dialog system are over 100 separate data bases allowing the user access to such diverse informational sources as the National Agricultural Library, The Foundation Grants Index, The Maritime Research Information Service (MRIS), the Social Science Citation Index (SSCI), and World Aluminum Abstracts (WAA).

Despite all of the excitement generated, very few Americans have computers, but their numbers are increasing at a staggering rate:

- From the beginning of time through 1980 there were only 1 million computers, estimates the president of Commodore International Ltd., a major manufacturer of personal computers. Commodore alone expects to match that figure in 1982.
- Dataquest, Inc., a Cupertino, California, market research firm, estimates that over half a million personal computers were sold in 1980, and that the total will grow *at least* 40 percent annually.
- Apple Computers, a pioneer in the field of personal compters, has sold more than a quarter of a million computers since its beginning in 1977, and currently is selling around 20,000 every month.
- In 1977, only 50 stores catered to computer hobbyists; by 1982 there were 10,000.

Lack of good software is holding back, for now, the widespread use of personal computers in our homes. Better software will eventually sell more hardware (computers), which in turn will attract more software. It will work the way the introduction of high-fidelity equipment worked in this country. When first introduced, there was little software (records), but as hardware sales grew, the market became large enough to attract the development of more software. With more wonderful software available, sales of hi-fi equipment took off. After a critical point the hardware and the software fed on each other, which is what will happen to computers.

The home computer explosion is upon us, soon to be followed by a software implosion to fuel it.

It is projected that by the year 2000, the cost of a home computer system (computer, printer, monitor, modem, and so forth) should only be about twice that of the present telephone-radio-recorder-television system. Before then, computers in homes will approach the necessary critical mass, first in California. Community-wide information services will work this way as well. At some point, some city in the United States will have a sufficient number of home computers (San Diego is a good bet) so that the local newspaper, say, the San Diego *Union*, will give up publishing the hundreds and hundreds of stock listings, on dearer and dearer newspaper stock, and offer self-selected stocks printed out by individual order each afternoon on individual home computers. Such services will sell more computers—which will encourage additional software offerings. Again, it is a shift from supply to selection.

In the future, editors won't tell us what to read: We will tell editors what we choose to read.

Anthony Smith in his 1980 book, *Goodbye Gutenberg,* has usefully pointed out that we are at the beginning of a period that will witness a shift from author to receiver in the "sovereignty over text." For hundreds of years, authors and editors have decided what to put in the packages they create for us—newspapers, magazines, television programs—and we pick among them, deciding what we want to read or watch. Now, with the new technologies, we will create our own packages, experiencing sovereignty over text. It will evolve over a long period of time, but the accumulated impact of people exercising sovereignty over text will undoubtedly have a strong effect on the new society we are shaping.

The Three Stages of Technology

Technological processes will first be applied to the old industrial tasks (the second stage of technological innovation).

There are three stages of technological development: First, the new technology or innovation follows the line of least resistance; second, the technology is used to improve previous technologies (this stage can last a long time); and third, new directions or uses are discovered that grow out of the technology itself.

During the first stage of technological innovation, technology takes the path of least resistance, that is, it is applied in ways that do not threaten people—reducing the chance that the technology will be abruptly rejected.

The way society handled the introduction of microprocessors is a classic example of this first stage. The first application of the microprocessor was in toys. Who could object? Robots were first used in jobs considered unsafe or too dirty for humans. Who could object? Robots (for dangerous tasks) and toys represented the unthreatening path of least resistance.

At the same time, this path has created a whole generation of computer-comfortable kids. In five years, young people entering the labor force will have had some form of information device in their hands most of their lives—from calculators to computer games to push-button telephones.

Today we have moved into the second stage of development: The microprocessor is being used to improve what we already have—cars, manufacturing, sewing machines. Today's word processor is nothing more than an improved typewriter, for example, and there are many other examples where computers are also improving what exists:

- The federal government used computers to match job seekers and private job openings under an experimental Labor Department program that may "soon be in coast to coast operation," reported the *Portland Oregonian.* Congress voted $30 million as the first step in a five-year plan to install the system in every state employment service office.
- An IBM computer is managing energy use in a 481-unit apartment house in Crystal City, Virginia. The $110,000 system cut annual electricity costs by $50,000, according to the building manager.

27

- Real estate offices in California provide potential buyers with instantaneous information about available housing, financial terms, ownership history. Videotapes show the property.

The list could go on and on. It may be some time, though, before we get to the third stage, where we will create things suggested by the microprocessor itself, inventions and applications that are unimagined now.

To a certain extent, society has readily accepted the technology only because we have been through the first stage of technological development. Only now is technology being introduced into old industrial tasks—the running of factories with information rather than workers—and that introduction is sending shock waves into a labor movement already weakened by the shift away from manufacturing itself.

Unions have been forced to fight automation in both industry and agriculture, sometimes accepting automation in exchange for job security.

One by one, local typographical unions are agreeing to allow newspaper management to automate as long as current union members are given job security. At the *Minneapolis Star and Tribune,* the union ratified a ten-year contract that requires the company to employ 130 printers, with nearly 400 printers subject to layoffs and reductions in the total workforce.

In California, where mechanization is fast replacing farm workers, the United Farm Workers have criticized the state-supported University of California for doing research and development of labor-replacing farm machinery.

The potential of microprocessors is awesome. The automation of factories and offices, once a futuristic pipe dream, is becoming a reality.

It is no wonder, then, that computers have inspired fear and mystery in workers ever since their powers were first uncovered.

Computer technology is to the information age what mechanization was to the industrial revolution: It is a threat because it incorporates functions previously performed by workers.

The most vivid example in recent technological history, of course, is the movement of robots from the first to the second stage of technological innovation. Robots have expanded beyond the dangerous jobs into the unskilled and skilled labor market.

28

At Ford Motor Company, robots test engines. General Motors uses robotic welders. And there are ten government agencies where robots pick up and deliver mail.

"Robots are coming: the question is how soon. They are going to mean erosion in employment opportunities throughout the industry," said retired UAW's international vice president, Irving Bluestone.

Unlike the Luddites, the antimechanization workers group that destroyed some 1,000 English mills during the early nineteenth century, contemporary workers are so far limited to staging nonviolent battles to fight off the advancing computer revolution. In Australia, microprocessors are called "job killers," and in England, a television program entitled "The Chips Are Down" portrayed widespread job loss and economic upheaval because of microelectronics.

Until now, however, the worst fears about automation-related job loss have not materialized. During the 1960s and 1970s, people lost jobs because of temporary recessions and because mature industries in developed countries became less competitive than new industries in Japan or in the more advanced developing countries.

But now labor planners are gritting their teeth again and dusting off the gloom-and-doom scenarios, largely because of the advent of the microprocessor:

- A French government report predicted the country would lose 30 percent of its banking and insurance workers within the next ten years.
- Britain's national trade unions have demanded that no new technology be introduced unilaterally by management.
- In negotiations with Ford in the United States, the United Auto Workers (UAW) demanded the right to strike over technological issues. (They didn't get it.)

Why is the microprocessor causing such widespread concern? The reason is simple: its widespread applicability. Earlier computer technology could be applied to some products, electronics, and large-scale office information equipment, for example, but not others. Microprocessors can improve almost anything, anywhere, and are consequently far more threatening.

In fact, there is virtually no limit to the sectors of the world

29

economy where microprocessors can be put to work. Writes Colin Norman, author of a World Watch Institute paper on microelectronics, "No technology in history has had such a broad range of applications in the workplace."

The British publication *New Scientist* offers more precise estimates: "The application market for microprocessing technology is about 38 percent of the world's present economy."

Newsweek magazine estimates that "from 50 to 75 percent of all U.S. factory workers could be displaced by smart robots before the end of the century."

Notice that all the above illustrations are rooted in the second stage of industrial development, the application of technological innovation to the old industrial tasks. It is clear that we are still in the second stage of technological innovation and that the introduction of technology into the industrial workplace is on a collision course with much of the workforce, organized or not.

Labor unions are quick to describe the negative dehumanized work environment after technological innovation. Such is the theme of an article appearing in *In These Times,* a prolabor Socialist newspaper published by the Institute for Policy Studies.

The article describes the operations of a local telephone company where, after new technology is introduced, jobs are reorganized to eliminate responsibility, initiative, and human contact—in short, nearly everything that makes work rewarding. Workers found their jobs dehumanizing and robotlike, the stereotype of what we have come to fear: Workers get their daily assignments from a terminal and spend most of their day doing routine monitoring work. Because these machines have no moving parts, they rarely break down. If something important goes wrong, management takes over to do the more interesting troubleshooting work. The article's sentiment is clear: This is where labor thinks we are heading.

One would be tempted to dismiss this discouraging forecast as just so much Socialist rhetoric. The problem is that the same scenario keeps reappearing in the research of technology experts with no particular ax to grind.

One such expert is Robert Lund, the assistant director and senior research associate at MIT's Center for Policy Alternatives. Lund recently conducted a study for the British Department of Industry on the impact of microprocessors.

He found that production and service jobs tended to become "deskilled" when technology is added. "Engineers' and supervisors' jobs, on the other hand," writes Lund, "tend to become more demanding."

MIT's Harley Shaiken, who comes from the labor side, concludes: "If labor does not find a way to control technology, then management will use technology to control labor."

Clearly, automation will remain a key labor-management issue in the coming decade. Yet, much of debate so far is based on the old industrial paradigm of labor-management relations. Technology is seen by labor as management's latest tool for harnessing workers.

The Education Mismatch

A 1980 report by the U.S. Department of Education and the National Science Foundation stated that most Americans are moving toward "virtual scientific and technological illiteracy." It concluded that science and math programs in U.S. schools lag behind the U.S.S.R., Japan, and Germany. Part of the problem is the shortage of qualified high school science and math teachers. But there is an even worse shortage of college-level computer science and engineering teachers.

On the sixteen-year decline of SAT scores (the tests to qualify for college), however, the report falsely consoled Americans that the brightest students *seemed* to be doing as well as ever on the college entry tests, even though the majority of students were learning less and less. But less than six months later, new data showed that the country's best students were following the lead of their less gifted classmates. The scores of the best and the brightest were beginning to slide as well.

The generation graduating from high school today is the first generation in American history to graduate less skilled than its parents.

The Carnegie Council of Policy Studies in Higher Education recently reported that "because of deficits in our public school system, about one-third of our youth are ill-educated, ill-employed, and ill-equipped to make their way in American soci-

31

ety." Estimates of the number of functional illiterates in the United States range from 18 million to 64 million.

What is perhaps even more discouraging is the growing number of high school dropouts.

- In the bellwether state of California the dropout rate increased 83 percent during the 1970s and now is three times the national average.
- Ohio's Citizens Council for Ohio Schools reports the dropout rate has increased dramatically during the last five years.
- Boston, New York, Cleveland, Washington, Baltimore, and New Orleans report chronic absenteeism—which usually leads to higher dropout rates.
- In Wisconsin, the dropout rate increased 50 percent during the 1970s. Governor Lee Dreyfus, "shocked" at the dropout data, told the *Milwaukee Journal,* "These people make up a city approximately the size of Madison and they will have to be supported by the rest of the state."

With the schools turning out an increasingly inferior product, corporations have reluctantly entered the education business. Some 300 of the nation's largest companies now operate remedial courses in basic math and English for entry-level workers, according to the Conference Board. Just when offices are demanding more highly skilled workers—to operate a word-processing machine, for example—what they are getting is graduates who would have a hard time qualifying for the jobs that are *already* technologically obsolete.

There's a bright side, even to discouraging news such as this. There will be a huge demand for teachers to tutor "students" with jobs in private business. Former teachers with an entrepreneurial bent will find a growing market for educational consulting services in the new information society. (There's an answer to the problem of what to do with the surplus of teachers generated by the baby-boom kids.)

But will we be able to acquire needed skills fast enough? Technology will help us manage the information society only to the extent that its members are skilled in utilizing it.

A powerful anomaly is developing: As we move into a more and more literacy-intensive society, our schools are giving us an increasingly inferior product. SAT scores have been going down each year for more than a decade. In 1980 scores hit an all-time low: 424 for verbal and 466 for math, down from 473 and 496 in 1965, the year before scores plunged.

It is more and more apparent that young high school—even college—graduates cannot write acceptable English or even do simple arithmetic. For the first time in American history the generation moving into adulthood is less skilled than its parents.

And without basic skills, computer illiteracy is a foregone conclusion. In the new information society, being without computer skills is like wandering around a collection the size of the Library of Congress with all the books arranged at random with no Dewey Decimal system, no card catalogue—and of course no friendly librarian to serve your information needs.

By one estimate, 75 percent of all jobs by 1985 will involve computers in some way—and people who don't know how to use them will be at a disadvantage.

The National Council of Teachers of Mathematics has said "computer literacy is an essential outcome of contemporary education. Each student should acquire an understanding of the versatility and limitations of the computer through first-hand experience in a variety of fields." Harvard University now requires graduates to demonstrate the ability to write a simple computer program.

Some observers believe computer illiteracy should be tackled with a massive top-down national computer literacy campaign—an approach that would surely fail. And one that may not even be necessary. Fortunately, computers are being designed to be simple to operate and will eventually be programmed in English. In the meantime, children are growing up interacting with computers, playing with computers, and learning to be comfortable with computers without even realizing it. Furthermore, the computer is slowly finding its way into the public school system. Although the cost is prohibitive for most school districts, computer use in schools is on the upswing for a variety of reasons.

First, computers offer a cost-effective albeit capital-intensive way of individualizing education. Second, computers simplify the extensive recordkeeping required for individualized instruction. Third, familiarity with computers is now considered a strong vocational advantage, a salable skill.

Finally, the computer is an enormously flexible tool that can and is being used in a wide variety of ways depending on local needs and available resources:

- Students in the Alaskan bush study Alaskan history and English using microcomputers hooked up to television sets. The pilot project demonstrates the ways to use computers in remote areas.
- Harrisburg, Pennsylvania, students use computers for instruction and to learn programming. Most of the instruction materials were obtained free from the Asbury Park, New Jersey, School District.
- Neighborhood centers in Wilmington, Delaware, offer after-school tutoring on computer terminals hooked up to a data bank at the University of Delaware.
- The Houston Independent School System says it plans to have as many as 30,000 microcomputers in use by 1985.
- Seven Arkansas high schools use a sophisticated guidance computer to help students select a career by programming likes and dislikes and strengths and weaknesses. It stores information on 875 jobs, nearly 5,000 colleges, and more than 300 scholarships.
- Ninety-five percent of all students in Minnesota are believed to have access to instructional computing services through the Minnesota Educational Computing Consortium, which claims it is the largest time-sharing network in the world.

Although computer use in public education is still in its infancy, schools around the nation are beginning to realize that in the information society, the two required languages will be English and computer.

In the business community, computer learning is flourishing. Executives are learning to program computers themselves because it takes too long to wait for the computer department. As a result, they are enrolling in basic courses in droves. *The Wall Street Journal* estimates that some 5 percent of the white-collar workforce have and use computers. California computer consultant Arthur Luehrmann calculates that ten to twenty hours of actual hands-on computer experience translates into a $1,000 annual advantage on the job market.

The American Management Associations' computer course

for noncomputer personnel is so popular, they offer it eighty times a year. At Boston University, 20 percent of the students in computer courses are business people trying to get a handle on the new technology. There are several reasons behind this computer literacy boom. In addition to wanting information right away, some business people complain that they can't communicate exactly what they want to the data-processing staff, who may spend weeks on a program, only to have it turn out wrong. It's not surprising many executives would rather do it themselves. It is estimated that fully one-third of the personal computer systems shipped up until 1980 have landed in private executive offices.

Nevertheless, many executives are resisting the computer. This is a holdover from the industrial era, where executives considered it beneath themselves to type. That attitude will have to change if an executive expects to survive in an information society where computers and keyboards are the tools of the trade.

The Human Side of High Technology

Many observers are betting that the major change for clerical personnel will be in *where* they work, rather than in what they do. With terminals and word-processing machines hooked up to an office miles away—so the scenario runs—tomorrow's secretaries and clerks will almost universally opt to work at home. So will other workers who create, process, and distribute information in industries such as banking and insurance. Pilot projects to accomplish this aim are already being set up in companies such as Control Data and Continental Bank in Illinois.

But workers report mixed reactions. Yes, it's fun for a while to escape the daily grind. No doubt about that. But after a time, most miss the office gossip and the warm interaction with co-workers. High touch. Alone in their electronic cottages, they feel a high-tech isolation. Yet, the attractions are still there—a chance for more time with the family, the choice to work at night, and, if one so chooses, the opportunity to eliminate the word commuting from one's vocabulary. What emerges from interviews with workers who have tried telecommuting and with their employers—who presumably are fairly flexible to begin with—is a multiple-option solution: signing on for a stint working at home, later rejoining the office staff for a while.

Employers report that it costs approximately $1,700 to install a terminal in a worker's home. As the costs continue to decline, the alternating home/office work schedule will become less of a financial consideration. Workers who want the home-stint option may elect to finance the hookup themselves, with the company footing the bill for the limited number of permanent home workers. Many of these will be handicapped persons for whom the home terminal is a boon to greater self-reliance and increased financial independence. The point is that *not* all of us will work at home.

My own sense of it is that not very many of us will be willing to work at home. People want to be with people; people want to go to the office. (This high-tech/high-touch consideration is fully treated in Chapter 2.) Even enthusiastic prophets of the electronic cottage estimate that by 1990, only 10 million of us will be telecommuting.

Finally, the transition from an industrial to an information society does not mean manufacturing will cease to exist or become unimportant. Did farming end with the industrial era? Ninety percent of us produced 100 percent of the food in the agricultural era; now 3 percent of us produce 120 percent.

Information is as necessary to General Motors as it is to IBM. In the information age, the focus of manufacturing will shift from the physical to more intellectual functions on which the physical depends.

Information is an economic entity because it costs something to produce and because people are willing to pay for it. Value is whatever people are willing to pay for. So even if an economy built around information seems less real than one built around automobiles and steel, it doesn't matter so long as people will pay for information or knowledge.

Sometime during the 1980s, electronics—undeniably an information industry—will become a $400-billion business, the largest ever created on the planet. Perhaps by then even the skeptics among us will for the first time grasp the reality—and the wonder—of the new information society.

In the new information era, all the information occupations will continue to grow for a long time. Systems analysts, programmers, and service technicians must grow at least 100 percent before the decade is over.

But whether you work with computers or not, it is important to become friends with the computer and become computer literate, because the computer will permeate the whole world of work. The rapid change ahead also means that you cannot expect to remain in the same job or profession for life, even if it is an information occupation. The coming changes will force us to seek retraining again and again. Business will have to play the key role, similar to the way IBM now spends approximately $500 million annually on employee training and education.

We are moving from the specialist who is soon obsolete to the generalist who can adapt.

We all know the computer is coming into our home and work environments. But how many of us thought it would affect our marriages? One of my friends reports that at her evening computer course, more than a third of the people there came only because their spouse had purchased a home computer. It can certainly be the third party that upsets the delicate balance of a marriage.

In connection with our national economy, it is important now not to get depressed about the latest gloomy business statistics, which are strictly industrial-based measures of economic well-being. The information economy and the other sunrise sectors are going well. They are the ones to invest in now. Small sunrise stocks versus large sunset stocks; buying Computer Software, Inc., selling U.S. Steel.

If, as predicted, electronics replaces the automobile as the most important industry in our economy, will we have to buy a home computer before buying a car? Steven P. Jobs, cofounder of Apple Computer, Inc., has said, "We subscribe to the mode that everyone wants his own computer." If that sounds far-fetched, look at the shift that has already occurred: We used to buy cars for fun; now we buy cars for good gas mileage and transportation and home computers for fun. We need cars now because we organized our society around them fifty years ago when we (or was it Detroit?) decided that since the economy was going to be built on cars, everyone from age sixteen up should want and need one. But what did the automobile ever contribute to society besides transportation? Without it, would we have moved so far apart and created such poor public transportation?

Of course, we need cars. But three-car families? Who live in cities? In addition to transportation, the automobile has brought us air pollution, 50,000 highway deaths each year, automobile insurance, and parking tickets. So far the computer looks relatively benign. The whole orientation of the computer is getting you to expand your brainpower through growth, education, and learning.

In the computer age we are dealing with conceptual space connected by electronics, rather than physical space connected by the motorcar.

2

From Forced Technology to High Tech/High Touch

High tech/high touch is a formula I use to describe the way we have responded to technology. What happens is that whenever new technology is introduced into society, there must be a counterbalancing human response—that is, *high touch*—or the technology is rejected. The more high tech, the more high touch.

The parallel growth of high tech/high touch took place during the last three decades, a period that appeared chaotic, but that really had its own rhythm and sense.

The alienation of the 1950s was a response to the most intensely industrialized period in our history. During this decade of the gray flannel suit and the organization man, fully 65 percent of our workforce were in industrial occupations, many in assembly-line regimentation. More workers, 32 percent, were unionized than would ever be again.

During both the 1950s and the 1960s, we mass-marketed the products of that industrial era—products whose regimented uniformities mirrored their industrial base. High tech was everywhere—in the factory, at the office, in our communication, transportation, and health care systems and, finally, even in our homes.

But something else was growing alongside the technological invasion. Our response to the high tech all around us was the evolution of a highly personal value system to compensate for the impersonal nature of technology. The result was the new self-help or personal growth movement, which eventually became the human potential movement.

Much has been written about the human potential movement, but to my knowledge no one has connected it with technological change. In reality, each feeds the other—high tech/high touch.

Now, at the dawn of the twenty-first century, high tech/high touch has truly come of age. Technology and our human potential are the two great challenges and adventures facing humankind today. The great lesson we must learn from the principle of high tech/high touch is a modern version of the ancient Greek ideal—*balance*.

We must learn to balance the material wonders of technology with the spiritual demands of our human nature.

High Tech/High Touch: TV, the Pill, and Hospices

Perhaps the most powerful technological intrusion was television, far more vivid and more engaging than either radio or the telephone. At almost exactly the time we first introduced television, we created the group-therapy movement, which led to the personal growth movement, which in turn led to the human potential movement (est, TM, Rolfing, Yoga, Zen, and so forth—all very high touch). Television and the human potential movement developed almost in lockstep, much of both in the bellwether state of California.

The first real television generation, the baby boomers, who started out in life with *The Howdy Doody Show* and who mellowed into *The Mickey Mouse Club* and *American Bandstand,* are without a doubt the strongest proponents of the human growth movement. The need to compensate for the years of being technologically bombarded is part of the unfolding of this high-touch phenomenon.

40

The gee-whiz futurists are always wrong because they believe technological innovation travels in a straight line. It doesn't. It weaves and bobs and lurches and sputters.

We show no signs of lessening the pace with which we introduce even more technology into our society—and into our homes. The appropriate response to more technology is not to stop it, Luddite-like, but to accommodate it, respond to it, and shape it. In the interplay of technology and our reaction to it, technological progress does not proceed along a straight course. That is why the gee-whiz futurists who said we are all going to pilot our own helicopters, or that home hookups will replace the newspaper, were mistaken. Technological innovation rarely goes the way of straight-line extrapolation, but proceeds as part of a lurching dynamic of complicated patterns and processes.

Examples of the high-tech/high-touch phenomenon are all around us.

- The high technology of heart transplants and brain scanners led to a new interest in the family doctor and neighborhood clinics.
- Jet airplanes, as far as I can tell, have led only to more meetings.

The pill is a good example of high tech/high touch. The high technology of chemistry and pharmacology led to the development of the pill, which in turn led to a whole revolution in lifestyles. Societal taboos against premarital sex are of course partly pragmatic since becoming pregnant can lead to all kinds of complications; the advent of the pill initiated widespread experimentation and adventurism, including living together, which became very widespread. Although marriage is coming back in the 1980s, during the 1970s there were days when I was sure that the only people in this society who *really* wanted to get married were priests.

The introduction of the high technology of word processors into our offices has led to a revival of handwritten notes and letters.

41

A very poignant example of what I mean by high tech/high touch is the response to the introduction of high technology of life-sustaining equipment in hospitals. We couldn't handle the intrusion of this high technology into such a sensitive area of our lives without creating some human ballast. So we got very interested in the quality of death, which led to the hospice movement, now widespread in this country.

The more high technology we put in our hospitals, the less we are being born there, dying there—and avoiding them in between.

The health field offers still more examples of high tech/high touch. The high-tech side has brought heart transplants into the medical mainstream; microsurgery to reattach severed limbs, and, recently, artificial pancreata; and "walking dialysis" to replace expensive and confining hemodialysis. At the same time there is a trend toward less surgery and less radical surgery.

And medical care is becoming far more high touch. Home care and home births are becoming increasingly popular, while in hospitals the staff is attempting to create a more homelike atmosphere. New low-tech birthing rooms are being added to hospitals, and freestanding birthing centers, similar to hospice centers, are proliferating. Primary nursing, for example, where a nurse is responsible for the total care of a few patients, is very high touch.

The immensely popular movie *Star Wars* is very high tech/high touch. It portrays a contest between characters who have used technology within human control and scale and others who have been dominated by it. The good guys are not antitechnology: When Luke Skywalker flies in on that final run, the Force with him, he turns off his computer, but not his engine.

The Computer as Liberator

I had thought earlier that we might rebel against the computer for dehumanizing us. But now I think we are beginning to understand just how liberating the computer is in a high-tech/high-touch sense. For example, a company with 40,000 employees has treated those employees pretty much the same for generations.

It had to because that was the only way to keep track of them. With the computer to keep track, the employees can be treated differently, with a unique contract for each of the 40,000. We are all slowly moving in that direction. In addition, companies are now offering a "cafeteria of compensations," for example American Can. An employee can now decide to have a certain combination of salary, pension, health benefits, flexitime, job sharing, and job objectives.

The technology of the computer allows us to have a distinct and individually tailored arrangement with each of thousands of employees.

Even pension plans are moving in this direction: Because we have the computer to keep track of it, an individual contributor to the pension plan can decide where that contribution is going to be invested. And that is one of the key reasons that unions are out of tune with the new computer-rich information society. The basic idea of a union is to ensure that everyone is treated the same. But now we all want to be treated differently.

High-Tech Backlash

Whenever institutions introduce new technology to customers or employees, they should build in a high-touch component; if they don't, people will try to create their own or reject the new technology. That may account for the public's resistance to automation and electronic accounting.

In 1975, when automatic payroll deposits were instituted at Spartan Industries in Detroit, three women assembly-line workers sued the company over the issue. They charged that they were fired for refusing to participate in the computerized system. Electronic Funds Transfer faced a far more substantial and widespread backlash. The vice president of the Bank of Hawaii, David Cheever, explains it this way: "We've done a lot of research and the customer simply feels better writing checks himself, knowing it will get done."

There is no high touch in the high tech of electronic funds transfer, so bank customers are rejecting it everywhere. The banks offering it are essentially saying, "We used to do business one way and now we are all going to do it another way—electronically."

The problem is with the customers. Some of us *want* to go to tellers. In fact, some of us want to go to *the same* teller every time. I don't know about you, but I feel outrageously virtuous writing out my own checks every month—and the banks want to take that away from me.

The banks are offering what amounts to an either/or formulation rather than an option. In a highly diversified, highly segmented society, options succeed and either/or formulations fail miserably.

When high tech and high touch are out of balance, an annoying dissonance results. There are many examples of high-tech dissonance:

- The backlash against high-tech polygraph tests, which were labeled "dehumanizing" and subsequently outlawed in nineteen states and the District of Columbia.
- The widespread concern about personal privacy that erupted just as computers were becoming widespread in society.
- Another example is as mundane as the telephone. You use the high technology of the telephone to dial 411 to get a phone number and, instead of a high-touch response, what you get is more technology: a record upbraiding you for not checking your directory.

High-tech dissonance infuriates people. It's even worse when you again use the technology of the telephone to call a warm friend and instead get more technology: "Hi there, I've gone out for a little while. . . ." That's why so many improbable messages are left recorded on those machines.

Many of us instinctively feel the metric system is too high tech. To make matters worse, it was imposed on us top-down by some Metric Council or other (presumably in Washington, D.C.) and consequently we do not want very much to do with it.

"Metric will be about as successful as Esperanto." That prophetic statement was made by Steward Brand, the editor of *Co-Evolution Quarterly* and head of California's Metric Council. The high tech of metric is being imposed on people without any high-touch tradeoffs and in the face of the comfortable, high-tech/high-touch balance of measures like the inch and quart. The inch, we all know, is about the size of the middle joint of our fingers, and the quart has been the traditional container of the ultimate higher-touch beverage—milk.

The genius of customary measure is its highly evolved inter-relationship of hand and eye. Metric works fine, technically. But when you try to cook, carpenter, or shop with it, as Brand has pointed out, metric fights the hand. In Japan, which has been trying to go metric for forty years, architects design in metric and the contractors blithely build (even skyscrapers) by the traditional shaku-sun measure.

The high touch of traditional measure is simply too well-ingrained for us to want to change without good reason to do so. High-tech metric has gone as far as it is going to go.

High Touch: The Need to Be Together

High tech/high touch. The more technology we introduce into society, the more people will aggregate, will want to be with other people: movies, rock concerts, shopping. Shopping malls, for example, are now the third most frequented space in our lives, following home and workplace.

About seven years ago, in 1975, after we invented those huge screens that you could have in your living room to watch movies, Arthur D. Little issued a report suggesting that by the year 1980 there would be almost no movie theaters in the United States. What they didn't understand was high tech/high touch. You do not go to a movie just to see a movie. You go to a movie to cry or laugh with 200 other people. It is an event.

Perhaps it is the high-touch need to be together that enables us to tolerate the high levels of density we experience in many crowded cities.

And what could be more high tech/high touch than an impossibly crowded nightclub dance floor with flashing strobe lights circling above?

Because we want to be with each other, I don't think many of us will choose to work at home in our electronic cottages as I discussed in Chapter 1. Very few people will be willing to stay home all of the time and tap out messages to the office. People want to go to the office. People want to be with people, and the more technology we pump into the society, the more people will

45

want to be with people. It is good for emergencies (like Mondays) and to be able to stay home on some days and deal with your office and work through a computer is an attractive occasional option. During certain specific periods—the late stages of a pregnancy, for example—it is useful to be able to continue work via a computer. But for the most part, we will seek the high touch of the office.

The utilization of electronic cottages will be very limited: People want to go to the office; people want to be with people.

The same may be said for electronic marketing. The same people who predicted we would all fly helicopters (those captives of straight-line, technological extrapolation) now say that with computers at home we will shop electronically and stores will become extinct. We will eventually do some shopping by computer, but only for staple items of which we have a very clear sense and experience. It will be no substitute for the serendipity and high touch of shopping for what we want to be surprised about.

Computer buying will never replace the serendipity and high touch of shopping for what we want to be surprised about.

Teleconferencing. That is another trend that will not happen. Talking with people via television cannot begin to substitute for the high touch of a meeting, no matter how rational it is in saving fuel and overhead. If it is of little importance, use teleconference. Be appropriate. But we have to face it: There is no end to meetings.

Teleconferencing is so rational, it will never succeed.

On the other hand, videotechnology works wonderfully in a high-touch situation:

- A Tahoe City realtor told the *Los Angeles Times* that videotapes are proving a useful marketing tool for vacation property: The tapes can be mailed to prospective buyers, who can then decide whether the property is worth the trip to see it.

- A Rockville, Maryland, talent agency shows engaged couples videotapes of the bands available to play at their wedding.
- A Washington, D.C., woman offers what amounts to "shrink selection service" whereby prospective patients can view psychologists and psychiatrists, taped at their offices, talking about themselves and their theories.
- Then, of course, there is the proliferation of videodating services. Not everyone's cup of tea, perhaps. But the services do appear successful.

High Touch: In the Schools

Readers of the *Trend Report*'s education section noticed a curious phenomenon for volume two of the 1980 report. During the exact same time period that articles on education appeared throughout the nation reporting widespread use of the computer in the schools, a wave of stories appeared about either reviving religion in the schools or about teaching values.

Twenty-five states were debating the questions of voluntary prayer, posting the Ten Commandments, and silent meditation at school.

And many schools incorporated values discussions into the regular curriculum:

- A Denver, Colorado, elementary school program seeks to "break sexual stereotypes limiting career opportunities."
- At a Kansas City, Missouri, school, students discussed whether or not a friend should turn another friend in for shoplifting.
- In Scarsdale, New York, moral questions are used to teach an "argumentative writing course."
- In Tulsa, Oklahoma, an elementary school is testing the positive-thinking theories of former Dallas salesman Zig Ziglar. The course's motivational message is "I can-ness."

Conclusion? Again it is high tech/high touch. As computers begin to take over some of the basics of education, schools will more and more be called upon to take responsibility for teaching values and motivation, if not religion.

47

High Tech/High Touch: Home and Factory

The need for compensatory high touch is everywhere. The more high tech in our society, the more we will want to create high-touch environments, with soft edges balancing the hard edges of technology.

As we moved through the 1970s, industrialization and its technology moved more and more from the workplace to the home. High-tech furniture echoed the glories of an industrial past. Kitchen tech, whose high point was Cuisinart, industrialized our kitchens as minimalism dehumanized our living rooms. And of course the ultimate intrusion of home-style high tech is the personal computer.

But the brief period of interest in high-tech furniture and minimalist design was just that—brief. It is now behind us. Ahead of us for a long period is an emphasis on high touch and comfort to counterbalance a world going mad with high technology.

Among other things, this means soft colors—pastels are becoming quite popular—coziness, plumpness, the unconstructed look, and links to the past. Folk art is the perfect counterpoint to a computerized society. No wonder handmade quilts are so popular. Even country music's popularity is partly a response to electronic rock.

Uniformity in style, whether it is traditional or modern, will give way to a great eclectic mix. Mixing furniture styles, accessories, and art can be a bold statement of individuality. The same goes for original art and one-of-a-kind furniture.

Granted, at this point few of us appear terribly original, what with our need to have a designer's initials on all our clothing, fabrics, sheets, towels. And now even chocolates.

But it is all part of a transition. We needed to buy designer this and designer that because we were not yet confident of our own ability to make an individual statement.

Even insecurity does not last long in a fast-changing world.

Now we are moving in the direction of putting our own imprimatur on our environment, allowing personal visions amid the technology.

High-tech robots and high-touch quality circles are moving into our factories at the same time—and the more robots, the more circles.

In our factories we are also moving in the dual directions of high tech/high touch: high-tech robots and high-touch quality control circles—groups of workers who discuss work-related problems and solutions.

As we restructure from an industrial to an information society, we are moving more information and more technology, in the form of quality circles *and* robots, into our factories. And (high tech/high touch) the more robots, the more quality circles.

Similarly, when we moved from an agricultural to an industrial society, we moved more industry into our farms. In about 1800, 90 percent of our population produced 100 percent of the food. Today, as mentioned in the previous chapter, only 3 percent of our population produces 120 percent of the food we need. The surplus is stored or exported.

That is the direction our industrial production is going. As part of this process, we will increasingly run our factories with information rather than laborers. Robots will play a big role in bringing this about. Conservative estimates predict that by 1990 we will be producing 17,000 robots per year and that the total robot workforce will reach 80,000. Most experts would double those figures.

Needed: High-Tech Skills

The skills to maintain high-technology systems are becoming as important as the creative skills that design the systems.

All across the country, buses, planes, utilities, even sewage treatment plants, miracles of modern science, are breaking down and proving unusable because we are unable to provide the companion miracle of modern maintenance.

The lack of skilled workers is most alarming in the area of nuclear power. Everyone is familiar with Three Mile Island, but numerous other dangerous incidents have been caused by carelessness or ignorance. In Virginia, the North Anna One nuclear plant was shut down when a worker's shirt snagged a circuit breaker; previously, employees at the same plant had jammed an emergency switch with a pencil and paper clip. At Florida Power's Crystal River plant, a potentially serious leakage of radioactive water may have been unknowingly caused by an electrician. At the Rancho Seco plant in California a similar incident occurred several years ago when a technician dropped a console light bulb into the wiring.

New safety requirements in the nuclear industry have created a need for more engineers and other technicians, while the fear of another Three Mile Island has led to greater emphasis on hiring qualified workers. But as the need has grown, the number of workers has not. The unpopularity of nuclear power on college campuses and its uncertain future have discouraged many students from entering the field. There was a 19-percent drop in the number of students receiving a bachelor of science in nuclear engineering in 1980, and a 10-percent drop in those taking a master's. Regulators fear that plants, unable to find qualified workers, will lower their safety standards; in fact, one of the Nuclear Regulatory Commission's regional offices recently ordered Toledo Edison Company to retract a series of promotions at its Davis-Besse nuclear plant. The promotions had gone to unqualified workers, they said, making the plant unsafe.

The panel studying the crash of the DC-10 in Chicago in 1979, which killed 273 people, listed improper maintenance as the starting point for the failures that led to the crash. That and similar findings have led the airline industry to worry that too many functions are being taken over by unqualified workers.

Both Houston, Texas, and Baltimore, Maryland, have plans to renovate old buses, at considerable expense, because the new "advance design buses" manufactured by both General Motors and Grumman's Flxible Industries (the only type currently available in the United States) have proved too difficult and expensive to maintain. In Connecticut electrical fires have started in the engine boxes of five Grumman Flxible's buses. Miami's new air-conditioned buses broke down when the air conditioning was turned on. Houston has 150 of the General Motors buses, which have lifts for the handicapped, wide seating, air conditioning, and windows that don't open. The city found itself in a crisis situation last summer when the air conditioning on dozens of the new buses broke down, making them unusable. Authorities solved the problem by removing the windows on forty of the buses, a short-term solution at best.

In 1979 a new sewage treatment plant at San Jose, California, broke down, flooding a billion gallons of partially treated sewage into San Francisco Bay and wiping out marine life. Floating bacteria had clogged the screens, and the bacteriologist, who might have corrected the problem, had resigned and not been replaced. In all, there were nineteen vacancies on the operating staff. Between September 1979 and March 1980, the state of Maryland ordered 24 malfunctioning treatment plants to cut back the flow of sewage. And when the Environmental Protection Agency checked 100 new sewage plants, it found 20 operating poorly at times. "It takes a lot of judgment to run these plants, but finding good operators is a nationwide problem," said Laurence D. Bory of the American Consulting Engineers Council. In an increasingly complicated area, one with the potential for causing massive pollution, the level of salaries is incredibly low, in some parts of the country falling under $10,000 a year. It's not surprising that a study conducted for the Water Pollution Control Federation shows operators often lack the experience and training to understand how the plants operate. "Operators are no longer people who should be thought of as coming to work in T-shirts," says Bill Parish of Maryland's sewage plant compliance section. "They need mechanical engineering and biological backgrounds."

Even the family automobile is becoming too complicated for most of us to fix. "There is already a competency crunch among the nation's 525,000 automechanics," says the president of the National Institute for Automotive Service Excellence, which certifies mechanics. "We may already have passed the day when an individual could work on his own car," asserts John Betti, a Ford vice president.

What's going to happen when we get artificial hearts? Unless we begin to fill the need for skilled technicians, we will be forced to abandon much of our technological infrastructure and return to older, simpler methods.

The high-tech repair problems we already face are testimony to the need for mechanically skilled engineers, technicians, and repair people. All of these are good occupational bets for the next twenty years. But better incentives will have to be created to attract and develop the skills needed to keep our technology viable.

Living in a High-Tech World

Generally speaking, most of us will want to develop our own ways to compensate for the high-tech influence of the computer in our work and home environment. Soft shapes and colors are some of the design responses possible. And parents will have to watch to see that children don't become completely wired to the computer (remember television?).

We will have a greater need to compensate for technology by being out in nature more often, going camping, going to the seashore. You may have to drag your children away from the computer or video games to take them fishing or bicycling.

In a high-tech information world, where we use our brainpower instead of performing physical labor, as did the factory workers of the industrial era, we will want to use our hands and bodies more in our leisure activities to balance the constant use of mental energy at work. You can see this already in the popularity of gardening, cooking, and home repair and renovation.

The balance between the high tech and high touch is one way to evaluate the usefulness and lasting value of the many high-tech (and high-priced) consumer gadgets that fill the marketplace. I for one wish I had not bought a food processor. I use it infrequently, preferring the high touch of chopping foods by hand, even though it takes longer.

The food processor is only one high-tech temptation, and there will be many more. We can probably all do with a little less enthusiasm for the latest technological wonder vying for our attention and our wallets, and seek a little more high-touch balance in our lives.

The Danger of the Technofix Mentality

"Man is a clever animal. There is no way to keep him from devising new tools. The error lies in thinking that new tools are the solution. It could be a fatal error," writes John Hess in a *GEO* magazine article entitled "Computer Madness."

When we fall into the trap of believing or, more accurately, hoping that technology will solve all our problems, we are actually abdicating the high touch of personal responsibility. Our technological fantasies illustrate the point. We are always awaiting the new magical pill that will enable us to eat all the fattening food we want, and not gain weight; burn all the gasoline we want, and not pollute the air; live as immoderately as we choose, and not contract either cancer or heart disease.

In our minds, at least, technology is always on the verge of liberating us from personal discipline and responsibility. Only it never does and it never will.

The more high technology around us, the more the need for human touch.

That is why the human potential movement that advocates both discipline and responsibility is such a critical part of the high-tech/high-touch equation. By discovering our potential as human beings we participate in the evolution of the human race. We develop the inner knowledge, the wisdom, perhaps, required to guide our exploration of technology.

With the high-touch wisdom gained studying our potential as human beings, we may learn the ways to master the greatest high-tech challenge that has ever faced mankind—the threat of total annihilation by nuclear warfare.

High tech/high touch. The principle symbolizes the need for balance between our physical and spiritual reality.

3

From a National Economy to a World Economy

The two most important things to remember about world economics are that yesterday is over and that we must now adjust to living in a world of interdependent communities. Some of us find those ideas hard to accept.

We in America have come to love playing the starring role in world economics. Perhaps we rightfully earned that place of honor. During the 1950s and 1960s, our growth and productivity rates and the quality of our products set the pace for the rest of the industrialized world:

- For two decades after World War II, American productivity growth increased more than 3 percent per year.
- In 1960 the United States had about 25 percent of the world market share in manufacturing.
- In the important U.S. market, American companies produced 95 percent of the autos, steel, and consumer electronics sold in 1960.

That was yesterday. Today, we no longer dominate the world's economy:

- Between 1973 and 1977, productivity growth decreased to about 1 percent per year. And in 1979, productivity growth declined 2 percent.
- In 1979 the U.S. share of world manufacturing slipped to just over 17 percent.
- In 1979 American companies' share of the domestic market dropped to only 79 percent of the autos, 86 percent of the steel, and *less than 50 percent* of the consumer electronics sold in the United States.

Japan has seized from us the position as the world's leading industrial power, having surpassed the United States both in steel and automobile production. On a per capita basis, Japan's GNP is about even with ours, with Japan having the growth edge. We are ahead only because of the sheer size of our economy.

Japan is number one, but that is like a new world champion in a declining sport.

But it is not so much that Japan is taking our place. For Japan, in turn, is being challenged by Singapore, South Korea, and Brazil—the dazzling economies of these newly developed Third World nations. Yesterday is over, and tomorrow is not going to last forever, either.

It is too late to recapture our industrial supremacy because we are no longer an industrial economy.

Nevertheless, how many of us realize that we continue to base our national policies, goals, and objectives on the implicit assumption of continued U.S. industrial leadership? How many of us admit that we have already lost that position?

"There are no passengers on spaceship *Earth*," Marshall McLuhan said. "We are all crew."

In the new economic era, all of the countries on the world scene are growing increasingly interdependent, despite the fact that in our home countries we are behaving in ways that are increasingly independent of our centralized governments. Hence the popular dictum "Thinking globally, acting locally." For instance, Illinois and Florida, among many other states, are trading directly with countries around the globe.

their wealth by advance knowledge of Waterloo. Carrier pigeons dispatched from the scene brought them the news of Napoleon's defeat. A few swift moves on the stock exchange and a fortune was amassed.

Advantages like that are hard to come by these days, because for all practical purposes there is no information float. Would-be Rothschilds in the United States or in Singapore, for that matter, have equal access—in real time—to knowledge about the value of the deutsche mark and the Japanese yen in world markets. (There is one interesting advantage, however. In the financial community, London will always have an edge because it is the only financial center in the world where you can call Tokyo early in the morning and the United States during business hours before you yourself go home for the day at a civilized hour.)

The information float collapsed because of a telecommunications infrastructure that grows more sophisticated, and more accessible, every day. By the end of this decade, for instance, this world will have one billion telephones, all interconnected and almost all capable of dialing direct to any other. More instantaneously shared information.

Industry: The New Pecking Order

As the nations of the Earth move toward a global economy, it is no longer clear who is going to make what. We are deeply in a process of a global redistribution of labor and of production: Spain and Brazil are replacing Japan and Sweden as shipbuilders; the United States is yielding on apparel, steel, and automobiles to Third World countries.

In turn, part of the redistribution process is that *all* developed countries in this world are deindustrializing. Whether they want it or not, their industrial activity is slowing down. Their growth rates tell the story.

The seven major industrial nations—the United States, Japan, West Germany, France, Britain, Italy, and Canada—averaged a skimpy 1 percent growth rate for the first half of 1980. During the second half, they did even worse. Together, their economies declined an average of 1.25 percent.

Japan fared the best by far. Without her impressive statistics to bolster up the average, the group would have looked much worse. Japan grew at a 5-percent rate for the first half of 1980 and at a rate of 2.75 percent during the second. Most forecasters believe Japan can keep up a 4- to 5-percent growth rate until the 1990s.

At a time when American businesses are frequently criticized for being too shortsighted and too quick to seek immediate profits, it is important to note that real economic strength is not built—or destroyed—in a matter of a few years of sharply fluctuating percentage points.

London's *Economist,* with a global view almost always more balanced than that of the American media, has pointed out that American economic dominance was achieved by a "small lead in productivity growth in the Grant-to-Truman years."

During that time, between 1870 and 1950, the United States held a slow, small, but consistent 0.6- to 0.8-percent lead over Britain, Germany, and Japan. It was this plodding but cumulative edge that begat the spectacular growth rates of the 1950s and 1960s.

Since 1950, however, productivity growth in the United States fell some 3 to 5 percent behind Germany and Japan. And it is that cumulative effect that hurts.

The United States must also be concerned about real growth, as well as productivity growth. The United Kingdom, by growing just 1 percent less than France, Germany, and the United States, managed in a couple of generations to transform itself from the wealthiest society on Earth to a relatively poor member of the Common Market.

When we think of deindustrialization, we tend to immediately think of our great negative model Great Britain. But even the Japanese are getting out of industries such as steel making and shipbuilding. They realize that in the future South Korea will make better and cheaper steel and Brazil and Spain will make better and cheaper ships.

Made in the Third World

While the economies of the developed world creep along and enter periodic recessions, several Third World nations have entered phenomenal boom cycles. Over the next decade, we will see a number of new "Japans."

Hong Kong, South Korea, and Taiwan were the new leaders at first, but recently Latin American countries, which tripled their collective Gross Domestic Products (GDP) during the 1960s and 1970s, have grabbed an increasing share of the production boom.

Mexico grew about 8 percent in 1981. By 1980, Brazil was the tenth largest economy and Mexico's economy was about the size of Sweden's or Belgium's. The twenty fastest-growing economies for the period 1970 and 1977 were *all* Third World countries. Some were oil exporting countries—Saudi Arabia and Iran, for instance. But the vast majority were not: Botswana was up an annual average of 15.8 percent; South Korea up nearly 10 percent; Singapore up 8.6 percent; and the Dominican Republic up 8 percent. The economic stars—Singapore, Taiwan, Hong Kong, South Korea, Mexico, and Brazil—averaged 9.4-percent annual growth in the 1970s. The economic powers of the Third World are growing with purpose and design: South Korea, Taiwan, Brazil, and Singapore invested between 25 and 35 percent of their GNPs into their economies, nearly twice the rate of the United States. During the past decade, the Third World has begun to take up most of the world's industrial tasks.

The United States and the rest of the developed countries of the world are on their way to losing their dominant positions in industries that include steel, automobiles, railroad equipment, machinery, appliances, textiles, shoes, and apparel. By the year 2000, the Third World will manufacture as much as 30 percent of the world's goods. That is only eighteen years from now, the same number of years ago that Lyndon Johnson defeated Barry Goldwater. It is just around the corner.

To the chagrin of many industrialists, the Third World appears competent in its new industrial role. For years, U.S. manufacturers have asserted that their products were superior to less expensive imports. But consumers have forced them to give up their rhetoric and face the truth; in many industries (tape recorders, auto parts, apparel) the products of developing countries are every bit as good as those made in the industrial world—and they are cheaper.

Recently, the Third World reached an important industrial

benchmark. For the first time, the non–oil-producing developing countries collectively exported more manufactured goods than raw materials; an added confirmation of the trend toward the Third World's new power in manufacturing:

- Singapore is second only to the United States in its current backlog of oil rigs.
- Hong Kong and Taiwan are moving out of textiles and light electronic assembly and into more complicated computer technology.
- South Korea is challenging Japan's position in home electronics. The reason we hear so little about it, though, is because their products are marketed in this country under familiar trade names, such as Sears, J. C. Penney, and Sylvania.

One key element fueling the Third World's industrial drive is its growing workforce, which is mammoth in size compared with that of the industrialized world. The U.S. Census estimates that the workforce in the industrialized nations (members of the Organization for Economic Cooperation and Development) will increase only 10 percent by the year 2000. In Asia and the Pacific, the workforce will increase by a stunning 55 percent. In Latin America and Africa, workers will increase by an incredible 80 percent.

What does the industrialization of the Third World mean for the United States and other industrialized nations? Simply stated, it will mean a heightening of the present trends: U.S. manufacturers will continue to produce less and less in the world market while foreign manufacturers will make even stronger inroads with American consumers.

Just since 1960 alone the U.S. share of the world export pie has dropped from 16 to 11 percent, a dramatic change. Clearly, this country has to wake up.

For Third World countries, changing conditions will bring about increased competition with *one another* for a share of the manufacturing trade. That competition has heated up considerably with the recent emergence of China as a new contender in manufacturing. Until the late 1970s, China aimed to fund its ambitious modernization plans by selling raw materials, primarily oil. But China's leaders have changed their strategy. The

Chinese will concentrate instead on light industry—textiles, baskets, bicycles, radio and television assembly. Production in these industries soared 23 percent during the first half of 1980. In the U.S. market, China has edged out other Third World countries such as the Philippines, Mexico, India, and Sri Lanka in imports of cotton handkerchiefs, trousers, and tea.

Not surprisingly, China will emerge as a textile leader. By the year 2000, it will probably be employing 4 million textile workers, whereas textile employment in South Korea and Taiwan will remain about steady, and in Hong Kong will decrease by 25 percent. In fact, textile employment decreased in Hong Kong for the first time ever in 1979.

Even the fast-growing Third World countries must learn the same lessons about the shifting global economy as the developed industrial nations: not only that yesterday is over, but that tomorrow isn't going to last forever, either.

Global Car Wars

The sorting out of global economic priorities is perhaps most dramatic in the auto industry, which has undergone a large-scale shake-up in global production sharing. Four major trends have emerged that will continue to shape the future of the world auto industry.

First, the United States lost its position as the world's premier auto maker. It takes Japan eleven hours to build a car; American workers do it in thirty-one. Japan's robot-equipped Zama plant builds an automobile in nine hours flat. In 1980 Japan became the number-one automobile maker in the world (with an output of 11 million vehicles), exceeding U.S. production by an almost unbelievable 40 percent.

The second key trend is the move toward global saturation in the auto industry.

What's really remarkable about Japan is that, even as it becomes the number-one automobile maker in the world, Japan does not see the automobile industry as a growth industry. Japan is well aware that, in the developed countries worldwide, we are reaching saturation and moving to a replacement market.

Half the American population owns a car already, and in Europe, where public transporation is superior to that of the

United States, the demand is satisfied with one-third of the people owning cars. The replacement market in automobiles that's left will fall far short of the dynamic growth market that we've known for the past thirty years.

Furthermore, if we think we are going to supply automobiles to satisfy the Third World's growing demand, we had better think again.

There are eighty-six countries in the world that have automobile assembly lines. Mexico, for example, is fast becoming a major auto producer. Volkswagen, Nissan, Ford, GM, and others operate plants in Mexico, which produced nearly 300,000 autos in 1979. Countries with their own auto plants will be in the best position to meet the local demand for automobiles as the developing world becomes rich enough to purchase them. Furthermore, many developing countries have clearly indicated they will act to protect their own growing auto industries from any invasion by big auto makers.

Incredible though it seems, it's in this environment that the United States government bailed out Chrysler. If we continue in that direction, this country will turn its automobile industry into an employment program, the way the British turned their automobile and steel industries into employment programs. And we will probably call it "reindustrialization." It was part of the conceit of the U.S. automobile companies that they never diversified. They thought they would go on forever, and then even Henry Ford II, whose grandfather gave the world the car, got out while the getting was good.

The globalization of the world's automobile industry is inevitable.

Many automobile companies are just not going to survive. That's the third important direction in the world auto industry. We have already seen a flurry of cooperative arrangements and joint ventures. Renault has agreed to purchase 10-percent interest in Volvo's passenger-car business, and the French auto firm's holdings in American Motors jumped from 5 percent to 46 percent after the American firm fell on hard times. GM owns 34 percent of Japan's Isuzu. Chrysler and Peugeot plan to produce a subcompact in the United States by late 1985, provided Chrysler lasts that long. Honda and B.L. Ltd. (formerly British Leyland) have agreed to produce Hondas in Great Britain. Nissan, which owns 37 percent of Spain's Motor Iberica, has a joint venture with Alfa Romeo to manufacture 60,000 cars per year in Italy.

But that is only the beginning. Expect the next round of auto ventures to produce mergers, buy-outs, and bankruptcies. The automobile industry is well on the way to becoming the first globalized industry.

The thirty automobile companies now competing on an international scale will, by the end of the 1980s, be reduced to as few as seven to eight companies or alliances of companies—perhaps just Volkswagen, Nissan, Toyota, and GM. The internationalization of the world's automobile industry is inevitable.

This environment is leading to production of the "world car," which has come to mean a line of autos made from components that are manufactured and assembled around the globe.

Ford's new world car, the Escort, is being put together in the United States, Britain, and Germany from parts made in Spain, Italy, Britain, Japan, and Brazil. General Motors' new J model is assembled in the United States, Canada, Australia, Brazil, and South Africa.

Although there is much talk about world cars, the internationalization of the automobile-components industry is already complete. American imports of automobile components have increased dramatically:

• Volkswagen provides engines for Dodge Omni/Horizon cars and Mitsubishi the engines for Chrysler's Dodge Colt, Plymouth Champ, Dodge Challenger, and Plymouth Sapphoro models. Of course, many of the components are made in the Third World. Volkswagen is building commercial vehicles with components made in Mexico and Brazil.
• South Korea and Taiwan manufacture everything from ignition wires to intake valves, while Brazil makes entire auto and truck engines.

The globalization of the auto industry has sparked serious reaction from U.S. labor leaders, who fear it will be used against workers in collective bargaining to play the workers of one country off against the workers of another.

Says UAW President Douglas Fraser: "All workers of the

world are going to be exploited unless we unite in solidarity. If you're going to have multinational companies, then you're going to have some kind of corresponding unit for the labor movement."

The fourth important direction is that Japan will have to bow to increased pressure to situate its automobile plants around the globe—especially in other industrialized countries. Generally speaking, Japan's auto makers have resisted going abroad, fearing they would lose production advantages there. Consultants have repeatedly warned Japanese firms that investments in the United States would be unwise because of difficulty in getting parts, problems in organizing production, and—to our embarrassment—low productivity on the part of American workers. When the Japanese did invest overseas, it was usually in Third World countries such as Brazil. But now the West is clamoring for Japanese factories to offset losses in local markets to Japanese firms. In 1981, Japanese auto imports alone held a 30-percent share of the U.S. auto market, and by spring 1982 imports accounted for 70 percent of the automobiles sold in the bellwether state of California. Every state in the Union except Alaska and Hawaii has invited Toyota to locate there. Americans are now reasoning: "If we are going to buy their cars anyway, let's try to get the jobs for our workers." The Japanese will have to give in eventually—and should have done so long ago. Protectionism, even in the form of President Reagan's seemingly benign "voluntary restraint," is the most dangerous threat to Japan's continued prosperity.

In the meantime, Japanese investment is trickling in. Nissan is building a $300-million plant in Tennessee that will begin making pickup trucks in 1983. Don't look for Japanese plants in Detroit, where the out-of-work auto workers are, but in the more attractive economic climate of the booming South and West. Nevertheless, Honda is trying out an old industrial setting near Columbus, Ohio, where—beginning in late 1982—they will eventually turn out 10,000 cars a month.

Production Sharing: A New Global Model

Production sharing, as Peter Drucker has said, will be the prevailing form of worldwide economic integration. Auto makers are not the only ones to recognize its potential. So have baseball mitt manufacturers: 95 percent of the baseball mitts used in the great American pastime are made in Japan. But they are made from American cowhide, which is shipped to Brazil for tanning before it goes to Japan to be made into baseball mitts. Shoes are often shipped among several countries in the course of production.

Before Japan began making microprocessing chips, the only thing made in Japan on a hand-held electric calculator was the nameplate that said "Made in Japan"; the electronic chips came from the United States. They were assembled in Singapore, Indonesia, or Nigeria, and the steel housing came from India. The "Made in Japan" label was tacked on the calculator when it arrived in Yokohama or Kobe.

An American architectural-engineering firm is building three hotels in Saudi Arabia. The room modules for the hotels—right down to the soap dishes in the bathrooms—will be made in Brazil. The labor to build the hotels is coming from South Korea, and we Americans are doing the construction management, the information side. That's a model we will see a lot in the future.

Companies like General Electric are beginning to think of themselves as world trading companies. They will tell you that their competition is not Westinghouse, but Japan's Hitachi and Germany's Siemens. General Electric won a $160-million contract—not very big for them, but still significant—from Romania to help build a nuclear power plant. They beat Hitachi and Siemens on that contract because they agreed to 100-percent countertrade transactions—in other words, barter. GE's price is taken out in Romanian cement that is being brokered by a German firm for use in Egypt.

Barter agreements used to be considered rare, if not downright odd. No longer. Some of America's largest firms—Occidental Petroleum, General Motors, and General Electric, among others—are bartering with countries that cannot afford to trade any other way, like Eastern bloc countries, China, and developing countries in Africa and Asia, which lack hard currency.

When U.S. firms barter, they usually end up brokering the commodity that the trading partner offers. Said the head of one countertrade department in a large U.S. firm: "I don't care what the product is, so long as I can find a market for it and move it."

Somewhat related to barter is the practice of selling developing countries secondhand plants that American companies consider obsolete. Both parties usually gain from the transaction: The seller gets rid of surplus equipment and the buyer gets good equipment for far less than it would cost new. For example, a used alkaline plant was dismantled in Canada and sent to India, where it was reassembled, at a total cost of $4 million. A new plant would have cost more than $10 million. Another model for a global economy.

Structural Adjustment: Learning to Bend

We have much to learn from both Japan and West Germany on the subject of structural adjustment.

After the Germans surrendered their lead in shipbuilding to South Korea, Taiwan, and Brazil, which collectively captured 30 percent of the recent new orders, Germany kept its shipyards busy by concentrating on repairs and on converting engines for better fuel consumption.

The German textile industry suffered the loss of some 100,000 jobs during the 1970s, but it went ahead and introduced unpopular new technology anyway. That move saved what textile jobs remained for the 1980s.

Germany and Britain, which are similar in size and industrial structure, provide contrasting case studies in dealing with structural adjustment. Britain invests twice as much in industry as Germany, but Germany gets far better results through its policy of picking winners, that is, concentrating on emerging industries such as computers and electronics.

The Germans are also more willing to invest in human resources. During a one-year period between 1974 and 1975, the Germans retrained eight times as many workers as did the British.

The Japanese and Germans, then, try to promote structural readjustment. The rest of us try to prevent it. And in so doing, we miss out on many opportunities.

What sort of structural-adjustment policy would work best in this country? Generally speaking, the government should stay out of the way of the sunrise industries (electronics, computer software, cable television, biotechnology) and allow the mature industries to level off.

The one exception is training: not that the government should do the training itself, but it could pay workers who have lost jobs in the old industries to obtain training in the new.

Presumably this is the responsibility of the Labor Department's Trade Adjustment Assistance Program. In truth, however, only a fraction of the program's monies is spent on training—most of the annual $1.6-billion program goes out in cash subsidies, over and above unemployment compensation, to workers who have lost their jobs because of imports. The idea behind the program is that recipients, mostly auto and steelworkers, deserve to "get something extra" to help make up for Washington's failure to protect their industries. With combined benefits, many auto and steelworkers collected $12,000 tax-free the year after they lost jobs—a very bad investment on the government's part, which produced no "adjustment" whatsoever. Several hundred thousand of these workers are now left with no jobs and no benefits either.

In contrast, the minuscule amount of money spent on training has produced results, so long as the funds were disbursed on a decentralized basis in response to concrete local initiative. Clearly, all the unemployed auto and steelworkers are not going to become computer programmers. But the Trade Adjustment Assistance Program can cite many examples of cases where a counselor at a local job service office helped a jobless worker from a dying industry to learn new skills in a growing new business, applied for funds to train the worker, and facilitated a successful transition. It's the big programs that don't work. Case by case, there are many successes. Otherwise unemployment would be far worse.

Global Economy/Global Investments

In this environment of a truly world economy, there are great opportunities to work and invest in each other's territory.

Helped by the decline of the dollar in the 1970s, the United States became a foreign-exchange mecca for European investors. The largest investors in America today are not from the

Middle East but from the Netherlands, Britain, Canada, West Germany, Switzerland, Japan, and France.

Foreign ownership of American property will continue to increase and Americans will learn to accept and even welcome it. The Commerce Department has tried to estimate how much money foreigners have invested here and came up with a figure of $52 billion, but that does not take into account the huge sums that foreigners have borrowed from U.S. banks to invest here. A U.S. congressional committee investigating foreign ownership put the figure at $350 billion.

By 1980 the Japanese alone controlled wholly or in part some 225 U.S. manufacturing companies with operations in forty-two states and a combined workforce of 60,000. And a Japanese firm (Nomura Securities International, Inc.) became the first Japanese member of the New York Stock Exchange in July 1981. Giant Hitachi got itself listed in April of 1982.

Business is replacing politics as the world's gossip.

Concern about OPEC taking over America fizzled out after a careful look behind the scenes. It's true that Abu Dhabi bought up 4 percent of Eastern Airlines and that a Saudi entrepreneur bought the largest building in Miami for $50 million. It is also true that Saudi millionaire Gaith Pharon bought up Bert Lance's stock in the National Bank of Georgia. But beyond these few visible, controversial deals, the total amount of investment by oil-producing interests doesn't amount to much. A Commerce Department–Office of Foreign Investment study found only seventeen OPEC-type investments totaling a paltry $156 million during 1979—less than 1 percent of the total foreign investment in the United States.

Along with the Commerce Department, the Conference Board has been tracking foreign investments or expansions in this country on a state-by-state basis. Their study showed that North Carolina had the most investors—thirty-six in 1980, compared with only thirteen in 1978. Runners-up were California and Pennsylvania with thirty foreign investments each in 1980. Foreign investors seem to be shying away from New York, however. Only twenty-three investments were made there in 1980, down from fifty the previous year.

In all, 174 manufacturing firms were sold to foreign investors in 1980, reports the Conference Board, nearly three times the number in 1975.

Not only is foreign ownership of U.S. properties increasing, it is being actively sought here. Forty states competed to get the $250-million Volkswagen plant that was eventually built in Pennsylvania. Thirty American states now have offices in major European capitals seeking investments in their areas.

A leading edge here is banking. The number of foreign banks with a U.S. presence jumped from 278 in 1978 to 315 in 1979. Foreigners now own 12 percent of U.S. banking assets. There is a large Japanese presence and also there has been a huge growth of Spanish banks in the United States.

More than 100 U.S. banks, whose assets total $77 billion, are owned wholly or in part by foreigners. Foreign banks hold 40 percent of all commercial loans in New York State. California, a state that often shows the way for America, has 20 of the 300 largest banks in this country. Ten of those 20 are now foreign-owned.

It goes both ways. Many U.S. companies now do as much as a third of their banking with European and Japanese banks. Both Citibank and Chase Manhattan derived 10 percent of their 1980 income (before securities and income transactions) from their operations in Brazil.

New Tasks, New Measures

We have two economies in the United States today: a sunrise economy and a sunset economy.

It's becoming clear that yesterday is over, and as the Third World prepares to take over the major industrial tasks, the developed countries must move on to the new enterprises.

Actually, we are in the midst of doing that right now. In the industrialized nations, we have two separate economies: sunrise industries and sunset industries. This dual economy is a new phenomenon that has caused a lot of confusion in analyzing our economic situation.

I do not believe that the United States is, or has recently been, in a recession. In the United States we have parts of the

71

country that are in prosperity and parts that are in depression, some business sectors that are doing very well, and some that are depressed. Economists have averaged the two together and declared the nation in a recession. In late 1981, the unemployment rate in Detroit was 12.4 percent; in Buffalo, 9.6 percent; in St. Louis, 7.9 percent; in Minneapolis–St. Paul, 4.9 percent; in Atlanta, 5.5 percent; in Austin, 4.1 percent; and in Denver, 4.7 percent. By averaging, we lose all that intelligence about what is going on. One of my clients has begun to look at the economic health of each state, state by state. What is the economic health of Texas? Michigan? Florida? The idea is then to look at and learn from the mosaic and not mindlessly average everything and be left wholly uninstructed.

We lose all intelligence by averaging: To understand the U.S. economy today, we have to look at the economic health of each of the states and each of the business sectors.

The problem is that economists continue to root their judgments in the old indexes, and most of those are buried in the dying industries. We need new concepts and we need new data if we are to understand what is going on today, to say nothing of what may go on tomorrow.

Economists predict gloom because they focus on industrial companies; that's like predicting a family's future by watching only the grandparents.

Instead of constantly bemoaning the loss of the old industries, we must explore the adventurous new technologies: electronics, biotechnology, alternative energy sources, mining of the seabeds, robotics, and more. Ten years from now, the electronics industry will be bigger than auto and steel are today. The United States alone will need a million or more programmers of software by the end of the decade.

The huge increase in small businesses in the United States will provide a huge market for computers as well. Sales of small computers to small businesses will increase from approximately $590 million in 1980 to $2.7 billion in 1985. Also around the mid-decade, sales of home computers are expected to take a sharp upturn—better software will be developed by then, right around the time prices are expected to drop. Both will be sales boosters. The United States must retain its technical and competitive advantage in computers, though, if we are to take full advantage of the new markets in the Third World. As is well known, Japan's highest priority is perfecting and fine-tuning its computer industry, with Fujitsu planning to go after both IBM and this country's successful small computer makers in every possible market—the United States, other developed countries, and the Third World—where a Japanese success can mean billion dollar losses for U.S. companies.

Then there's the biotechnology revolution. Biology will be to the twenty-first century what physics and chemistry were to this century.

In this field, there are three main areas of interest: (1) fermentation technology, from which the Japanese have produced new drugs and chemicals; (2) the production of enzymes or "living catalysts," which act the same way as chemical catalysts, that is, they drive chemical reactions further than they would otherwise go without themselves changing; and (3) the aspect we have heard most about—gene splicing.

Gene splicing: more important than atom splitting—unless, of course, we blow ourselves up.

Gene splicing is the most awesome and powerful skill acquired by man since the splitting of the atom. If pursued humanistically, its potential to serve humanity is enormous. We will use it to synthesize expensive natural products—interferon, substances such as insulin, and human endorphins that serve as natural painkillers. We will be able to create a second "green revolution" in agriculture, to produce new high-yield, disease-resistant, self-fertilizing crops. Gene splicing has the potential to synthesize new substances we can substitute for oil, coal, and other raw materials—keys to a self-sustaining society.

Biology is replacing physics as the dominant metaphor of the society.

The next twenty years will be the age of biology in the way that the last twenty years have been the age of microelectronics. Other areas that offer tremendous opportunity are alternative energy sources and conservation products, robotics, and seabed mining. This last technology will require innovative new conglomerates of companies and countries. Hundreds of new energy devices will be commercialized and marketed extensively throughout the decade: new types of power plants; new automobile fuels; new uses for electricity, alcohol, flywheels, and fuel cells, to name a few.

In the area of robotics, the Japanese have pulled far ahead of us. In Japan robots are building robots. In the Yamazaki machine-tool plant, only robots work the night shift, along with one solitary night watchman.

Despite some human worker opposition, we are entering a period of automating our factories. There are only about 1,000 robots in the U.S. auto industry today, but they are earning their keep and gaining a reputation for productivity as well. Quality robots that cost $50,000 each can work two shifts a day for eight years. That figures out to about $5 per hour—quite a bit less than an auto worker's $15 per hour for salary and benefits.

In the United States the guest workers will be robots.

In the area of robotics, Chrysler is ahead of its American competition. Probably because of its financial problems, the auto maker has been forced to experiment with robots. In newly refurbished plants in Delaware and Detroit, 128 robots make K-cars as fast as Japan's robotic Zama plant.

Of course sunrise industries will not account for all future growth. Established businesses, where we are still competitive and where demand remains strong, will continue to grow: aerospace, all of the information processing and telecommunication industries, health care, and medical technology. Information will be the new economic good, and as of now, at least, the United States is the world's leading supplier of information. But America has no manifest destiny to maintain its lead in information. We will still have to work at it.

Global Interdependence

It is especially critical that the industrial countries forge a new relationship with the Third World. The United States, in particular, must move out of that old role as the world's dominant economic and political force. In a genuinely interdependent world where there are several strong countries, it is absurd for this country to assume such a position. Yet, at times we still do.

As some developing countries test the limits of a shifting global balance of power, we are likely to call their political acts "terrorism" and their economic stands "blackmail." Out of habit, we attempt to respond in the old ways. "If the Arabs won't sell us their oil, we'll starve them!" "If the Iranians take our hostages, we'll bomb them back to the Stone Age." Those ways worked back when we ran the world. The problem, of course, is that we don't anymore.

The truth is that the industrial world is confused about the role it should play in relationship with the Third World, which encompasses three-quarters of the human race, most of which is impoverished and hungry. In *Foreign Affairs*, the distinguished political journal, the late British economist Barbara Ward wrote that the "North," the economically advanced countries, have "no strategy and no vision when it comes to their dealings with the . . . developing South."

In an increasingly interdependent world, the developed countries must deal with the Third World. In the past, perhaps the only reason the North had for taking its poorer neighbors into account was that it was morally right to do so. And it still is. Yet, now there is another, perhaps more compelling, motivation: the North's own self-interest.

Only by developing the Third World will the North be assured of adequate markets for its goods. In an interdependent world, aid is not charity; it is investment. And it is an especially strategic investment, considering that traditional markets are quickly becoming saturated.

Caught up in its own economic woes, however, the developed world has failed to recognize the importance of aid. There are a few exceptions, notably the Dutch and the Scandinavians. But in the United States, for example, aid has fallen from 0.50 percent of GNP in 1965 to 0.20 percent of GNP in 1980. Barbara Ward argued that it is in the interest of the developed world to increase aid to at least 0.70 percent of GNP, as recommended by the 1980 Brandt Commission report, drafted by a distinguished group of world citizens from both North and South.

Wrote Barbara Ward, "The whole boom of the 1950s and

1960s would have been inconceivable without the launching pad of the Marshall Plan, which, in giving away for over five years a goodly *two* percent of a much poorer America's GNP, ensured its own prosperity along with that of its neighbors in the North."

The more economically interdependent we become, the more we will do the human thing, in my opinion, and become more assertive about our distinctiveness, especially our languages.

The globalization of our economies will be accompanied by a renaissance in language and cultural assertiveness.

About 125 years ago, when the steam engine and railroads really came on the scene, the writers of the day said we would become one world with one language: English. That didn't occur then and it is not going to happen now, although English will continue to grow as a business language off to the side.

In everyday life, however, as we become an increasingly interdependent global economy, I would look for a renaissance in cultural and linguistic assertiveness.

In short, the Swedes will become more Swedish, the Chinese, more Chinese. And the French, God help us, more French.

Thinking Globally

For Americans, it is self-evident that this is the time to learn another language—and learn it well. The size, proximity, and economic promises of Latin America make Spanish an attractive choice. If you were in the Peace Corps, or have other overseas experience, that will become increasingly valuable.

To be really successful, you will have to be trilingual: fluent in English, Spanish, and computer.

We can expect to buy more quality goods from abroad—not less, as the protectionists would want us to believe. This is the time for business, even small business, to think exports. And isn't it provincial to consider buying stock only in the New York Stock Exchange or the American? There's a whole global economic village that beckons. What about the Tokyo Stock Exchange? The Singapore Exchange? Or the Berlin Exchange or the Mexican Exchange, one of the world's fastest growing.

World Peace Through World Trade

Instead of resisting increased economic interdependence, we should be embracing it wholeheartedly. In my view, it is our great hope for peace.

If we get sufficiently interlaced economically, we will most probably *not* bomb each other off the face of the planet. For example, I suggest that we are so economically intertwined with Japan that if we have any problems with Japan today, we are going to work them out. I think the same will be true globally. We should welcome increased trade with the Soviet Union, all the developed nations, and the Third World, as world trade moves us closer to world peace.

4

From Short Term to Long Term

There is unprecedented criticism of American business management throughout the world today. A great deal of this criticism is because of the short-term orientation of American managers. It is remarkable how willing American business people are to make the current quarter look better at the expense of the future, to sacrifice the future to make this year's bottom line a little more attractive or less embarrassing. The American approach stands in sharp contrast to Japan's sophisticated business leadership, which often does just the opposite, sacrificing now in order to have a healthy future.

There are many signs, however, that American managers are beginning to change. Long-term planning has become a familiar theme in many business circles, particularly for companies operating in global markets. American Standard, Inc.—the transportation and building-products maker—for instance, made a dramatic short- to long-term shift after the 1974 recession, a time when the company was in very bad shape. In 1975 American Standard's board of directors added long-term incentives to the standard annual bonuses for top executives and tied the bonuses to increases in earning per share over a four-year period. Since 1975 profits have grown at an annual rate of 30 percent and the company now has three concurrent long-term executive bonus plans.

Learning from the Environment

Although Japan's example inspired part of the shift to long-range thinking, there is another important factor behind the changes American business is beginning to make.

During the past decade, the debate over the environment and nonrenewable resources has raised our collective consciousness about the dangers of the short-term approach. As a general proposition, we have become much more sensitive to the longer-range implications of our short-term actions. It has become apparent to most people, for example, that the short-term convenience that encouraged us to pollute the air and water was not worth the long-range damage done to the quality of our lives and our environment. All the forest-products companies now have impressive reforesting programs as a result of the shared realization that if we just kept cutting down trees without replanting, few would be left for our children and their children.

The ground is right for a shift to long-term: Values and necessity are coming up on the same side. We experience change when there is a confluence of changing values and economic necessity. The change in values from short-term to long-term was amply articulated in the environmental resources debate. Now economic necessity is crashing in on us in the form of striking and perilous inability to compete as well as Japan, indeed as well as we used to in the world economic market. We basically have to reconceptualize what we are up to. And that is what we have begun to do.

Short-Term Rewards, "Numbers," and the B-Schools

During the past two decades there has been a lot of support for the short-term; the reward systems are all structured that way.

All the judgments of Wall Street are short-term—oriented; executive salary and bonus plans are almost all geared that way; chief executive officers' tenure averages only five years, and they

80

all want to make their mark during that short period when they are heading up their company.

Reginald Jones, after retiring as board chairman and CEO of the General Electric Company, said that "too many managers feel under pressure to concentrate on the short-term in order to satisfy the financial community and the owners of the enterprise—the stockholders. In the United States, if your firm has a bad quarter, it's headlines. Real trouble ensues. The stock price falls out of bed. That's far different from Japan and Germany."

In the United States, Wall Street puts up the capital and demands (short-term) results. One of Japanese industry's strengths (and Germany's, too, to a lesser degree) is that 80 percent of its permanent capital is provided by banks, with companies grouped around each major bank like satellites.

Executives in America, says Julian Scheer, a senior vice president of LTV, "try to deal with long-range problems in the short run. They want to demonstrate . . . that they'll meet this year's targets this year. What gets lost is the strategy that will take the company over 25 to 30 years."

"One of the problems in the United States, with government and business," says Bendix Corp. Chairman William Agee, "is the very short-term, expedient approach to problems—this quarter's earnings, this year's budget: 'Get me through the next election or the next board meeting.' "

The short-term drives out the long-term.

Not one American corporation in ten has truly long-term (six to ten years) compensation plans for its executives, and year-end bonuses are almost universally larger than long-term incentives.

"What short-term CEO will take a long-run view when it lowers his own income?" asks economist Lester Thurow. "Only a saint, and there aren't very many saints."

Also, in most corporations, middle-management executives are responsible for identifiable profit centers and are promoted or demoted based on quarterly profits. The product-manager system is notorious for this. The sum of it is that everybody works to get immediate results, not only ignoring the longer-range future, but often at the expense of the future.

Japanese managers, by contrast, pursue long-term strategies *despite short-term costs.*

In American business "the numbers" are pervasive. *Numbers* is in fact the term we use to talk about business. We also focus on the numbers because we always focus on what we can measure. And numbers are short-term. We have seemed to be totally pre-occupied with the financial successes, the short-term numbers: Prices are raised to enhance the return on investment—with hardly a thought to whether the customer will pay.

As Lewis H. Young, the editor-in-chief of *Business Week,* has pointed out about the automobile industry, the "top managements were blinded by numbers—the profits on large cars, the advantages of big numbers of production models—and penny-pinching on the fits and finishes."

What is called long-range planning (sometimes strategic planning, although that is an entirely different thing) is close to meaningless in most companies because they are for the most part momentum-driven and nobody pays much attention to them after they are completed.

America's business schools must accept a large share of the responsibility for the short-term numbers orientation of American business. For years they have been turning out MBAs who, because of their training, fancy they could manage anything because they know the numbers.

Michael P. Schulhof, vice president and director of the Sony Corporation of America, points his finger at the business schools. "The short-term and frequently shortsighted positions win out with disturbing regularity because American business is top-heavy with the ever-expanding numbers of business school graduates who are trained advocates of the short-term profit." Schulhof hits it pretty hard. "It is not entirely coincidence," he says, "that the same years that have seen industry increasingly, almost exclusively, run by financially oriented business school graduates have also seen the worst productivity performance since the Depression."

Long-range plans must replace short-term profit or our decline will be steeper still.

America's No-Tech Managers

It seems almost simpleminded to say it, but American business managers are the cause of our national economic decline. We hear a lot of alibis, but their preoccupation with short-term results and quantitative measurements of performance were responsible for the neglect of the kinds of investments and innovations necessary to increase the nation's capacity to create wealth.

Kenneth Mason, former president of Quaker Oats Co., before an audience of business school educators in July 1981 ridiculed many corporate leaders who insist on the value of regular profit increases, quarter after quarter, year after year.

> The top executives of an incredibly large number of America's best-known corporations spend hundreds of man-hours a year, year after year, making sure not only that this year's annual earnings increase is consistent with last year's, but that this year's third quarter doesn't fall below last year's third quarter, or that this year's third quarter isn't so good that next year's third quarter won't be able to top it, or that this year's third quarter won't embarrass this year's fourth quarter, and so on and on.

This, in Mason's view, is irrational behavior, unsound economic activity, and an almost totally unproductive use of real assets.

Corporate executives themselves are not unaware of these shortcomings. In a recent poll, one out of three said they think that most of the managers in charge don't know enough about technology and do not push innovation. (Technology and innovation have no numbers, and they are future-oriented.) The only country with executives less trained in technology than the United States is the United Kingdom, which should tell you quite a bit.

David Vogel, who teaches in the school of business administration at the University of California at Berkeley, asks the provocative question "Why are the nations with the most developed systems of professional management education, the United States and Great Britain, performing so poorly, when two nations that provide almost no professional management training, Germany and Japan, have been the outstanding successes of the postwar period?"

Signs of Change

Amid all this criticism, there are signs of change—a shift from the short-term to the long-term, or at least the longer-term.

Reginald Jones again: "Boards of directors have to understand that they must shelter management from these pressures. In the interest of the corporation itself and in the interest of the nation, the board has got to concern itself with the long-range future of the business and not be that upset by a bad quarter so long as productive and cost-effective spending is going on for the long range."

Business Week editorializes that "companies can change the signals that push their own people away from long-term vision into short-term myopia. They can reaffirm the need for basic research, for taking risks, for planning for the long haul. And they can create a climate in which educated risk takers feel that their jobs are secure and that their willingness to take risks is appreciated."

According to Edwin Murk of Arthur Young & Co., "We are finding more concern, particularly at the board level, for structuring compensation packages to motivate executives to think long-term."

But some managers get mixed signals at best. Thomas V. Jones, chairman and CEO of Northrop Corporation, says that "we tell our guys they are supposed to take care of the short-term profits with their left hand and long-term performance with their right."

The criticism about short-term management is becoming widely accepted by the business community itself. Of nearly 1,000 top executives surveyed in 1981 by the Chicago management research firm, Heidrick and Struggles, 76 percent said there has been a damaging overemphasis on immediate financial goals.

Law of the Situation: The Railroads Did Not Understand

The kinds of changes that are forcing us to think long-term, however, are so pervasive and so powerful that what is really required is that we completely rethink our businesses as part of the shift to the long-term.

One way to do this is by applying "The Law of the Situation."

The Law of the Situation is a term coined in 1904 by Mary Parker Follett, the first management consultant in the United States. She had a window-shade company as a client and persuaded its owners they were really in the light-control business. That realization expanded their opportunities enormously. The Law of the Situation asks the question "What business are you really in?"

The question for the 1980s is "What business are you really in?"

When the business environment changes, a company or organization must reconceptualize its purpose in light of the changing world. And now, with situations in constant flux, we must apply the Law of the Situation to present-day businesses.

One business that did not understand the Law of the Situation was the railroads.

We all now know that the railroads should have known they were in the transportation business and not just railroading. It was not so long ago that the railroad industry was the largest in the U.S. economy, and we were celebrating the Pennsylvania Railroad as the best-managed institution in the country. But times changed. We started to build big trucks and highways for those trucks and then jumbo jets. Even when the evidence was overwhelming that trucks and airplanes were the wave of the future, railroad men (and they were all men) remained, as Harvard Professor Theodore Levitt has written, "imperturbably self-confident." They thought they would go on forever. So did the people who continued to hold railroad stock.

The great business lesson of unrecognized obsolescence is not buggy whips, it's the railroads.

Suppose that somewhere along the way a railroad company, sensing the changes in its business environment, had engaged in the process of reconceptualizing what business it was in. Suppose they had said, "Let's get out of the railroad business and into the transportation business." They could have created systems that moved goods by rail, truck, airplane, or in combination, as appropriate. "Moved goods" is the customer-oriented point. Instead, they continued to be transfixed by the lore of railroading that had served the country so well—until the world changed.

Of this phenomenon Walter B. Wriston, chairman of Citicorp, in 1981 said:

> The philosophy of the divine right of kings died hundreds of years ago, but not, it seems, the divine right of inherited markets. Some people still believe there's a divine dispensation that their markets are theirs—and no one else's—now and forevermore. It is an old dream that dies hard, yet no businessman in a free society can control a market when the customers decide to go somewhere else. All the king's horses and all the king's men are helpless in the face of a better product.
>
> Our commercial history is filled with examples of companies that failed to change with a changing world, and became tombstones in the corporate graveyard.

Railroading is, I think, the great lesson for business. And today's appreciation of that lesson is to see that other great industries that have served us so well in the past are in the process of being replaced by the new tasks.

As with the railroad industry, it is difficult for us to believe that we are in process of losing the automobile industry that has served so well and has in fact been the economic underpinning of this society for so long.

How Some Companies Have Reconceptualized

"Big companies can't prevent change." The Harvard University business historian Alfred D. Chandler is quoted in *The Wall Street Journal* as saying: "Even they will be bypassed unless they keep on top of changing markets and technology." The article then goes on to take a look at three former Chicago giants that are today embarrassing shadows of their former selves: Swift, Pullman, and International Harvester.

Companies, like people, find it difficult to change, mainly because people run companies. "You get stuck in your ways," says historian Chandler. "It's a complicated process, but the key point is that you have investments in equipment and in people that do things a certain way. Then how do you change?"

I would argue that you can't change *unless* you completely rethink what it is you are doing, unless you have a wholly new vision of what you are doing.

"Economic power changes," says Chandler, "as markets and technology change." And that is certainly going to be the story of the 1980s.

Nevertheless, some exceptional companies have seen change with a clearer eye and done something about it. Their examples serve as apt models for instructing the reconceptualization process elsewhere.

A dozen years ago, when big steel was riding very high, the management of Armco Steel Company took a look around and decided that the good times for steel were not going to last that long. Armco decided to "get out of the steel business," which sounded crazy at the time. Using its high-flying profits to buy into other business, the company was by 1979 less than 50 percent in steel, and that year at their annual meeting changed their name from Armco Steel to Armco, Inc. The other steel companies were by that time in big trouble and were beginning to reconceptualize what business they were in. But some were too late, such as U.S. Steel's purchase of Marathon Oil in late 1981.

The big-business mergers and the big-labor mergers have all the appearances of dinosaurs mating.

Sometimes, when a company asks what business it is in, there are surprising answers.

In its 1981 annual report General Electric Company's outgoing Chairman Reginald Jones and the incoming Chairman Jack Welch signed a joint letter to stockholders saying GE was "in the business of creating businesses." That is a little sweeping but the awareness of the necessity to reconceptualize a company's direction is right. (From 1970 to 1979, GE's earnings from electrical equipment dropped from 80 percent to 47 percent of total earnings.)

Also in 1981, Xerox announced that it was in the "automated office business," although less than 5 percent of its sales were there. The 95 percent of sales in the copying business was subsumed by the new sense of what business Xerox thinks it is really in. Here is a case where a company, taking into account the changes in the society and the world, conceptualizes what business it would be useful for it to think it is in, in order to give vision and clarity to its overall direction.

If you don't know what business you are in, conceptualize what business it would be useful for you to think you are in.

Singer Co., whose name has been synonymous with the sewing machine, is becoming an aerospace company. As women abandon home sewing machines (and the home during the day while they are at work), Singer is moving more and more into aerospace and electronics, to flight simulators for both airplanes and spacecraft, sophisticated military communication equipment, and radar systems. Singer's Linkflight simulator was used to train the space shuttle Columbia's astronauts. This is all coming after a disastrous period when Singer stock went from $93.00 a share in 1972 to $6.50 in 1980.

The trick, of course, is to be alert to changes around you, to anticipate their impact on your institution, and then to respond: to reconceptualize what you are up to. Disastrous results tell us something is very wrong. But we ought to be able to hear the signals before they get quite so strong.

Schlumberger Ltd. is a very successful, fast-growing $5-billion-a-year business that has just rethought what business it is in. Since the 1920s, when two French brothers, Conrad and Marcel Schlumberger, invented an electronic process that depicts underground geology in oil wells, this company has been in the well-logging business. Now Schlumberger has decided it is in the "data collection and processing business." Says Schlumberger's chairman, Jean Riboud, "it just happened that the first data we collected and interpreted were on an oil well."

Last year this highly profitable French company acquired Manufacturing Data Systems, Inc., a computer services company in Ann Arbor, Michigan, and Applicon, Inc., of Burlington, Massachusetts, a company that makes computer-aided design systems, each for about $200 million. Two years earlier Schlumberger had bought Fairchild Camera and Instrument Corporation of early semiconductor fame (but not performing wonderfully at the moment) for $425 million. Schlumberger is also talking about getting into factory automation.

Schlumberger says it is taking the long-term view, keeping in mind the time when the oil-drilling business will have receded. It has a plan for the future. It used to be (and was thought to be) in the oil business. But instead of extending the oil direction or enlarging it for the company's future growth, it has set out to extend what it knows about measuring. After all, anyone in the oil business will, with time as the only variable, eventually be out of business.

Schlumberger's main business, well-logging, is extraordinarily profitable and still growing rapidly, but Schlumberger is using those profits to purchase a future.

Sears, Roebuck & Co. provides a dramatic example. It has been unable in recent years to grow in retailing (see comments on the decline of department stores and chain stores in Chapter 10). In late 1981 it embarked on a daring new strategy: Remain the top retailer *and* become the country's number-one (what we used to call) bank by moving into consumer financial services. Having decided on this strategy, Sears moved quickly and dramatically to buy big in stock brokering, real estate, and money-market funds. The appearance is that Sears continues to see itself in the retailing business, but with a very more widely cast net. To banks, stock brokers, and realtors, it will very much feel as though Sears is in their line of work.

Libbey-Owens-Ford has for fifty years been making quality glass products, mostly for General Motors Corp. Now, like all auto-dependent companies, LOF has got to unhitch itself from that dependency. In 1980 LOF's glass business for GM, nearly half the company's total revenues, went into the red for the first time in recent history. Now the new emphasis is on export, aerospace, and architectural glass (against tough industry leader PPG Industries). The hope is to end the long period when, according to CEO Don T. McKone, "General Motors drove what we built, where we built it, and what kinds of plants we built it in." Auto industry–dependent companies—rubber, steel, parts, among others—will court disaster if they wait around for the U.S. automobile business to get better. It won't. They must reconceptualize their businesses or perish.

Utilities, so often under highly regulated mandates, have been in the business of winning rate cases; now they must re-examine what business they are in as the industry is deregulated and decentralized. As in so many other industries, diversification is the early direction: Utilities are increasingly involved in real estate, fish hatcheries, insurance, oil drilling, coal mining, pipelines, and barge transport. So far, it is not very significant, partly because they don't know how state regulatory agencies are going to respond. The big question is whether earnings from nonutility businesses will have the effect of reducing requested rate increases.

What Business Are Banks In?

Banks and savings and loans are examples of institutions that have weathered much change in recent years and therefore serve as instructive examples of the problems faced by many other businesses during times of dramatic change.

What happened in the case of banking is that inflation and electronics made old-time banking obsolete—virtually overnight. In times of inflation, the value of money goes down and the value of goods increases, and since banks are in the business of money itself, their equity decreased.

The other problem for banks is "margin equity squeeze." In 1958 equity equaled 9 percent of reserves. That meant banks had a lot of room for error. As much as 9 percent of loans could go sour and only the investors—stockholders—would get hurt; today, there is a much thinner margin of error, since equity is down to only 3.5 percent.

As a result of the equity squeeze, banks are taking bigger risks and extending loans for longer periods of time. In 1960 loans were rarely made for more than one year. Today, loans are regularly made for as long as ten years. Banks are now using very expensive overnight money to finance long-term loans. What it means is that the banks are committing the classic error of borrowing short and lending long, with the short getting shorter and the long getting longer.

One way to think of banking is as information in motion. Now computers and communication satellites are moving money around the world so fast that customers each night can take all their money out of all of their bank accounts and lend it until the next morning. That hits the banks pretty hard; that's what they used to do with their customers' money. In the past, banks improved their productivity by creatively operating on the float, increasing that productivity perhaps 100 times during the last century. Now, with the collapse of the information float—owing to instantaneous communications—customers are using the float against the banks.

Money is information in motion.

The collapse of the information float is as important to finance as was the shift from barter to money. Imagine how much simpler transactions became after everyone had a common unit of exchange. Imagine how much transactions were speeded up. The shift from money to electronics is just as fundamental. It does not mean that we are suddenly going to do away with money, any more than we gave up bartering when we shifted from barter to money. We didn't. But in the world of finance the shift from money (and checks, notes, and so forth) to electronics is profound. Now banking is information in motion and we move it around the world at the speed of light.

The shift from money to electronics is as important as the earlier shift from barter to money.

Another thing to think about: After the shift from barter to money, people created businesses that had only to do with money as money, and we have been very inventive about that for centuries, charging interest being the primary example. Now, with the beginnings of the shift from money to electronics, people are going to create businesses that have only to do with electronics as electronics. For example, the Bank of New York is selling something it calls "Checkinvest" to companies with sales between $500,000 and $10 million. The service automatically—and electronically—transfers every dollar every day over an agreed minimum to a money-market fund and automatically transfers dollars from the money-market fund back to the checking account whenever it falls below the minimum. For this service, Bank of New York charges $100 a month. This is just the beginning. There will be no end to the inventive ways to make money on the electronics side of the shift from money to electronics.

At the end of the 1970s and the beginning of the 1980s, when the price for money went so high and electronic manipulation became so available, the buying-and-selling-of-money business became an irresistible attraction and many new players got into the "banking" business. In just four years Merrill Lynch's money-market business had $2 billion *more* in deposits than Citibank, which had been at it for 117 years. No wonder Citicorp's Chairman Walter Wriston said out loud that Citicorp was considering getting out of domestic banking.

Unless banks reconceptualize what business they are in, they will be out of business.

In the next few years we will witness many bank mergers and bank failures. When I was a young person growing up with the memories of the Depression all around me, bank failures meant *the end of the world.* Today bank failures only mean that, like the railroaders, some bankers are just waiting around for their virtue to be rewarded. There will still be abundant banking services available from many kinds of institutions.

With the death of the thirty-year fixed-rate loan, companies in the life-insurance industry must reconceptualize what business they are in, or many of them will be out of business.

In discussing the shift from short-term to long-term and the need for almost universal reconceptualization, I have used business examples because the relatively swift and harsh judgments of the marketplace allow us to see what is occurring more clearly. Business knows about change sooner than the rest of us.

But this need for reexamination and reconceptualization applies throughout the society. Here are some examples from other areas:

- Labor unions are now entirely preoccupied with survival. All of their actions are short term and defensive in nature. Unless labor unions reconceptualize their role in the society, they will continue on their dramatic downhill slide.
- The two national political parties will continue in name only unless they reconceptualize their role in the light of all the changes that have occurred in the last three decades. Because Ronald Reagan is in the White House, what is left of the Republican party has little incentive to examine its status. What's left of the Democratic party is at this writing just waiting for it all to come down on President Reagan, and then they believe they'll just pick up the pieces; that is the

road to disaster and continued decline. And the spectacle, beginning in 1981, of the AFL-CIO giving money directly to the Democratic party (under George Meany contributions were made only to favored candidates) and becoming its key source of financing has all the appearances of dinosaurs mating.

- Universities—with substantial cutbacks in federal funding, changes in their student populations, and the heavy blows of inflation—are hooking up right and left with companies for joint ventures in bioengineering and telecommunication: a new era of university-industry cooperation and a new concept of what a university is.

- Short-term solutions in dealing with the dumping of toxic wastes are catching up with us in all parts of the country.

- And the long-term implications of short-term decisions involving many of our nonrenewable natural resources have been the subject of national debate for a decade. The reconceptualization here is moving from conquerors of nature to a partnership with nature.

- Beginning with the granola ethic in California a dozen years ago, and moving through new concerns about nutrition and physical well-being, there has been evolving a reconceptualization of health care from a sickness orientation to a wellness orientation, and from short-term to long-term.

- In energy during the last two decades, we have moved from "nuclear is the answer" to an emphasis on a diversity of fuel sources, with the mix of fuels varying geographically—all of this, of course, instructed by longer-term considerations.

- In education we are moving from the short-term considerations of completing our training at the end of high school or college to lifelong education and retraining. The whole idea of what education is will be reconceptualized during the next decade.

- As the Southwest part of the United States booms, it is clear to everybody that longer-term steps must be taken to assure water for all.

Rethinking: A Constant, Long-term Process

Building on Mary Parker Follett's Law of the Situation, I would say that when the situation changes, we must: (1) reconceptualize what business we are in, or (2) conceptualize what business it would be useful for us to think we are in. Furthermore, when the situation is constantly changing—as it is in today's world—the process of reconceptualization must itself be a constant process.

The word *process* should be emphasized. What I am talking about is not a produce you get or buy from the outside. It is something that occurs inside an institution (well instructed by what is going on outside). It is the hard work of colleagues rigorously questioning every aspect of an institution's purpose—and the questioning of the purpose itself. The purpose must be right, and it must be a shared vision, a strategic vision.

Strategic planning is worthless—unless there is first a strategic vision.

A strategic vision is a clear image of what you want to achieve, which then organizes and instructs every step toward that goal. The extraordinarily successful strategic vision for NASA was "Put a man on the moon by the end of the decade." That strategic vision gave magnetic direction to the entire organization. Nobody had to be told or reminded of where the organization was going. Contrast the organizing focus of putting a man on the moon by the end of the decade with "We are going to be the world leader in space exploration," which doesn't organize anything.

In a constantly changing world, strategic planning is not enough; it becomes planning for its own sake. Strategic planning must be completely geared to a strategic vision and know exactly where it is going, with a clarity that remains in spite of the confusion natural to the first stages of change.

Too often a shared vision or purpose is absent. Drawing from the public sector, let me suggest how important it is to have a shared sense of a common purpose: What business are we really in?

In the area of the law and justice system in the United States, for several decades we operated under a framework, a paradigm, of rehabilitation. Admittedly, we never did do it very well, but until the 1970s, our common rubric was rehabilitation. That changed. During the 1970s, the operating framework slowly changed from rehabilitation to punishment, and that is today's prevailing paradigm. That's why we see—in many or most of our states—mandatory sentencing, the death penalty coming back strongly, more adolescents treated as adults, more prisons being built, and so forth. Now, throughout our vast law and justice system involving the police, the courts, and the prisons, the millions of decisions and judgments that are made every day are greatly influenced by the operating framework. If that framework is rehabilitation, those millions of decisions tend to be shaped in that direction. If on the other hand, as is the case today, those judgments are made under a punishment paradigm, they move the law and justice system in an altogether different direction.

In a large company, if the business it is in is railroading, all the decisions and judgments down the line will be greatly influenced by that shared perception. However, if that same company has decided it is in the transportation business, and if that is a widely shared perception in the company, then all of those collective judgments and actions will be very different indeed.

If you want to move a company or some other kind of institution in a new direction, people within that institution must share a sense of that direction. This brings up the question of who decides on a new direction, a new vision for a company or institution. For best results, the people in the institution must have "ownership" in the new vision. And as I will discuss in Chapters 5 and 7, more and more these decisions will be made from the bottom up in a participatory fashion, rather than top down.

There are cities and companies, unions and political parties, in this country that are like dinosaurs waiting for the weather to change. The weather is not going to change. The very ground is shifting beneath us. And what is called for is nothing less than all of us reconceptualizing our roles.

The short-term to long-term shift will transform the way you look at education and employment. The notion of lifelong learning is already replacing the short-term approach to education, whereby you went to school, graduated, and that was that. For the first time on the American scene, many large corporations are considering offering employees lifetime employment, the way America's Type Z companies (which are discussed more fully in Chapter 8) have informally done.

The long-range perspective may signal the need to return to

95

the ideal of a generalist education. If you specialize too much, you may find your specialty becoming obsolete in the long run. As a generalist, committed to lifelong education, you can change with the times.

Make sure the company you are working for has a long-range view of the future or you may find yourself in one of the next dying industries—or in a company that is dying in a growing industry. Skills in long-range forecasting will be increasingly valued.

There will be an increased demand for quality in all the items we purchase, buying for the longer term. Quality goods will present opportunities for growth and investment.

The shift to longer term may even result in some political changes: all states shifting from two- to four-year terms for their governors and a lengthened term of the presidency from four to six years.

5

From Centralization to Decentralization

Centralized structures are crumbling all across America. But our society is not falling apart. Far from it. The people of this country are rebuilding America from the bottom up into a stronger, more balanced, more diverse society.

The decentralization of America has transformed politics, business, our very culture.

In politics, it does not really matter anymore who is president, and Congress has become obsolete.

My neighbors in Washington, D.C., don't believe it, of course. But the reality remains: State and local governments are the most important political entities in America. The Ninety-Seventh Congress (1981–82) will introduce some 15,000 bills and pass only 500. Meanwhile, the states will introduce 250,000 in all and 50,000 will become law. American business in particular should shift its focus from the federal to the state level. Strengthening the trend still more, America's local governments have grown increasingly assertive vis-à-vis the federal government.

In business, the once almighty home office no longer governs regional divisions with an iron hand. Advertisers in New

York in many goods and services can no longer design a top-down national campaign and expect it to succeed all across the country. Even McDonald's, that ubiquitous American institution, no longer builds the exact same restaurant in each new location. The pull of decentralization extends to the nation's most conservative industry, banking, where some local banks are pulling out of the Federal Reserve System, an unthinkable move until recently.

American culture is decentralizing as well. Americans are spreading out to small towns and rural areas and leaving the old industrial cities as decaying monuments to a past civilization. As we decentralize, we diversify and tend to stress our differences instead of our similarities. Remember the people who boasted that wherever you traveled in America, you could see the same homes and office buildings and shop at the same chain stores? Not anymore. The 1970s witnessed a return to regional architecture. And many of those chain stores have gone out of business, to be replaced by highly individualized boutiques. Contemporary Americans have discovered geography as a way to distinguish themselves from one another. Now we identify with the cities, states, and regions where we live.

We reject the notion that we are a homogeneous nation. America is diversity itself. Politically, we have evolved into a human conglomeration that is too varied for central government. Culturally, we seem to have lost the desire for centralized institutions of any kind.

That is what decentralization is all about, yet there is more. The growth of decentralization parallels the decline of industry. America's industrial machine was probably history's greatest centralizing force. The mechanical blueprint of industrial society required enormous centralization—in labor, material, capital, and plant. This is because mass industrialization was organized according to the principle of economies of scale, that is, the more you produce in one place, in one way, the cheaper each individual unit will be. Agricultural and information societies are decentralized societies. Farmers could grow crops wherever the right field was; today you can start an information business with a telephone and a typewriter. Not so in the industrial society: All the workers have to go to the same place, the centralized plant or factory. But the decline of American industry and the rise of the new information economy neutralized the pressure to centralize and we began to decentralize.

Furthermore, I would argue that decentralization is America's natural condition, with centralization emerging only in our recent industrial past. The country's sheer size is certainly one factor favoring decentralization. But more importantly, strong central leadership is anathema to democracy. And Thomas Jefferson's "the less government, the better" is back in fashion. Early America was a community of farmers, and agricultural society lends itself to decentralized government.

But by the nineteenth century the spread of the industrial revolution brought America's agricultural era to a close. When the North won the Civil War, centralization and industrialization also won out over decentralization and agriculture. Centralization continued to flourish as industrialization gained further momentum in the twentieth century. Recent history brought two additional centralizing events—the Great Depression, when citizens first looked to Washington for centralized programs such as Social Security, and World War II, where only centralization could achieve the full mobilization needed for victory.

Since the postwar economic boom and the golden age of American industry in the 1950s, the need to centralize has receded, gradually at first, then more dramatically.

By 1976, America's two-hundredth anniversary, we had turned the corner: The growing strength of the decentralization trend surpassed the receding tendency to centralize.

Yet, the pull of decentralization extends far beyond politics and geography.

It is structuring the transformation of social relationships and social institutions as well.

Life, Look—*and* Runner's World

What is happening in America is that the general purpose or umbrella instrumentalities are folding everywhere. An instructive analog was the collapse more than a decade ago of the great general-purpose magazines, *Life, Look,* and *The Saturday Evening Post,* with their 10 million circulations. The same year those great mass-audience magazines folded, 300 new special-interest magazines were born. Soon there were 600, 800, and more. We now have 4,000 special-interest magazines and no general-purpose magazines. That is the analog for what is happening throughout society.

The American Medical Association, a large umbrella organization, is getting weaker. (Half the doctors belonged in 1970; only one-third did in 1980.) Meanwhile, the specialty medical groups within it—the brain surgeons and the pediatricians for instance—as well as the county and local medical organizations, are getting stronger and stronger. This is happening with most trade associations in America. The locals and the special sections are getting stronger and stronger at the expense of the nationals.

Several years ago the National Association of Manufacturers and the U.S. Chamber of Commerce announced they were going to merge for all kinds of wonderful reasons, none of which was true. They were merging for survival. A year later they announced the merger attempt had failed. Now presumably they will die separately.

The meat cutters and the retail clerks merged in 1979, becoming one of the largest labor unions in the United States. This growth is like the sunset. The sun gets largest just before it goes under. Remember the brontosaurus? The brontosaurus got so huge just before its demise that it had to stay in the water to remain upright. There were thirty-five mergers of labor unions between 1971 and 1981. In late 1980, the machinists and the auto workers announced merger talks that would make them the largest, most powerful union in the United States. If it comes off, it will appear that big labor is getting its act back together again. The reality will be the sunset effect.

America is moving toward an almost union-free society.

National network television is on a long, downward slide. In the analog, ABC, CBS, and NBC will be the *Life, Look,* and *Post* of the 1980s, their audiences drawn away by the increasing options of cable television. In the analog, the endless array of cable stations will be the special-interest magazines: You can tune in *Runner's World* or *Beehive Management* or whatever. There will be thousands of lower-powered broadcast TV stations. In 1950, when television started, there were 700 radio stations. Now there are 9,000, and that is the direction television is going.

Then there are all the new networks—Spanish networks, black networks, BBC in America, all-sports networks, and the all-news network. There are two childrens' networks (not to mention the gavel-to-gavel coverage of the House of Representatives). My own guess is that by the end of the 1980s, ABC, CBS, and NBC will have half the viewers they have today.

I think the same analog illustrates what is happening with leadership in America. We have no great captains of industry anymore, no great leaders in the arts, in academia, in civil rights, or in politics. That is because we followers are not creating those kinds of leaders anymore. And, in the analog, we are creating leaders along much narrower bands and much closer proximity.

Followers create leaders. Period.

I am constantly surprised, as I speak around the country to business audiences, by business people who grouse for three-and-a-half years about Washington and in the fourth year want strong leadership. What they seem to forget is that strong leadership is anathema to a democracy. The whole idea is that our democratic system itself creates a strong, viable society, and that has been our history. We don't need strong leaders, and we have not attracted strong leaders except in times of crisis.

In a crisis we choose Lincoln and FDR. In between we choose what's-his-name.

In the old Taoist model of leadership, you find the parade and get in front of it. What is happening in America is that those parades are getting smaller and smaller, but of course there are many more of them.

From the White House to Our House

The reason it doesn't matter anymore who is president is that real political power—that is, the ability to get things done—has

101

shifted away from Congress and the presidency to the states, cities, towns, and neighborhoods.

It is the smaller political units—cities, counties, and individual communities—that are claiming local authority over, and taking responsibility for, social issues that hit hard at the local level. What is surprising is their success rate. Local communities are tackling difficult problems and achieving solutions where the federal government with its vast but clumsy resources has failed: in energy, transportation, waste disposal, even in the controversial area of genetic research.

Ronald Reagan is riding the horse in the direction the horse is going.

The power shift away from Washington has energized state government. The states have grown more independent and more assertive vis-à-vis the federal government, especially federal regulatory agencies. Federalism and a new version of states' rights are reemerging in the daily newspaper.

In policymaking, we are giving up the grand, top-down strategies imposed from above and substituting bottom-up approaches, that is, limited, individual solutions that grow naturally out of a particular set of circumstances.

For example, we have no national urban policy because the old top-down, master-plan approach is completely out of tune with the times. It is inappropriate to ask: "Are we going to save our cities?" We are going to save some of our cities and we are not going to save others. We are going to save parts of some of our cities and allow other parts to decline. And the whole process is all going to turn on local initiative. The only "national urban policy" that is in tune with the times is one that is responsive to, and rewarding of, local initiative. The same can be said for energy, national health, and scores of other considerations.

Decentralized policymaking comes in the wake of the failure of centralized strategies to effect social change. Enrique Arroyo of New Jersey's Puerto Rican Congress echoed the frustrations of many when he wrote in a *New York Times* op ed piece in January 1981: "If, 80 years ago, the Federal Government had developed a deliberate plan to destroy our cities, it would not have been more successful than has been the case."

What the American Voters Are Really Saying

The way Americans vote says a lot about political decentralization.

In 1976 only 54 percent of those eligible voted. The standard reaction was "My god, this is scandalous!"

But what are the people telling us? Simply, that the outcome of the election doesn't matter. If you live in Eugene, Oregon, what does it matter whether Jimmy Carter or Ronald Reagan is president? I guessed that in the 1980 national election only 50 percent of the people would vote. I was wrong: 53 percent of the people voted. Forty-eight percent did not. Ronald Reagan got 27 percent of the votes of the eligible voters—hardly a mandate. Forty-two million people voted *against* Ronald Reagan, making his 43 million victory seem less impressive. None-of-the-above won by a landslide.

The main point here is that national political contests are a distorted barometer of political participation. In reality, we are participating in politics in this country at a more and more local level. The number of people voting for the president and Congress continues to decline—from 62 percent for president in 1952 to 54 percent in 1976—and from 42 percent for Congress in 1954 to 35 percent in 1978, the last congressional year. But totals for local initiatives and referenda are going up—as high as 75 and 80 percent in some areas.

In contrast, Congress is going the way of the presidency. Our congressional representatives are spending almost no time in the lofty statesmanlike tasks for which we presumably elected them. During the last Congress (1978–1980), for example, *20,000* bills were introduced and only *600* were passed (mercifully).

"I recognize now that Congress does very little," former Senator Adlai Stevenson recently said.

Increasingly, Congress has become an obsolete institution with its members and their growing staffs spending almost all of their time running errands for constituents and special-interest groups. This is not to be despised; it is a new role.

For the States: A New Assertiveness

Meanwhile, the states are seizing political power in the wake of presidential and congressional weakness. No longer waiting for federal leadership, the states are initiating local solutions to national problems. Should the state plan conflict with Washington's agenda, the states are ready and willing to challenge federal authority.

The new assertiveness of the states did not happen overnight. It follows a period of two decades during which state government quietly grew stronger.

State government has changed significantly in the last twenty years, according to a recent study by the National Advisory Commission on Intergovernmental Relations. Twenty years ago the states were considered inefficient, unrepresentative, racist, and corrupt. Now, says the report, the states are "structurally and procedurally stronger, more accountable, assertive, and perform a major intergovernmental management role." In addition, the states have upgraded tax systems and modernized legislatures, as well as the executive branch (partly the result of federal legislation and federal court decisions). Better qualified, more public-spirited representatives are being elected to state office. This new breed of state officials, in turn, are surrounding themselves with more professional legislative staffs.

During the 1970s, most states moved from two-year– to four-year–term governors. State legislature replaced short sessions every other year with longer annual sessions. Some states drafted new constitutions, and many increased aid to local governments.

Simultaneously, the states increasingly used their power to levy income and sales taxes. Most states achieved financial solvency during the late 1970s, precisely the time when the federal deficit—and the public's resentment toward it—seemed to increase outrageously each day. In contrast to the federal government, every state except Pennsylvania balanced its budget or had a surplus in fiscal 1978. By 1979, some state governors proposed politically popular tax cuts—$5 billion worth. This newfound financial respectability reinforced the states' political clout, enabling them to resist Washington and tackle their own problems.

To be sure, the states' financial picture has changed rapidly in a few short years. Heavy cuts in federal aid to the states and other budgetary problems have eroded sizable state surpluses. Almost all show small surpluses however, because all but two (Connecticut and Vermont) must by law balance the budget. At the same time, energy-producing states are amassing huge surpluses. Alaska's was $1.4 billion in 1980 and $850 million in 1981; Texas, Oklahoma, Hawaii, North Dakota, and Kansas had surpluses of *well* over $100 million both years. The point is that the state finances were uniformly strong during the 1970s. The combined effect of economic power and streamlined political structures guaranteed the further movement of political power from Washington to the states.

Now the nation's governors declare the states are better able to serve citizens than the federal government.

Liberal or conservative, most governors believe the country is too diverse for the federal government's centralized policy-making. Pennsylvania's Republican Governor Dick Thornburgh summarized the mood in spring 1981:

> Washington should end its preoccupation with hundreds of questions meant for local decision-makers and its tendency to impose unrealistic mandates that undermine public support for such worthy goals as helping the handicapped and cleaning air and water.

More impressive is the fact that the states are reviving their traditional function as the laboratories of democracy, experimenting with society's most intractable problems. Recent examples of state assertiveness and inventiveness abound:

- Alaska, Nevada, Texas, and Arizona have neutralized the FDA's federal authority by legalizing the controversial drug Laetrile.
- Six Minnesota counties joined together to manage a 200-mile stretch of land along the Mississippi River in order to keep the federal government from declaring it a federally managed Wildlife and Scenic River.
- Seven states levied additional gasoline taxes in mid-1980, after Congress had rejected former President Carter's 10-cent-per-gallon fee to reduce imports. "Apparently the politicians on the lower level are not afraid to raise the taxes," said American Petroleum Institute's deputy director, William Mahoney.

- Georgia, Alabama, Kentucky, Virginia, Indiana, New York, and Pennsylvania thought the Justice Department was dragging its heels on an investigation of organized crime, so the states joined together to go after loansharking, bribery, extortion, and kickbacks in the coal industry.

- The Environmental Protection Agency took four years, 1976–1980, to write hazardous-waste regulations, plenty of time for organized crime to get into the illegal hazardous-waste-disposal business. New Jersey, Delaware, and Pennsylvania tightened regulations in the interim. Ten eastern states sought a Law Enforcement Assistance Administration grant to share information and chase dumpers across state lines.

- In Missouri, Governor Joseph P. Teasdale asked the State Department of Natural Resources to deny a permit to the U.S. Department of Energy, which sought to dump radioactive water into the Mississippi River.

- Ohio, Michigan, Illinois, Indiana, Kentucky, Pennsylvania, and West Virginia are considering building a 150-mile-per-hour train based on Japanese and West German technology and in direct competition with Amtrak. The plan is significant not only for its pioneering new technology, but because "it strikes at the very heart of federalism," says Pennsylvania's *Harrisburg Patriot*.

- San Diego, California, is constructing a streetcar system entirely without federal money. The decision to build the system was hailed as a "local Magna Carta from dependence on federal construction grants" by California State Senator James Mills. Denver is considering following San Diego's lead with a locally funded transit system.

States' Rights

These actions suggest that governors and state legislatures are gearing up for new states' rights battles.

Says Colorado Governor Richard Lamm, "The day of the state has come and gone—and come back again."

"I am fighting to keep state control," says another new-age Colorado politician, Democratic Senator Gary Hart. Hart dislikes the term *states' rights,* he told the *Denver Post,* because of its old racist connotation. On a critical issue like water resources, though, a states' rights stand is appropriate, he said.

In fact, today's states' rights rhetoric reemerges most frequently in connection with energy and environmental issues.

The present-day argument for states' rights is a simple one, and no one has said it better than North Dakota State Engineer Vernon Fahy in an interview with the *Fargo Forum:* "North Dakota and the people of this state should make the decisions, not the federal government and not the energy companies. This philosophy is not something that will be worked out overnight. It takes conflict."

Carried to extremes, the issue of states' rights suggests secession—or the threat of it. Threats, at least, have already popped up here and there.

"My vision is that we might need a new western nation from the MacKenzie River to the Rio Grande," says Kent Briggs, administrative assistant to Utah's Governor Scott Matheson.

Prior to Ronald Reagan's election, some westerners thought their problems would be solved with a western president rather than by secession. A western Republican quoted in the *Idaho Statesman* accused President Carter of "waging war against the West" because the West had voted for Gerald Ford. The West's solution, Wyoming State Secretary Thyra Thomson told the *Wyoming State Tribune* in 1977, is to elect a western president to protect regional interests. Of course, one of the West's own is now president. It is not yet clear to what extent President Reagan will look out for the western states.

But as the states' rights battle reemerged in a variety of new issues, the National Governors Association asked the president and Congress to convene a national commission on federalism to determine which functions are best served by the states and which by the federal government.

Federalism, like *states' rights,* is now part of the vocabulary of political decentralization.

Governor Bruce Babbit of Arizona has said, "It is long past time to dust off the Federalist Papers and to renew the debate commenced by Hamilton, Madison, and Jefferson."

With the election of Ronald Reagan, governors like Babbit believe the White House will encourage the flow of political authority from Washington to the states and localities.

It was Reagan, after all, whose inaugural address seemed to resound the governors' demands from the previous summer:

"It is my intention," said the President, "to demand recognition of the distinction between the powers granted to the federal government and those reserved to the states and to the people."

President Reagan's call for old-fashioned federalism, for example, his *plan* to convert scores of federal grant programs in education, health, transport, and urban aid into several broad block grants to be spent as the states see fit, meshes perfectly with the decentralization trend and the demand for states' rights.

States' rights—the 1980s version—is usually associated with the now famous Sagebrush Rebellion, the western states' challenge to federal authority over lands within state borders. Nevada is spearheading the battle by demanding state control over the four-fifths of its land now under federal jurisdiction.

What is less publicized is that the rebellion is somewhat of a hoax. Privately, the western governors concede it would be almost impossible to marshal the resources needed to manage the huge chunks of land at stake—collectively about half of the territory of the Rocky Mountain states—even with federal funds to help. Nevertheless, the states find it an effective way to antagonize the federal government.

President Reagan established a task force to explore turning over some of the federal government's hundreds of buildings and millions of acres of land to state control or at least to ease restrictions on their use. Should that occur, it may diffuse the loud though somewhat insincere cries of the Sagebrush Rebellion.

The New Regionalism

The logical extension of states' rights is the notion that the states within a region should band together to protect their mutual self-interest. This is not the benign regional loyalty where we stress our differences for the fun of it. It is a tough new brand of economic regionalism, a geographic chauvinism that grows out of the unique problems and resources common to a group of states. Perhaps the best name for this phenomenon is the *new regionalism*.

One of the first signs of this new regionalism was the Sunbelt/Frostbelt controversy, beginning in 1977. Ostensibly the feud was over which region would get the most federal dollars and defense installations. At the core of the dispute, however, was the North's growing sense of loss—of population, businesses, and therefore economic power. The fears of the North were confirmed in the 1980 census, which documented the megashift from North to South.

But even before census figures were released, the U.S. Department of Labor reported that an impressive two out of three new jobs were created in the South or West.

Hard feelings in the North grew more resentful when a presidential commission under President Carter advocated that public policy encourage large-scale migration in the United States from the cities of the North to the South and West, where the jobs are.

As the North and South straighten out their differences (or become involved with more productive issues, depending on how you look at it), a far more divisive regional battle is brewing between the East and West. The key element is not defense spending or public works projects, but the precious commodity of energy that divides the United States into have and have-not states.

The energy-rich western states have found a new regional cohesiveness in this critical issue. Those states will earn well over $100 billion during the 1980s. Energy consumers, located mostly in the East, will be the ones reaching into their pockets.

No wonder consumers are calling the West the "new OPEC" and muttering about a new "energy war between the states." Westerners, of course, have a different viewpoint. They feel the energy windfall will help protect them from the boom-bust development cycles that debilitated Appalachia.

Much of the West's new energy wealth—and antiexploitation insurance—depends on mineral severance taxes levied on exports of oil, gas, coal, and other minerals.

The old North/South controversy and the Sagebrush Rebellion will pale in contrast to the coming brouhaha over state export taxes, which will have a multibillion-dollar impact on the energy industry, all energy-consuming states, and each American consumer.

From the West's viewpoint, of course, the high economic and environmental costs of energy development more than justify the taxes. The commitment to help meet national, rather than just local, energy goals often means a state must surrender its agricultural base and provide the costly but critical infrastructure for development. Westerners obviously feel the tax can help them avoid "colonial exploitation" by the East.

At this juncture, the West is still savoring a recent mineral tax victory. In June 1981, the Supreme Court ruled that Montana's 30-percent tax on coal export was legal.

Ironically, the challenge to Montana's tax was led by energy-rich Texas. The city of Austin, Texas, which was locked into a long-term purchase of Montana coal, mounted the assault, despite the fact that Texas treasury brings in $2 billion in oil and gas taxes—twenty-five times what Montana receives in coal taxes. Texas Representative J. J. Pickle, who in 1980 introduced legislation to limit coal severance taxes to 12.5 percent, said congressional action was necessary because the Montana tax—the highest in the nation—was so exorbitant.

Representative Samuel Devine (R–Ohio) complained that "Montana and Wyoming have become a domestic OPEC, earning millions of dollars at the expense of other states."

Wyoming's severance tax is 17 percent. Several other states have the taxes as well. North Dakota's tax is 20 percent. New Mexico is expected to increase its severance tax, and although attempts to increase the tax have failed in Michigan and Wyoming, severance taxes can be expected to increase.

States' Wrongs

For all the assertiveness of the states, the drama of the Sagebrush Rebellion, the pettiness of the North/South controversy, and the self-interest of the state export taxes, it is becoming more and more difficult for the states to appear noble. But given the cynicism toward Washington, many of us continue to believe the governors' contention that the states serve us better.

Nevertheless, it is naive to think the states are automatically aligned with the local community or the individual citizen against the federal government. Sometimes the federal government is actually on the "right" side of the issue, at least according to someone's point of view.

How many Californians supported their state's refusal to enact tougher air-control standards in a show of states' rights? Air quality in Los Angeles worsened considerably during the 1970s (despite earlier predictions that air would be cleaner by 1980). Even so, California was one of seven states that refused to enact a mandatory annual vehicle-inspection program by July 1979, as required by federal law.

Along with the decentralization of power has come, if not corruption, then at least an increase in mischief.

During the 1970s, for example, Congress enacted 3,359 laws, but the state of New York passed 9,780. All fifty state legislatures passed some 250,000 laws in the 1970s.

Those figures confirm that the burden of regulation has shifted to the states, a trend that was powerfully underscored with the advent of the Reagan presidency. The business people who applauded the Reagan victory as a sign of the demise of government regulation are in a bit of a quandary now. The single set of hateful, costly, yet standardized, national regulations has disintegrated into a labyrinth of contradictory state regulations—even more time-consuming and equally hateful.

State government has followed Washington's misguided lead in another direction—the tendency to serve as an employment program. Few of us have noticed that the increase in the much ballyhooed government jobs has occurred in the states, not in Washington: In 1968, there were 2.7 million federal employees; by 1980, only 2.8 million. Between 1968 and 1979, however, the ranks of state and local government workers swelled by 4 million.

But states' wrongs are not going unnoticed. As power is decentralized to the states, it is further challenged by local communities.

Connecticut, Maryland, and Michigan recently claimed the new authority to override local vetoes of hazardous waste dumping sites. But how many local communities go along with the states' new power? Ann Arundel County, Maryland, does not. When Maryland overrode the local veto, Ann Arundel County took states' rights down to the local level. The county closed down travel routes to trucks hauling the unwanted wastes. A bill reaffirming the county's right to check the state authority got a respectable 68-to-42 vote in the Maryland House of Delegates, just short of the three-fifths majority required for passage.

Many local communities are demanding that the state fund any programs it mandates. The Pennsylvania Senate passed a bill requiring the state to share the local cost of state programs. In Massachusetts, local officials demanded the state stop passing laws mandating local programs without providing reimbursement. In December 1981, the California County Supervisors' Association voted 41 to 2 to sue the state because it did not provide the funds to cover state-mandated programs.

Not all states are willing to share funds with localities. In Wisconsin, city officials were disturbed that Governor Lee Dreyfus vetoed $14.8 million in state revenue sharing for cities and $8.9 million for school districts. Local communities claimed the state was shifting the burden to local property taxpayers. Michigan refused to loan Wayne County funds to meet its payroll and allowed the county to operate in the red, against state law.

As the states continue to battle the federal government, local officials are taking up their own battle positions, challenging the states as well as the federal government, and in many cases forging new solutions to general problems.

Reversing Centralization: Building from the Bottom Up

The key to decentralization of political power in the United States today is local action. Localized political power is not delegated from the federal level to the state, municipal, or neighborhood levels. Rather, it stems from the initiatives taken by the state or neighborhood in the absence of an effective top-down solution. A good example is the way cities and states took the lead in energy (discussed later in this chapter), while the federal government floundered. Power that is bestowed from the top down can be withdrawn if the donor's priorities change. Successful initiatives hammered out at the local level have staying power. Local solutions are resistant to top-down intervention and become models for others still grappling with the problems.

The U.S. Department of Energy, for example, often reached down to the states for ideas and inspiration.

"We've stolen a lot of our legislation from the states," said a top DOE administrator during the Carter administration. DOE used California's appliance and building codes as guides in drawing up federal standards.

The failure of centralized, top-down solutions has been accompanied by a huge upsurge in grassroots political activity everywhere in the United States. Some 20 million Americans are now organized around issues of local concern. Neighborhood groups are becoming powerful and demanding greater participation in decision making.

Demands for greater bottom-up participation in policymaking have led to the restructuring of many political processes all across the country:

- In Madison, Wisconsin, for example, the City Planning Department no longer asks citizens to rubber stamp a completed master plan. Instead, city planners now present citizens with an array of alternatives in informal neighborhood sessions.
- Illinois has passed a new constitution granting home-rule powers to local governments.
- California's Governor Brown has expanded citizen participation in state regulatory agencies.
- In Providence, Rhode Island, Mayor Joseph W. Walsh has increased the use of citizen advisory groups.
- Ballot proposals in New York City and Grand Rapids, Michigan, successfully ended at-large election of representatives. Now councilmen and supervisors must be elected from established wards or districts.

Neighborhoods are using this newfound political power to tackle, at the local level, society's most persistent problems—education, crime, equal access to capital, and solid-waste disposal.

Because of a long tradition of local control, education is a natural issue for community activism. With the debate over the decline in the quality of education in this country and the recent history of federal and state intervention in local education, the education issue is ripe for increased local initiative.

Advocates of public education walk a tightrope between the demand for local control and the need for additional funding. Inflation and tax reform have made locally funded education a thing of the past. Consequently, state funding of local education has increased greatly during the past decade. But educators and parents have learned, to their dismay, that outside funds can also mean outside control. Many local education groups have now rallied around the sentiment "State (or federal) aid without state control."

The result is more political activism at the state and local level in education issues.

The Bismarck, North Dakota, school board considered forming a political action committee to endorse and fund state legislators who would favor their educational aims, including state aid without state control. In Arizona an education lobby of teachers, parents, and others is pushing for more state aid per pupil.

After Proposition 13, the National Education Association renewed its call for federal funding of one-third the costs of public education. But many citizens fear it will mean trading more local control for federal dollars.

At least one proposed federal program was stopped by local opposition—bilingual education. Responding to local constituents, seven groups—including the National School Boards Association and the National Association of Secondary School Principals, as well as many local officials—protested the program's "big brotherism," charging it would stifle local creativity and ignore the unique circumstances in each area. Acting in alignment with decentralization, the Reagan administration canceled the program outright.

On another issue, crime, citizens are responding to the 1980s crime wave with fear, anger, and activism. No longer willing to delegate the responsibility for their safety to the government or the police, citizens are taking matters into their own hands. Once an innovation, crime-watch groups and crime-stopper programs are fast becoming commonplace across the country and are compiling an impressive track record. Burglaries in Cocoa, Florida, for example, decreased 41 percent between 1980 and 1981. The reason, says the local police chief: "vigorous crime-watch groups." Nevada citizens through the state's thirty-two crime-stopper programs helped solve 1,275 major felonies, convict 670 out of 683 defendants tried, and recover six million dollars' worth of stolen property.

Residents of Washington, D.C.'s Logan Circle adopted a novel plan to discourage prostitution in their area. Local citizens put bumper stickers on the automobiles of people patronizing area prostitutes. The stickers read: "DISEASE WARNING: Occupants of This Car Have Been Seen with Prostitutes."

Neighborhood loyalty and concern are reflected in another trend: the tendency for neighborhood groups to become more professional. In Pittsburgh, Buffalo, Chicago, Indianapolis, and in twenty other cities, churches are sponsoring grassroots organizational efforts of paid professional organizers from the Industrial Areas Foundation. This group was founded by the late Saul Alinsky, the 1960s activist who trained people in the pragmatic aspects of neighborhood organizing.

All across America, neighborhood groups are making themselves visible with a variety of political actions:

- A Chicago coalition of 100 neighborhood associations took to the streets for a day-long street drama protesting that more money is being spent on downtown projects than on housing.
- New England's Section 8 Coalition set up a tent in downtown Providence to protest the "unjust distribution of federal rent subsidies."
- Residents of Bordentown, New Jersey, have organized a group called HOPE (Help Our Polluted Environment) to oppose a Love Canal–type plan being considered by the state.
- Local opposition in Minnesota forced the state to return a $3.7-million federal grant for a toxic-waste landfill and chemical-disposal facility.

The battle lines extend to rural areas as well. "Our biggest concern is the government's interference in land use," says Ruth Anne Ruehr, leader of a Michigan residents' group. The object of their protest? A Navy Seafarer communications proposal to bury 500 miles of low-voltage cables in nearby forests.

- North Carolina's Warren County residents are loudly protesting the state's decision to bury 40,000 cubic yards of contaminated soil in their area.

- In West Virginia's Lewis County, the Upper West Fork River Watershed Association has mounted a sophisticated attack against the construction of the $117-million Stonewall Jackson Dam. They have challenged the Corps of Engineers' economic calculations, questioned proposed compensation for underlying coal, and criticized the plans for recreational development. The association's latest maneuver is selling square-yard chunks of land within the proposed area for $10 apiece in an attempt to snarl the Corps's condemnation proceedings in paperwork.
- In perhaps the most active protest, Minnesota residents have toppled four powerline towers, compiling a vandalism bill of $140 million.

Neighborhood groups gained valuable experience while working on the issue of *redlining*, the practice whereby banks refused loans to inner-city neighborhoods they believed were deteriorating (no matter how credit-worthy the applicant). When state and local governments passed antiredlining laws, neighborhood groups demanded more: They forced banks to disclose virtually *all* loan information.

The Pennsylvania legislature held hearings on a bill requiring banks to publish reports every six months on down-payment rates, appraisal values, and interest rates, and to pinpoint the location of every mortgage and home-improvement loan.

Boston banks must prove they *green line*, that is, actively make loans to inner-city residents, before mergers or additional branch offices will be approved.

Neighborhood groups took on insurance companies as well as banks in the redlining fight. Chicago's Metropolitan Housing Alliance, a coalition of twelve community groups, charged that Allstate imposed stiffer fees on insurance buyers living within twelve local ZIP code areas. Allstate denied the charges, but the local groups retaliated with a boycott of Sears, Allstate's parent company, and disrupted a Sears stockholders meeting.

Solid-waste disposal is another issue of paramount concern at the local level. About half the cities in the United States have exhausted local dump sites, and garbage costs are second only to education in most local budgets. The efforts of local recycling groups have therefore proved invaluable of late. By the late 1970s some 200 jurisdictions had pickup and recycling programs, which are more successful than voluntary drop-off centers.

In Cambridge, Massachusetts, housing authority tenants operate a recycling program with block grant funds. A community development program in The South Bronx sells organic compost. In rural Minnesota, handicapped workers recycle garbage from a 17,000-square-mile area. And in Washington, D.C., the National Black Veterans Organization collects the federal government's major waste product—paper.

Energy—Catalyst for Local Action

Throughout the 1960s and 1970s, Washington's top-down, master-plan approach to social issues compiled a horrendous track record. In the meantime new solutions were flourishing closer to home, especially in connection with energy.

While special interests, political partisans, and regional coalitions carved up the Carter administration's ill-fated energy plan, the states and cities quietly took the initiative to analyze local needs, establish local energy policies, and even secure energy supplies.

Because the energy issue emerged after we were already well along in the decentralization process, it was natural we would attempt to resolve energy questions at the local level.

Perhaps, because it affects more of us individually than any other social issue, energy is a catalyst for local initiative. For one reason or another many of us are insulated from concerns about housing, education, or transportation. While many of us do not get too excited about environmental concerns, we all use energy.

If the cost of heating oil does not trouble you, the price of gasoline probably does. Should neither concern you, there's always electricity. No matter what state we live in, we all use electricity and telephones. That simple fact explains why most new consumer issues emerge in the bellwether utilities industry.

But that is where energy uniformity ends for Americans. Each region, state, even city, has a unique set of energy needs, problems, resources, and human values. Nowhere is the inappropriateness of centralization more apparent than in the notion of a "national" energy policy.

Precisely because we lacked an energy policy during the last decade, the states and localities filled the gap with local initiatives and geographically based plans of action. In reality, a "national" energy policy has already been hammered out from the bottom up across the country, and its key principles are decentralization and diversification. At this point, if the federal government ever decides on a policy, it had better conform to local initiatives—or it will be rejected.

The local energy initiatives are plentiful and diverse. Some communities formed municipal utilities and tried out cogenerative facilities. Trash into energy plants multiplied. Conservation measures were passed in local, state, and county ordinances. Tax incentives were offered for alternative energy projects. Some local governments set up various energy plans to release themselves from the tyranny of heavy dependence on one particular energy supply. Oregonians burned firewood; Wichita considered building a coal gasification plant, while in Columbus it was a trash and coal plant. A number of municipalities bought into the electrical power industry.

All across the American landscape, local innovators fought their way through the energy maze. Some experiments were successful; others were not. But state and local administrators tried to find the mix of programs that fit their own local energy picture: bicycle paths and nuclear power? Conservation and natural gas? Solar tax credits and more coal development? It all depended on local conditions.

Even people who branded the national energy crisis an outright hoax took an active interest in whether or not their town was going to take over the local public utility.

While Congress and the oil companies battled out Washington's energy war, the states learned to look out for themselves. Individually or regionally, the states moved toward a decentralized brand of energy independence.

California Governor Jerry Brown negotiated with both Mexico and Canada for future natural-gas supplies. The New England states explored entering an electricity collective with Eastern Canada and held an "Energy Summit" to develop a common policy toward the federal government.

Diversification was the byword. Communities invested in the kinds of energy sources that fit best with local needs and resources. For example, Springfield, Vermont, voters decided to spend $58 million restoring the use of six local dams, while three

Texas communities banded together to mine coal and produce electricity at affordable prices.

Ten states, mostly in the West, experimented with geothermal energy, deriving energy from hot water or steam from beneath the earth's surface.

In Oregon, where woodland is plentiful, 58 percent of all homes have turned to wood for some of their fuel needs.

The city of Wichita, Kansas, on the other hand, studied a plan (which was later voted down) to build a coal gasification plant financed with tax-free municipal bonds. The ambitious goal was that the plant become "the keystone of a regional energy network affecting nearly every home and business in Kansas."

Garbage-burning plants, once considered exotic, were judged an attractive energy option in many localities.

Dade County, Florida, was one. Officials there signed a $14-million contract with Florida Power and Light Co. to construct a garbage-powered generating plant to serve some 40,000 homes.

A Columbus, Ohio, referendum approved floating a $118-million bond issue to build a ninety-megawatt trash- and coal-fired plant. Some 64 percent of the voters approved the plant, which will fuel Columbus's streetlights.

Not surprisingly, California leads the states in solar energy development. Some thirty California cities and towns are considering requiring solar hot-water heaters in all new homes; several already require them. Santa Clara County has drawn up requirements for passive solar equipment in all new homes.

Although solar power is strongest in the Sunbelt, it is popular as far north as Wisconsin, where some 1,200 new solar units were installed shortly after that state introduced a solar tax credit.

Despite the popularity of solar and the more esoteric energy sources, the top energy priority for many communities was conservation.

One of the most ambitious conservation programs is in Seattle, Washington. That city aims to save 230 megawatts, or 18 percent of its total energy usage, by 1990. More energy-efficient building codes alone can achieve much of that goal.

And if the example set in Davis, California, is any indication, Seattle will probably reach its target. In Davis, total electricity consumption declined 18 percent since 1973, the year energy standards for new construction were adopted. The Davis code

119

requires that the glass area in new buildings be proportional to the floor area. If not, the builder must use thermal glass or situate additional glass areas on southern exposures.

One of the nation's toughest building restriction codes is in Portland, Oregon, which requires insulation in all homes, apartment buildings, and offices, not just new ones. That means the cost of weatherization will fall on homeowners, not just developers and builders. Average per home: $1,350, a sizable sum. By 1985, it will be illegal to sell an uninsulated home. Portland predicts that this measure and others will jointly save some 35 percent of the energy that city will need by 1995.

Finally, where do the states and localities stand on the sensitive issue of nuclear power?

The direction is by no means uniform, but an antinuclear feeling continues to grow in the states.

Though proponents of nuclear power consider it the most important alternative in energy diversification, the states have a long history of cynicism toward industry and government-backed nuclear projects in their states. Because of the huge scale involved, nuclear power is centralist by definition. Yet, nuclear power is not a single issue. It is at least three distinct issues—each of vital interest to the states and localities and each, I would argue, increasingly unpopular. The first is building and operating nuclear plants; the second is nuclear waste disposal; the third is the transportation of nuclear waste.

The first is in many ways simplest. Some states favor building nuclear plants; some do not. At this point, the trend is against nuclear power plants. In November 1980, two states, Oregon and Montana, passed initiatives effectively banning the construction of new nuclear plants. An antinuclear measure was defeated in South Dakota, but by a slim margin. In Maine and Missouri, antinuclear measures were also defeated, but there the issues were extreme—the possible closing of already operating or nearly on-line plants. Even so, some 40 percent of the voters cast anti-nuke ballots.

Residents of the towns and communities near nuclear plants felt they were not getting enough state and federal support, so they formed their own national network to deal with evacuation plans, relationships with utilities, and other common concerns.

The second issue, nuclear waste disposal, is less controversial and more important in terms of decentralization. Although some states favor operating nuclear plants that are genuinely needed, nearly all the states oppose nuclear waste disposal within their borders. The states' viewpoint crystallized during the late 1970s.

In 1976 Colorado, Connecticut, Indiana, Wisconsin, Montana, and several other states were surprised, and in some cases outraged, to learn the federal government was considering them as sites for nuclear waste disposal. Montana Governor John Melcher formulated the state's quintessential question: Why should a state with no nuclear plants have to bear responsibility for waste produced elsewhere? (It is a good question. Perhaps the solution is to offer some tradeoffs favoring the state that accepts nuclear waste.)

By 1978 at least nine states were considering legislation to ban nuclear construction until the waste issue was settled.

More recently, in 1980, seventeen states reacted unfavorably to an Energy Department report listing desirable locations for nuclear waste disposal.

The nuclear waste disposal issue will surely continue in this decentralized direction. Since nuclear waste hits the states in their own backyards, they can be counted on to argue that the federal government should not act unilaterally.

Instead, the states want to decide where to situate waste disposal dumps. The National Governors Association has proposed the formation of six regional associations to deal with low-level wastes. The governors propose leaving standards and technical matters in the hands of the federal government, while giving states siting authority.

Nuclear waste disposal will remain controversial because industry will triple the amount of low-level radioactive waste generated in the next ten years.

Finally, the third issue, nuclear waste transport, may well become the strongest focus of the nuclear debate. In many ways, transport is the most troubling nuclear issue, because of the number of people that stand to be affected by it right now. You and I may be indifferent about nuclear waste stored thousands of miles away in Nevada, for example. But suppose that en route to Nevada the same waste is transported on a road a few miles from your home. Multiply your individual concern by that of the

121

millions of people in communities along nuclear transport routes all across America. It adds up to a politically explosive issue.

And just where are America's nuclear transport routes? In 1980 a citizens group sued the Nuclear Regulatory Commission, forcing it to release the rail and road shipping routes for nuclear wastes. Several governors and state officials expressed surprise to learn where the routes were located and questioned their close proximity to population centers such as Philadelphia, Hartford, Trenton, New Jersey, and Oakland, California.

There is a growing trend, however, toward stronger action. Local governments are questioning Washington's traditional power to preempt local decisions on waste transport.

In 1979, for example, Charlestown, South Carolina, passed an ordinance banning the shipment of commercial nuclear waste through the city. Thirty-six towns in Vermont have banned the storage and transport of nuclear wastes. But Charlestown's action is especially noteworthy because South Carolina is considered conservative and pronuclear.

At local hearings all across the country in 1980, citizens expressed strong sentiment against federal regulation of nuclear waste transport. About 182 jurisdictions have now passed outright bans. Another 211 have required advance notice of shipments.

One participant in Eugene, Oregon, summed up the decentralist position of many Americans on the issue of nuclear power, whether transport, disposal, or operation of nuclear plants: "It is a matter," said the man in Eugene with grave simplicity, "too dangerous to leave in the hands of the federal government."

For many Americans that is equally true in the whole matter of energy, a bellwether issue of decentralization and local initiative.

Personal Geography: You Are Where You Live

In the 1970s, America began to celebrate geographic diversity. We celebrated it the way we did cultural and ethnic diversity in the 1960s. We have gone from "Black is beautiful" and "Polish is beautiful" to "I love Minneapolis!" Ordinary American citizens became fiercely loyal New Englanders, Californians, New Yorkers, and so on. Bumper stickers in Texas proclaimed, "Freeze a Yankee" (to protest the Northeast's reluctance to drill their own offshore oil).

Fifteen years ago, who would have predicted we would carry tote bags that pledge "I love New York," or that anyplace would inspire such powerful sentiment?

The regional differences we enjoy stressing are not imaginary. The people within a region have similar values and attitudes, a sort of geographic state of mind. New Englanders, despite the proper Bostonian stereotype, are the nation's most liberal group, with Pacific Coast residents running a close second—so say social scientists who polled the regions over an eight-year period. Forty percent of the New Englanders were willing to tolerate homosexuality and extramarital sex; 60 percent felt abortion was a woman's right. Southerners were far more conservative, as expected. In the Southeast, more than 80 percent thought extramarital sex was "always wrong"; only one-third went along with abortion.

Celebrating our geographic roots as part of the decentralization megatrend has inspired the phenomenal rise of state, city, and regional magazines. Some 200 of these have sprung up across the country over the past decade: *Columbus, Twin Cities, Texas Monthly, Washingtonian,* and many others. Most became financially successful, though similar magazines launched in the 1950s and 1960s had failed. They were ahead of their time. Some, notably *Seattle,* won journalistic acclaim. The next wave of geographic publishing—already under way—is a boom in local and regional business magazines.

Book publishers are catching on to regional diversity, too. One house trying to cash in on the trend is Bantam Books, which published an anthology, *West Coast Fiction,* in 1979. In early 1981, another Bantam collection, *Southwest Fiction,* followed. One editor predicted a Midwest anthology will be next.

The 1970s also witnessed the reemergence of regional architecture. Before World War II, buildings were constructed with available local materials and designed according to a region's climate. It was easy to guess the region where a building was located just by its design.

But the advent of air conditioning and cheap energy changed all that. Architects designed all buildings the same way

123

no matter where they were to be built. Now higher energy costs are bringing a return to regional architecture. Changing values are meeting up with economic necessity.

"Universal formulas, which we used for so long, don't work anymore, and architects are realizing they have to adapt buildings to local characteristics," says Paul Kennon, president of Caudill, Rowlett & Scott, the Houston architectural firm.

Still another example of regionalism and economic decentralization is the spectacular growth of regional airlines following industry deregulation, which was precipitated by a strong bottom-up pressure to decentralize power away from the big airline companies.

Many small communities, however, were not sold on the values of deregulation. Small cities and towns feared losing air service if the larger airlines were no longer required to serve less profitable routes. After deregulation in late 1978, those fears materialized. Major airlines pulled out of the shorter routes, as expected. What was not expected was the interest on the part of smaller commuter lines and larger regional airlines to jump into the newly abandoned market, not to mention the entrepreneurs who created new airlines.

Take the example of Providence, Rhode Island. Immediately after deregulation, National and American Airlines pulled out of Providence. Within two months, though, three new carriers— Pilgrim Airlines, EJA Newport, and the now defunct Air New England—were flying from Providence to New York and other cities. Rhode Island ended up with more seats and more service than it had prior to deregulation.

By 1980, after a full year of deregulation, the smaller regional airlines had realized substantial financial success. Regional airlines earned a combined profit of $150 million during 1980. That same year the larger national airlines collectively lost approximately $200 million, and blamed it on fuel price increases, strikes, and stiff price competition on key long-haul routes. Meanwhile, the regional lines enjoyed lower labor costs, flew smaller fuel-efficient 737s and DC–9s, and were able to raise prices with hardly a complaint from consumers grateful for good service at last.

But perhaps the most visible aspect of the whole decentralization trend is the decentralization of *people*. Many of us, along with demographers and social scientists, suspected that large numbers of American city dwellers were moving to small towns and rural communities.

The 1980 census made it official, confirming huge losses in city populations, mostly in the Northeast and Midwest: St. Louis down 27 percent, Buffalo down nearly 23 percent, and Detroit down nearly 21 percent. And many newspaper accounts expounded the long litany of social and economic woes that have beset the cities in the wake of losses in population, business, and tax base. (These will be discussed more fully in Chapter 9.)

At the same time there was a flood of feature stories telling the joys of the new small-town lifestyle as national publications started to sense what was going on. Former city dwellers are said to be opting out by the hundreds of thousands in search of clean air, safe streets, more time for family—in short, a simpler, slower pace of life.

> "It's utopia. It's God's country," says Florence Welton, who left New York City with her husband twelve years ago for an acre and a half of Pennsylvania hillside.
> *Newsweek,* "America's Small Town Boom," July 6, 1981

> "I may not be making as much money out here, but I'm making a better life," explains Ronald Amrein, who recently moved from Chicago to a small community in Illinois.
> *U.S. News & World Report,*
> "What Lures Americans Back to the Land?"
> November 26, 1979

> "The city people come up here with a 'whatever's here, it's got to be better than down there' attitude," said James Davison. "They're tired of the crime, they're tired of the race problem, tired of taxes, tired of the whole concrete jungle." He ought to know. Five years ago Mr. Davison gave up a job in Saginaw, as Michigan representative for Winchester Arms, for life in the northern woods of Michigan's Lower Peninsula.
> *New York Times,* "Rural Michigan Booming
> as Many Flee Urban Ills," July 8, 1981

In the long term, how will the small-town boom influence the shape of the American landscape? And how does this graphic form of decentralization fit into the decentralization megatrend?

First the basics: The small-town boom is not the figment of some news editor's imagination. It is one of those unusual trends that is noticed first and then statistically proven to exceed every expectation. That is not the case, however, for many trends—for example, the return of the well-to-do to the cities. In certain areas, such as Washington, D.C., gentrification is real enough. But the movement of the wealthy into the cities remains statistically insignificant because the tide is generally flowing in the opposite direction.

The statistics on the rural and small-town boom are significant to the overall pattern of American life. For the first time since 1820, rural areas and small towns are pulling ahead of cities in population growth. During the 1970s, small towns and rural areas grew 15.5 percent faster than cities. There are still more Americans living in the cities or close-in suburbs—approximately six in ten—than in the country. The point is that population is growing faster in the country.

With some 95 million Americans, around 42 percent of us, living in rural areas or small towns, it is not surprising that the country-living boom has spawned or strengthened organizations that cater to or lobby for rural interests. There is the 115-member Congressional Rural Caucus, the National Association of Counties, which is gaining as a lobbying force, the Rural Coalition, the Small Cities Study Group of the National League of Cities, and the Small Town Institute.

What makes the country boom so phenomenal is that it is not regional, but national, in scope. Small towns and rural areas are growing faster than metropolitan areas in *all* parts of the country, though the increase is smaller in the Midwest (up 7.8 percent) and largest by far in the West (up a whopping 31.8 percent). In the South, small-town growth is up 17.1 percent and in the Northeast it is up 12.4 percent.

The small-town boom is statistically valid and widespread, but most commentators have misunderstood its implications. It is not a nostalgic return to the agriculturally based economy of the past. Farmland and farmers are increasing a little in some areas too, but at a much slower rate. The farm trend is really not part of the small-town boom, although it is frequently portrayed as such.

No one has understood and interpreted the small-town boom with more clarity than *New York Times* reporter John Herbers, who, in my view, is one of the only three or four great

American journalists. Herbers has the ability to place his individual news stories within the context of changing social, economic, and political realities, thereby offering the reader not just the facts but an interpretation of the way those facts relate to the rest of what is going on.

More than a year before magazines like *Newsweek* were stringing together anecdotes of individuals who had moved to the country for a descriptive feature account of "America's Small Town Boom," Herbers was out in the small towns, using census estimates to analyze the overall factors behind the new rural boom.

Herbers points out that it is the decentralization of business itself that supports the small-town and rural boom—the tendency for companies to situate new facilities away from the cities and in the wide-open spaces.

Douglas County, Colorado, is typical of the counties that grew quickly during the 1970s. A rural area south of Denver, it had a population of only 8,400 at the beginning of the decade. The population there is now 23,500 partly because Johns Manville Corporation located its world headquarters in Douglas County, and several factories moved in as well.

According to John Kasarda, chairman of the Department of Sociology at the University of North Carolina, metropolitan areas suffered a net loss in jobs between 1970 and 1978, while there were some 700,000 new manufacturing jobs created in nonmetropolitan areas. In addition, estimates Kasarda, there were approximately 3.5 million new "service" (read information) jobs in nonmetropolitan areas during the same time frame.

The second most important factor, after the decentralization of business plants themselves, according to John Herbers, is America's strong highway system. It has helped foster the city-to-country shift by enabling workers to live far way from offices or factories, which are nearly always located alongside highways.

Furthermore, Herbers correctly perceives the dual nature of the country boom. Growth has occurred both in small towns away from major metropolitan areas and in the rural counties beyond those suburbs that surround the big metropolitan areas. The 1980 census reports that the fastest-growing counties are those located adjacent to metropolitan areas.

This is not the abrupt change in lifestyles that is presented in the popular press, but is actually a deconcentration, a *spreading out* or thinning out, a blending of lifestyles that is partly urban, partly suburban, and only partly rural in nature.

Viewed as a spreading out of the urban and suburban cultures, geographic decentralization is much easier to understand. Ex-urbanites are simply spreading their culture out to rural counties and small towns. The aspects of the small-town boom that seem to mystify or amuse the feature-story writers become perfectly logical: City people have brought the best and the worst of city life to the country. That is why liquor stores along country roads stock French wines, why rural crime increased 131 percent during the 1970s, and why small-town and suburban newspapers are flourishing (city folks have brought writing skills, education, and a taste for Pulitzer Prize–winning journalism). Finally, is it any wonder that the nouveau rurals have the audacity to expect the services they enjoyed in the city—good roads, waste disposal, and water?

This is all appropriate to a thinning out. The educated city immigrant is placing a layer of city culture on top of the country landscape. And, as the feature stories report, the country folks are often resisting the intruding culture, as native populations are wont to do.

But America is a country accustomed to great migration and the conflict that often follows. During the 1980s the new and old country dwellers will have the opportunity to work out their differences. The result will be a society that is richer, offers even more geographic lifestyle options, is more sophisticated, and draws an even greater sense of identity than in the 1970s, from wherever its people choose to live.

As our top-heavy, centralized institutions die, we are rebuilding from the bottom up.

Decentralization creates more centers. That means more opportunities and more choices for individuals. Because business is decentralized, you can find a job close to where you want to live in a rural area—or almost anywhere else. Your home computer and word processor will enable you to work at home in an isolated area, if you are one of the few who takes that course. On the other hand, the cities that some leave will become less crowded and more pleasant for the others who stay.

In the city *or* the country, decentralization empowers you to tackle problems and create change at the local level. Because political power is decentralized, you can make a difference locally. In fact that might be the only way you can make a difference. Besides, you don't need a lot of money in local politics. Decentralization is the great facilitator of social change.

6

From Institutional Help to Self-Help

For decades, institutions such as the government, the medical establishment, the corporation, and the school system were America's buffers against life's hard realities—the needs for food, housing, health care, education—as well as its mysteries—birth, illness, death. Slowly we began to wean ourselves off our collective institutional dependence, learning to trust and rely only on ourselves.

During the 1970s, Americans began to disengage from the institutions that had disillusioned them and to relearn the ability to take action on their own.

In a sense, we have come full circle. We are reclaiming America's traditional sense of self-reliance after four decades of trusting in institutional help.

It is important to recall that the Great Depression was the most traumatic event that America experienced in this century. During the 1930s our traditional faith in ourselves was badly shaken. We began to think that only with the strength of large institutions behind us could we effectively counter life's blows.

More and more, we relied on government to provide for basic needs. Government's traditional function is to safeguard citizens. We also asked that it provide food, shelter, and jobs. But by the 1960s, government's role had grown to testing toys and regulating the environment and much of the economy.

We allowed ourselves to act as passive bystanders, handing over to the medical establishment not only the responsibilities it could handle, healing traumatic wounds and grave illnesses, but also the responsibility that in reality belonged only to ourselves, the responsibility for our health and well-being. We revered doctors as our society's high priests and denigrated our own instincts. And in response, the medical establishment sought to live up to our misplaced expectations. Placing all their trust in the modern voodoo of drugs and surgery, they practiced their priesthood and we believed.

We gave our children over to the schools, relieved perhaps of our own uncertainties about the best ways to teach and raise them.

And we went to work in corporations, which became central to our daily life. To corporations, we assigned the most personal of our responsibilities. They had only to provide us with a salary, at first. But as the influence of other institutions (family, neighborhood, churches) waned, the corporate role expanded, and we made it responsible for our social contacts, self-esteem, even sense of identity (as in "I'm an accountant with IBM"). In short, we assigned the corporate institution the task of helping us achieve and fulfill our need for belonging (through social contacts) and for self-worth (through our success at work).

But at various points during these last four decades, those institutions have failed us. And about ten or fifteen years ago, we began to realize this, when a string of institutional failures became blatantly apparent. At around the same time we admitted to having lost the war on poverty as well as the war in Vietnam, we began to mistrust medicine as well. We read what were then simply incredible stories about the medical profession's routinely prescribing addictive drugs such as tranquilizers and diet pills and performing unnecessary operations.

We had suspected that the schools were failing to educate our young. By the 1970s there was proof. At that point it became clear that the trend toward lower SAT scores was not a temporary reversal, but a long, slow, and steady decline.

As we became more disillusioned we asked, "What, or whom, can we trust?" The resounding answer was "Ourselves."

We began to grow more self-sufficient. Motivated by mutual self-interest, we started to help each other and ourselves.

Self-help has always been part of American life. In the 1970s it again became a movement that cut across institutions, disciplines, geographic areas, and political ideologies. Self-help means community groups acting to prevent crime, to strengthen neighborhoods, to salvage food for the elderly, and to rebuild homes, without government assistance or at least with local control over government help. Medically, self-help is taking responsibility for health habits, environment, and lifestyle, and is demanding to be treated wholistically. It is asking to be treated as a whole person—body, mind, and emotions—by medical practitioners. It is people reclaiming personal control over the mysteries of life and death from the medical establishment through the hospices movement, natural childbirth, home births, and an increase in midwives and birthing centers where whole families participate in the birth experience in a homelike, low-technology setting. Self-help is the blossoming of America's entrepreneurial movement, which rejects large corporations in favor of self-employment and small business. In the schools, it is increased parental activism along with questioning of the public school system—and in some cases the rejecting of it for private schools or (more radically) home education.

The New Health Paradigm

America's loss of faith in the medical establishment gave a strong symbolic push to the paradigm shift from institutional help to self-help. When we entered the 1970s without the long-promised cure for cancer, people began to question the omnipotence of science. It was during the 1970s, of course, that interest in diet and nutrition soared. Adelle Davis's nutrition books began to attract a following beyond those who were considered health nuts. The importance of nutrition was being seriously entertained for the first time as a preventive measure against cancer.

Shortly thereafter, America's romance with running began. From cult, running and jogging became a budding mass movement. The benchmark was when the now enormously popular

Runner's World went from a modest newsletter to a glossy magazine.

In time, we seriously considered alternatives to the medical establishment's program of annual physical exams, drugs, and surgery. We talked and wrote about a wealth of new-age remedies—acupuncture, acupressure, vitamin therapy, charismatic faith healing, and preventive health care through diet and exercise.

My friend and colleague Rick Carlson, chairman of California's Wellness Council, has a concise way of explaining what was happening. There are three basic ways to improve health care, says Rick. You can introduce outside agents such as drugs and surgery (which we have been doing since the 1930s), or you can try to improve either the human being or the environment. What began happening in the 1960s is that we shifted over to working on the human side, the idea being that a stronger population can better resist disease. (The next big shift will be to focus more on the environmental influence on health, Rick predicts.)

The new emphasis on the human angle shows up in three major trends behind the move from institution help (the medical establishment) to self-help (personal responsibility for health): (1) New habits that actualize our newfound responsibility for health; (2) Self-care that illustrates our self-reliance in areas not genuinely requiring professional help; and (3) the triumph of the new paradigm of wellness, preventive medicine, and wholistic care over the old model of illness, drugs, surgery, and treating symptoms rather than the whole person.

New Habits and Self-Care

The change in personal habits is central to medical self-help. And there is no doubt that our habits have changed monumentally. A few statistics tell the story:

- At least 100 million Americans, almost half the population, are now exercising in some way—up from only about one-quarter of the population in 1960. That is a 100-percent increase in regular exercisers.
- We've reduced our fat intake mightily: Butter consumption

is down 28 percent—milk and cream, down 21 percent—since 1965.
- Smoking, long blamed for poor health, is down substantially, 28 percent, among adult men and down 13 percent among adult women since 1965.
- We've switched from hard liquor to wine. In 1980, for the first time, Americans drank more wine (475.8 million gallons) than hard liquor (455 million gallons).
- The number of health food stores in the United States increased from 1,200 in 1968 to more than 8,300 in 1981. Health food sales went from $170 million in 1970 to $2 billion in 1981.

One of the strongest allies in America's health habit transformation is the business community. If corporate America turns its nose up at kooky ideas like health food and acupressure, its reaction to the physical fitness craze is quite the opposite. This is one component in the new wellness picture that American business can identify with and get behind. And it has done so with a passion.

More than 500 companies across the country have fitness programs managed by full-time directors. Membership in the American Association of Fitness Directors in Business and Industry has grown from 25 in 1974 to 1,800 in 1980. Exxon, Xerox, Chase Manhattan, Johnson & Johnson, Pepsico, and Mobil Oil, just to name a few, currently have in-house fitness centers. Disease prevention programs have become increasingly popular in every area of the country:

- Republic Steel Corp. tests workers in its Alabama plant for high blood pressure.
- TRW, Inc., is testing employees in their Ohio valve division for early signs of health problems.
- Four Iowa companies offer comprehensive medical screening and between 60 and 95 percent of employees participate.

One small public employer has devised a simple but effective method for encouraging employee wellness. The Mendocino (California) County Office of Education sets aside $500 per employee per year; medical costs are deducted and the employee is entitled to the rest. The "stay well" program, as it is called, has reduced medical claims by 60 percent, and the office has been besieged with inquiries about it.

Along with new habits, the medical self-help movement has brought an upsurge in self-care. No longer do Americans feel they must run to a doctor for every minor ailment: 75 percent of the people can successfully deal with medical problems without ever walking into a clinic or doctor's office.

The advent of the self-care phenomenon has brought a boom in home medical tests. With a simple kit or medical device, you can now monitor your blood pressure, find out if you are pregnant, examine your urine to see whether you are a diabetic or have an infection. New York residents can send $1 to The American Cancer Society and receive a bowel-cancer test kit.

By 1981 home health care was a $2.5-billion-a-year business, up from a $500-million-a-year business in 1970. And its future looks bright. By 1990, sales should reach $10 billion. A New York research firm, Find/SVP, estimated the annual sales of all types of do-it-yourself diagnostic kits reached $100 million in 1980—and are continuing to grow. Sales of pregnancy kits alone will probably reach $100 million in 1982.

With self-care on the increase, the health care focus has shifted from medical facilities to the home. One of the major reasons, of course, is cost. A pilot project in New Jersey sponsored by the Veterans Administration is fostering home care, contrasting the high costs of hospital care with $15 per day for home care. In Connecticut, Blue Cross/Blue Shield will cover home care for the terminally ill. Again, because it is cheaper.

Says Frank Zorn, vice president of Marshall Electronics, in typical self-help fashion, "We are taking the medical instruments from the doctor and putting them into the hands of the layman." A Washington, D.C., medical supplier did 90 percent of its 1980 business with the general public.

And laymen who want to treat their illnesses at home can find like-minded souls. More than 500,000 self-help medical groups have been formed to support home self-care.

Says Dr. Tom Ferguson, author of *Medical Self-Care*, "I think we are on the edge of a very major change in our health care system. People are learning to make decisions about their own symptoms and to take care of themselves."

That's the essence of the shift from institutional help to self-help.

Central to the whole self-help concept is the redefinition of health from the mere absence of disease to the existence of a positive state of wellness in the whole person.

Wellness and wholistic health are often incorrectly linked with experimental and alternative medical treatments. That is a misnomer. Wholistic health simply means dealing with the body, mind, and emotions as a whole. Surgery can be thoroughly wholistic, provided surgeon and patient are full partners in the enterprise.

What constitutes a basic wellness program is simple and uncontroversial: regular exercise, no smoking, a healthy diet (with low-to-moderate intake of fat, salt, sugar, and alcohol), adequate rest, and stress control. Personal habits are the key element in the new health paradigm, so personal responsibility is critical. And that represents a real turnabout. In the past, we believed our health was the doctor's responsibility—that seems incredible now—and that the insurance company's responsibility was to pay the bills when we got sick. California's Governor Jerry Brown articulated the underlying assumption of the new paradigm when he said: "It bothers me when people smoke three packs of cigarettes a day for thirty years and then try to stick me with their health bill."

In the new self-help paradigm, prevention is clearly more sensible and cheaper than cure: We are practically blaming people for their own sicknesses, and wellness is becoming more respectable—a growth industry. The American Wholistic Health Association membership has doubled since its creation in 1978. It now boasts 500 member doctors and other medical professionals who believe in treating the emotional as well as physical causes of illness, using fewer drugs, advocating proper diet, and learning to deal effectively with stress.

The new wholistic health approach has opened up a new area in the search for health and wellness: the human mind. At the radical end of the spectrum is the belief that there is no disease that cannot be cured through the powers of the mind and a positive attitude.

But even traditional medicine has acknowledged that the mind has a role in the prevention and healing of disease. This was dramatized when Norman Cousins shared with millions of readers the story of how with his doctor's help he healed himself of what was thought to be an incurable disease with vitamin C and laughter.

Now wholistic and alternative cancer treatment programs have broken into the medical mainstream:

- In Ohio, Blue Cross/Blue Shield approved for insurance coverage a wholistic cancer treatment program founded by Dr. Ivan Podobnikar, director of the Ohio Pain and Stress Treatment Center and Cancer Counselling Center, in Columbus. Dr. Podobnikar approves of traditional cancer treatment—drugs and surgery—but his main approach is to help patients feel better about themselves by overcoming negative feelings.
- Another believer in alternative cancer treatment, Dr. Bernard Siegel, believes that many patients do not really want to participate in alternative programs, and really want to die. This "patient heal thyself" attitude would earlier have been unthinkable. For patients who really wish to become healthy, Dr. Siegel has created ECAP, Exceptional Cancer Patient program. Even five years ago, under the old institutional help model, this would have been rare.
- Dr. Gerald Jampolsky's Center for Attitudinal Healing in Tiburon, California, a similar program, has been duplicated in sixteen independent centers, and there is a new Menninger Foundation program in Kansas City that uses biofeedback and visualization for healing.

Although many doctors and medical practitioners reject the medical self-help movement as unscientific and amateurish, others encourage patients to participate as much as possible in their own well-being.

The Helping Hand Health Center in St. Paul, Minnesota, encourages patients to learn about their bodies. During medical examinations, patients learn step by step what the staff is doing and why, and how to take their own blood pressure.

In Excelsior, Minnesota, Dr. Milton Seifert's patients participate in his practice through a Patient Advisory Council, which determines office procedures, sets fees and salaries, handles debt collection, and investigates patient complaints. Dr. Seifert believes patients should share the responsibility, not only for medical care, but for the way health care is delivered. The patient council, organized in 1974, meets quarterly. About twenty-five of the council's fifty members attend each meeting; the rest get a copy of the minutes.

The Wholistic Health Center of Hinsdale, in Hinsdale, Illinois, emphasizes stress control, exercise, proper nutrition, and examines whether illness results from emotions, lifestyles, or habits. The center, founded in 1973, has opened thirteen other similar centers in Chicago, Cleveland, Minneapolis, Washington, D.C., and in cities in Indiana and Colorado. It also provides technical assistance in the wholistic health area.

The Hospices Movement

The medical self-help movement has helped people deal with the mysteries of birth and death, with the hospice movement and a variety of alternative, more natural ways of giving birth. We are reasserting personal control over the beginning and the end of life.

As previously mentioned, part of it is high tech/high touch—the rejection of too much medical technology, especially at the highly personal events of birth and death. The other part is self-help. For centuries people were born and died at home and among family, without either doctors or impersonal hospital procedures. Now we are again saying we are perfectly capable of handling birth and death by ourselves without the help of institutions.

Hospices provide a network of support services for terminally ill people and their families. Some hospices operate actual facilities; many more assist people to live out their final days at home as comfortably as possible. The goal is to give patients the power over their own care and a sense of dignity to their lives and deaths.

The original hospices were resting places during the Middle Ages for pilgrims on the way to the Holy Land. Present-day hospices began in the mid-1800s, when the Irish Sisters of Charity opened the first hospice for terminal patients in Dublin, Ireland.

The New Haven–based Connecticut Hospice pioneered the American movement. Since 1974, the Connecticut program has assisted some 1,000 terminally ill patients.

Now, according to the National Hospice Organization in

McLean, Virginia, there are more than 1,000 organizations in all fifty states and the District of Columbia.

There were two important reasons why the hospice movement gained in the 1970s: the illusiveness of a cure for cancer, and the increased willingness to discuss and confront death.

The popularity of books by Dr. Elisabeth Kübler-Ross and others has created an environment where death is no longer the last taboo subject. It is even being taught in the schools. Reports about high school courses on death have appeared in the *Seattle Times* and the *Grand Rapids Press*.

The failure to find a cancer cure has forced a shift in the treatment of terminally ill patients. In the past, the medical establishment had always encouraged patients to believe there was always hope, even up until the very last minute—another example of the mythic high-tech fix that will instantly solve all our problems.

But to the extent that people have given up on the medical establishment, they have sought a spiritual/humanistic approach, one where the emphasis is on living out one's final days in a comfortable, dignified, peaceful environment.

Birth Alternatives

The alternative birth movement began when women rejected the use of drugs in birth and turned to so-called natural childbirth, a perfect illustration of the shift from institutional help to self-help. The mother consciously lends her energies to the birth process rather than handing the experience over to the medical institution. From this beginning, parents have claimed greater and greater participation in the birth process, so that now there are birthing centers, more midwives, and more home births.

The appearance of the midwife is an example of American self-reliance having come full circle. Midwives were prevalent earlier in this century, but their numbers decreased as people relied on doctors and hospitals for their care. The great midwife comeback has occurred because their services fit the self-help model. Midwives provide more patient care and favor family participation in the birth process.

Currently in the United States, there are more than 2,100 nurse-midwives certified by the American College of Nurse-

Midwives. About 200 more graduate each year from accredited schools including Columbia University.

The *Lansing State Journal* ran a lengthy interview with a local midwife that discussed the personal values and economics that would lead a mother to select a midwife, while the *Dallas Morning News* reported that Brownsville, Texas, passed an ordinance for licensing midwives. As many as 80 percent of that city's Mexican-American community's babies are delivered by midwives.

Along with midwives, home births have become increasingly popular with American mothers. Between 1973 and 1978, there was a three-fold increase in the number of home births, with hospital births declining from 99.3 percent to 98 percent during that time period. In the bellwether state of California, home births increased to 3 percent of the total in 1980, while in Oregon the figure is 4 percent.

But for many parents the answer is somewhere in the middle. They do not wish to give birth at home but in a more home-like setting. They want to participate in the birth, but they want birth to occur near a medical facility. That is the reason behind the increase in birthing centers, birthing rooms, and shorter hospital stays.

In Rochester, New York, a new program combines one day in the hospital for childbirth with home care from community health nurses, technicians, and even housekeepers. The cost: $70 per day versus $300 per day for conventional care. No wonder it is being sponsored by Blue Cross/Blue Shield.

Hospitals are also adding more birthing rooms where mothers experience labor and delivery in a more homelike setting. Three hospitals in Louisville, Kentucky, opened birthing rooms in 1980. New birthing rooms were also reported in Austin, Denver, Detroit, and Indianapolis.

The *Portland Oregonian* says birthing rooms are "cropping up in Oregon like spring crocuses."

Birthing centers, freestanding facilities that provide comfortable low-technology care, are also becoming more popular. There are thirty-eight of these centers around the country today and many more birth centers within hospital settings.

One of the most successful is New York's Childbirthing Center, where 600 babies have been delivered since it began in 1975. The center limits services to women expecting normal deliveries;

its services are full maternity care, including natural childbirth, education classes, and pre- and postnatal checkups. Total cost: between $600 and $900.

Most of the deliveries are uncomplicated, but the staff is prepared for problems. About 18 percent of the mothers are transferred to nearby hospitals during labor. But, says a spokesperson, there have been no emergencies and no infant deaths. Approximately 5 percent of the center's mothers get medication during delivery.

The center was founded by New York's Maternity Center Association, which offers technical assistance to others wishing to start a birth center.

Education: Self-Help Comes to the Schools

The 1970s were not the best years for the public school system, but rather may have been the system's darkest hour. There was a widespread belief that the quality of education in America was declining mightily.

As we entered the 1970s, the SAT test scores (which students are required to take for college entrance) had declined from the 1965 level of 473 (verbal) and 496 (math) to 460 and 488 respectively. Obviously, no one was happy about the decline. But few would have been pessimistic enough to guess that the 1970s would produce a continued steady decline or that in 1979 scores would have sunk to an all-time low of 427 and 467.

Although many defenders of the education system deny test scores can measure education, there were many other indications that we were indeed losing faith in the school system, one of our country's most important resources.

In 1979, for example, respondents to a Gallup Poll on education expressed very little confidence in the schools. For the first time in the nation's history, adults considered themselves better educated than young people.

It is important to note that the disillusion with education occurred during the 1970s. Even in 1973, the schools were still well thought of: Half the respondents in the same poll thought young people better educated than themselves; one-quarter believed they—the adults—were better educated than the young people of the day. By 1979 the numbers were exactly reversed:

Half believed themselves the better educated, while only one-quarter thought young people were better educated.

In addition, school enrollment decreased 16 percent in the 1970s. Partly because of fewer students, the schools faced enormous financial problems. In some communities, for example, only a small percentage of the taxpayers has children in the school system. The result is an erosion in local financial support, coupled with the effects of a generalized taxpayer revolt.

There have been a variety of self-help responses to the continued disillusionment with the school system. Parent activism has increased and private-school enrollments have increased dramatically. In its most radical form, the new educational self-help movement has produced a steady stream of new alternative schools and attempts to move the education process from the schools into the homes, either as a supplement to the regular school curriculum or as an outright threat to the compulsory education laws.

Curriculum programs involving parents received increased publicity during the late 1970s:

- The National Committee for Citizens in Education proposed creating a citizen/parent office in what was then to be the new Department of Education. The National Committee passes out wallet-sized cards informing parents of their rights in the education system.
- In New Jersey, a group sued the local school board for "effectively excluding" parents from the educational goal-setting process.
- Parents in Palo Alto, California, pushed for a role in collective bargaining between teachers and the school board.

For some parents and other interested citizens, activism was not enough. They decided to seize control of the education process by creating their own schools.

"It is heresy to start your own school. We are heretics," says Dr. Anyim Palmer, founder of the Marcus Garvey Preschool and Elementary School in Los Angeles's predominantly black Crenshaw District.

"We have shown that it doesn't take elaborate facilities, it doesn't take credentialed, degreed, certified teachers, and it doesn't take mammoth salaries to give children a good education," says Palmer, who founded the school in 1975 with $20,000 and has been involved in the day-to-day education of its students ever since.

Only a few miles away, near Santa Monica, there is another alternative school, called Crossroads, for predominantly upper-middle-class students. But it too began on a shoestring, with $2,000 in seed money in 1971. Now its graduates attend MIT, Princeton, and Yale.

Both are examples of the new self-help approach to education: If you don't like the institution, help yourself and start your own school.

Or educate your children at home, if you can. Home education represents the most radical approach to educational self-help, and more and more parents are becoming interested in the idea.

Says Boston-based educator and author John Holt: "I used to say reform the schools. Then I said start your own school. Now I say take the children out entirely." In the 1960s and 1970s the self-help approach to education took the form of creating alternative schools; in the 1980s it will be home education.

Several years ago, Holt estimated there were at least 10,000 families educating their children at home. In 1982 the figure was estimated at one million. Holt's latest venture in home education is "Growing Without Schooling," a bimonthly twenty-four-page magazine for people who have taken or want to take their children out of school and have them learn at home. It features articles by Holt, legal information, and success stories of parents who are teaching children at home. With home computers, home education can increase even more dramatically.

The main obstacles, of course, are compulsory education laws. The not very bellwether state of Mississippi is currently the only state where home education is legal. But compulsory laws are being challenged by parents.

During a brief period in 1979, the *Trend Report* recorded that court cases involving these challenges had surfaced in at least six states. In addition:

- Two state legislators in Maine proposed a law to abolish compulsory education laws there.
- The Utah state superintendent said he witnessed more cases on home education in 1979 than ever before.

- In the late 1970s two Michigan families were charged with truancy for educating their children at home.
- A New Hampshire school board had to drop its case against the parents of a nine-year-old girl being educated at home, because it would have cost $2,500 to bring them to court.

Although most parents are not willing to take such drastic action, a great many feel they must supplement their children's education with more home teaching.

Sales of the Calvert School Home Study program—which would probably become astronomical if compulsory education laws were revoked—have increased substantially as more parents use the system to supplement school curriculum.

Washington, D.C., parents supplement their children's education through a unique self-help program designed by Dr. Dorothy Rich, author of *Families Learning Together*. Rich does not believe parents should keep children out of the schools, "but schools have a more limited role than we thought," she says.

Rich's methods, a series of "learning appetizers" for home use, are imaginative and inexpensive. For example, using water and a paint brush, parents can help children draw disappearing letters and numbers on city sidewalks.

Recently she taught her program to eighteen Los Angeles–area counselors. They in turn were to teach the course to 1,000 families. Cost per family is $133.

Rich's self-help program works for a variety of socioeconomic groups. "We get a good response from college-educated parents as well as those parents who didn't finish high school," she says.

Entrepreneurial Explosion

In the business world, people are seeking self-reliance and self-help by becoming independent of large corporations through entrepreneurship, self-employment, and work in small business.

As I have mentioned previously, the past thirty years have witnessed a phenomenal increase in the number of American entrepreneurs. In 1950 we were creating new businesses at the rate of 93,000 per year. By December 1980, it was running at the rate of 600,000 per year.

Dun & Bradstreet Corporation believes much of the increase occurred in the late 1970s. D&B estimates there were 533,500 incorporations annually by 1980. By D&B's count, that represents a 63-percent increase over 1975.

In the Silicon Valley alone, more than 100 new companies emerged during 1979.

Self-employment is booming as well. After two decades of decline, it increased 25 percent between 1972 and 1979, says the U.S. Department of Labor.

Small business is all around us: Of America's 11 million businesses, 10.8 million are small business. Sixty million of the nation's approximately 100 million workforce are in small business.

With the increase in business start-ups has come a new appreciation for the contributions of small business to the U.S. economy.

It seems that America's collective thinking is shifting to "What's good for small business is good for America."

Recent studies have convinced government and business observers that small businesses, not big corporations, are responsible for most of the new jobs created and most of the nation's economic growth, and that they are more productive and innovative as well.

The most widely cited study is by David Birch of MIT's Program on Neighborhood and Regional Change. The study, which surveyed approximately 80 percent of all business enterprises in the United States between 1969 and 1976, showed that nearly two-thirds of all the new jobs created were generated by businesses employing twenty people or less. During the 1970s, by contrast, the *Fortune* 1,000 produced virtually no job growth, according to Birch. (The National Federation of Independent Businesses, however, is willing to acknowledge that the *Fortune* 1,000 created 10.6 percent of all jobs during the 1970s.)

A U.S. Department of Commerce study parallels MIT's findings. The Commerce Department grouped U.S. companies into clusters of mature companies, innovative companies, and young high-technology companies, and attempted to measure their sales and job growth between 1969 and 1974. The young high-tech firms were way out ahead. Mature companies averaged only a 1-percent job growth, innovative companies a 4.3-

percent job growth, while young innovative high-tech companies created an almost unbelievable 40.7-percent increase in jobs.

Sales growth showed a similar pattern. Mature companies increased sales 11.4 percent; innovative companies, 13.2 percent; but the young high-tech firms registered a huge 42.5-percent sales increase.

The Dow Jones Industrial Average—the stocks of thirty large, mostly industrial companies led by General Motors and U.S. Steel—is an absurd way to measure economic health. George Gilder has pointed out that, although the Dow Jones declined throughout most of the 1970s, other indexes that included many small companies did quite well during the decade. The Value Line Composite Index, for example, rose 140 percent since 1974. The American Exchange grew 260 percent since its 1974 low and 63 percent in 1979 alone.

A weighted index published by Wilshire Associates of Santa Monica, California, which includes nearly every American stock, grew at about the same pace as the Dow until 1977. Then, when the Dow plunged, the Wilshire index took off. During 1979, for example, it increased 20 percent to 1,056. (The Wilshire index, incidentally, is heavily weighted to favor the large companies. Hundreds of small companies must increase in value to counter a downward plunge by one of the big companies.)

American entrepreneurship has gotten a big boost in recent years with the abrupt increase in venture-capital money. Most businesses, of course, get their start on a shoestring. Usually entrepreneurs use their own savings for start-ups. Venture capitalists back only the most sophisticated business plans.

The venture-capital pool has increased dramatically: In 1977, $39 million was committed to venture-capital firms. The following year it jumped to $570. After a temporary decrease in 1979, the pool was up to $900 million in 1980, a record year.

What was behind the impressive upsurge in venture capital? For one thing, small business can thank government policy—in 1978, the capital-gains tax was reduced from 49 to 28 percent. That certainly helped.

(By contrast 1969 to 1977 were very rough years for entrepreneurs seeking start-up money. The capital-gains tax was hiked from 25 to 49 percent in 1969, which virtually dried up venture-capital markets. For example, about 300 new high-tech companies were founded in the United States in 1968, but not one was started in 1976. Now the capital-gains tax is down to 20 percent under the Reagan administration.)

But there are other reasons behind the new abundance in venture capital: More and more people are learning that entrepreneurship pays off. Sophisticated venture capitalists are willing to take a calculated risk in return for a possible 20- to-25-percent return. When stock market returns average below 10 percent and even money-market funds can barely keep pace with inflation, backing new businesses starts to look more attractive.

In recent years, even institutional investors are returning to entrepreneurship after pulling out of the market around 1969, when it really was too risky. Now, fifteen years later, institutional investors are back.

Says Janet Hickey, manager of investment research and head of capital commitment at the General Electric Pension Trust: "You've got teams of people now who are cycle-tested, who have managed venture capital during the past decade, which were turbulent times for financial assets. Confidence in venture-capital partnerships has grown."

Furthermore, venture capitalists can now choose from a great number of more sophisticated, more experienced entrepreneurs who are better managers and whose ideas are well thought-out.

All totaled, entrepreneurial self-help is an idea whose time has come again, and the 1970s were its debut decade.

But it was not always so popular. In the 1950s the entrepreneurial spirit was nearly dead. With memories of the Depression and World War II still vivid, we continued to look toward the institutions of big business and big government to protect us. Old-fashioned American self-reliance lay dormant beneath the simple fact that, at the time, big business and government were doing a pretty respectable job of assisting us. It was the heyday of industrialism and institutional help.

But the generalized disillusion with institutions that surfaced during the 1960s changed all that. One of the major institutional dependencies we sought to escape was the corporation. There was a basic anticorporate sentiment in the 1960s among college students, especially with respect to the environment, civil rights, and Vietnam.

But much of that anticorporate feeling went underground during the 1970s as graduates went to work—where else?—in big business. Many of us thought that was the end of it: Another generation of idealists wised up to the real world.

The baby boomers were not just another generation of idealists, though. Their numbers made them a megageneration, an army that was not easily absorbed in society. And the 1970s, when their ranks hit the job front, were not exactly booming times. Consequently, some baby boomers were forced into self-employment, even entrepreneurship, by a weak job market. Others who had cherished independence in the 1960s and given it up for high-paying corporate jobs in the 1970s were, all the while, saving, learning, and plotting their escape into entrepreneurship.

In the late 1970s it all exploded into an entrepreneurial boom.

We are shifting from a managerial society to an entrepreneurial society.

Now even parents of baby boomers are giving small business another look. The president of one New York recruiting firm told *The Wall Street Journal* that the number of executives he moved from big to small firms doubled during the last half of the 1970s.

Executives who have made the switch report greater job satisfaction, more independence, and in some cases a better financial deal: In smaller companies, employees escape the rigid salary structures of big firms and are free to negotiate higher pay. The reduced capital-gains tax often makes it worthwhile for an executive to accept a smaller salary in exchange for stock in growing companies.

Writing in a *New York Times* op-ed piece, former radical Jerry Rubin, who served a stint as a Wall Street securities analyst, sums up the feelings of many of his generation about the new entrepreneurial boom:

> The challenge for American capitalism in the 1980's is to bring the entrepreneurial spirit back to America. The large organizations have discouraged people's expression and ambition. America needs a revitalization of the small business spirit.

149

Self-Help: Personal and Community

Fifteen million Americans now belong to some 500,000 self-help groups, according to the National Self-Help Clearinghouse at City University of New York. These people have decided to bypass the traditional avenues of institutional assistance—churches, social service agencies, the mental health establishment—in favor of dealing with people like themselves who have conquered or are trying to solve the same problem. It is a telling illustration of the shift from institutional help to self-help.

There are self-help groups for almost every conceivable problem: retirement, widowhood, weight control, alcohol and drug abuse, mental illness, handicaps, divorce, child abuse, and many more.

The credit card boom triggered the creation of one of the latest self-help groups, Big Spenders Anonymous, for compulsive debtors. The main premise is that overspending is a disease.

Support groups like this often follow the successful Alcoholics Anonymous model, avoiding elaborate structures, expenses, or therapy, in favor of sharing information and experiences in an informal atmosphere.

"Self-help groups bring peers together for mutual assistance in satisfying a common need," write Alan Gartner and Frank Riessman, co-directors of the Self-Help Clearinghouse. The guiding principle is helping one's self by helping others.

Why did the self-help movement grow so rapidly during the 1970s? Gartner and Riessman believe it is because "people feel unable to control 'big government' and the distant bureaucracies and so are drawn to mutual-aid groups that enable them to deal directly with some immediate problems of everyday life."

When the self-help model is adapted in neighborhoods or communities, however, personal self-help becomes social activism. And socially oriented self-help groups are active all across the country.

Social and business critic Peter Drucker summed up the philosophical backbone of this new social self-help movement. "Nobody really believes anymore that government delivers," Drucker told *U.S. News & World Report.*

"Even in matters of defense—the purpose for which government was instituted among men—no government can promise any longer that it can protect civilians and that they are not going to be harmed by war," observes Drucker.

Drucker is on target, as usual. And his comments suggest we must rethink the very purpose for which government was created and the relationship of citizens to it.

In the meantime, the large-scale movement away from reliance on the government to solve problems continues unabated. People everywhere, especially the poor who have relied on government in the past, are acting en masse to secure food and supplies, to build and repair adequate housing, to conserve energy, to increase community and consumer activism.

"The self-help movement is one of the few promising developments in poor urban communities," says a *New York Times* editorial lauding the cooperation between two Brooklyn self-help groups, one Hispanic and one Jewish. The two groups will renovate 243 housing units with the help of a grant from Local Initiatives Support Corporation, a creation of the Ford Foundation.

Astronomical housing and energy costs have brought scores of community self-help groups into the renovation, rehabilitation, and retrofitting business.

During the 1970s new home prices rose 127 percent and rents doubled. In 1979, the average new home cost $79,000, far more than many Americans can afford. By early 1982 the average new-home cost had jumped to $86,700. But, over the years, self-help groups have found a variety of techniques to make housing affordable:

- The Kentucky Mountain Housing Development Corporation has helped nearly 200 families to purchase new homes and 500 others to renovate their houses. Family incomes averaged under $5,000 per year.
- In South Bend, Indiana, Renew, Inc., which began when a local priest raised $1,000 for a down payment on an old house, has sold renovated houses to low-income families since 1972. But because the program includes financial counseling, the homeowners' default rate is only 2 percent.
- In Washington, D.C., Jubilee Housing, Inc., which began as a local church group, renovated ninety units in two deteriorating apartment houses. Tenants then converted them into cooperatives.

- Denver's Brothers Redevelopment, Inc., has completed more than 700 repair and renovation projects since 1973. Mutual self-help is its core: Those who benefit from the group's efforts pitch in on the next project. Brothers, Inc., has gotten some government funding, but has also obtained loans from the Colorado Housing and Finance Authority, the United Bank of Colorado, and other local banks and foundations.

Adequate buildings in good repair are one of the most important elements in a strong community, and self-help activists have put their efforts into achieving both goals:

- St. Louis's Jeff-Vander-Lou, Inc., has renovated $15 million worth of housing, brought in low-cost medical care, and attracted a shoe factory to its community. The group started in 1966 with an upholstery-shop owner, two ministers, and a retired school teacher.
- In Georgia the Savannah Neighborhood Action Project is remodeling homes in a historic district for low-income residents who already live there. A similar effort in the Paterson Park section of Baltimore has turned tenants into homeowners.
- A grassroots organization in Astoria, New York, went into action when a handful of vacancies and a fire seemed to imperil the area's downtown district. "We convinced the neighborhood that our stores and their mortgages are equally important," said one store owner. "If the stores are boarded up, then the $80,000 homes around here would be worthless," he said.
- When downtown Miami began deteriorating, the chairman and CEO of Knight-Ridder newspapers summoned twenty-seven community leaders to an action meeting. "If it's not being done by elected people, then non-elected people have to do it," he said in typical self-help fashion. The result was the creation of the Miami Citizens Against Crime, composed of business and professional groups, including the Black Miami–Dade Chamber of Commerce and the Latin American Chamber of Commerce. A similar statewide group, Florida Citizens Against Crime, was established in 1982.

Food: Gardeners and Gleaners

Self-help in the food area means more home and urban gardening, food cooperatives, and farmers' markets.

- A 1979 Gallup Poll showed that more than 33 million American households grew some of their own food. Gardens cost about $19 and yielded up an average of $325 worth of produce, according to the survey.
- Boston Urban Gardeners (BUG) has helped hundreds of people transform vacant urban land into flourishing gardens. BUG now operates more than 120 community garden lots, each with between 20 and 400 individual plots.
- New York City's Greenmarket began in 1976 as a self-help attempt to attract fresh local produce and help area farmers. It now boasts eight locations that together handle $1 million a year in produce and serve as many as 30,000 New Yorkers each week.
- The Tucson Cooperative Warehouse, which began in 1973 when three groups merged their assets—a truck, a bookkeeper, and a good credit rating—now does a $1.5-million-a-year business and operates fifteen storefront cooperatives in four states.

Other Americans, especially senior citizens, are helping themselves by salvaging the vast food resources usually wasted in production and harvesting (about 20 percent of all food produced, according to the U.S. Agriculture Department).

"Gleaners" groups in Arizona, California, Michigan, Oregon, and Washington State go into the fields and find food passed over by the harvest, then distribute it to community groups.

St. Mary's Food Bank in Phoenix, Arizona, which collects cast-aside and gleaned food, sent 2 million pounds of food to schools and social service groups and fed 48,000 emergency victims for three days during 1979. Now St. Mary's helps other groups all across the country to learn the self-help approach to cutting waste and feeding the poor.

In Portland, Oregon, Tri-County Community Council Food Bank sent 700,000 pounds of salvaged food to eighty social service agencies.

153

Blue-Chip Self-Help

But low-income groups and middle-income consumers are not the only Americans attracted to the self-help concept. Some of its strongest advocates are among the rich. Well-to-do people, of course, are in a position to upgrade services by substituting private funds for inadequate government assistance.

In the wake of Proposition 13, for example, wealthy Beverly Hills residents raised $100,000 in a matter of weeks to make up the slack in education funds and community services.

San Marino's Blue Ribbon Committee asked residents to pledge 15 percent of their Proposition 13 savings to "maintain the quality of life in the area." Hundreds of thousands of dollars were raised.

Later some California citizens decided to bypass clogged courts by paying retired judges between $500 and $700 a day to hear cases.

Crime: Responding with Self-Help

When crime increased dramatically during 1980 and 1981, one response was to shift from institutional help to self-help. Grassroots interest in crime prevention showed up in the creation of neighborhood watches, civilian patrols, and an enormous increase in private security police.

Although citizens responded to crime with anger and fear, they also expressed a greater willingness to fight back. Neighborhood watch groups organized rapidly in many parts of the country. New groups included WHOA (Wilton Homeowners Alert) in Wilton, California; SNAP (Safe Neighborhoods Are Possible) in Bucks County, Pennsylvania; and SOS (Save Our Society) in Birmingham, Alabama.

Civilian patrols, such as the famous Guardian Angels of New York City, are another self-help response to crime. The Guardian Angels now have local branches in nineteen cities, including Los Angeles, San Francisco, Albuquerque, Cleveland, Boston, Newark, and San Juan, Puerto Rico. Other groups have copied the Angels' approach: the Guardians of Peace in Richmond, Virginia, the Young Dillingers of Washington, D.C., and the Red Berets in Cleveland. The guardians patrol without weapons and make citizens arrests, but defer to police.

Convinced that the government can no longer protect them, thousands of citizens, businesses, and communities are taking responsibility for their own crime prevention program.

- Churches, apartment buildings, and stores are hiring their own security guards in record numbers.
- Private police represent one of the fastest-growing occupations in the country, and the private police force in the United States is now three times the size of the public force.
- A Kansas City business group has hired a private security force to patrol the downtown area.
- Three new private security agencies have opened in Cheyenne, Wyoming, within a short period of time, despite the state's sparse population.

In communities across the country, people are volunteering to supplement police efforts.

- About 6,000 volunteer civilian police are at work in New York City.
- In St. Augustine, Florida, citizens want to reinstate a civilian police force that was disbanded a few years ago to augment what they say is an "impotent, lethargic, and openly disinterested" police force.
- Volunteer "citizen-officers" will patrol the streets of Charlotte, North Carolina.
- The Baltimore Police Department is creating a new uniformed, unarmed voluntary auxiliary force.

Survivalism

The most radical elements of the self-help movement are the militant survivalists. As Peter Drucker said, no government can any longer guarantee to protect citizens in the event of war.

Convinced that total self-reliance will be required to meet the years ahead, survivalists have created a $150-million business in survival gear. Most follow the advice of author Howard Ruff

(*How to Prosper During the Coming Bad Years*), who cautions readers to stockpile supplies before production and distribution lines are broken down. Bee Hive Foods in Redlands, California, which produces dehydrated and freeze-dried foods, reports that its market doubled in 1980.

Builders of fallout shelters report a brisk business again, and two Oregon architects have designed twenty luxury survival homes priced between $100,000 and $800,000. In Dalton, Georgia, the American Survival Training Center offers a four-day course for $550 that covers hand-to-hand combat and weapons use, as well as more conventional topics like food supplies and medical information.

Consumer Self-Help

On a more upbeat note, Americans are discovering the self-help answer to high prices, less disposable income, and soaring interest rates. Consumer self-help comes in a variety of packages.

Wholesale meat buying has recently increased 100 percent, according to *The Christian Science Monitor*. And higher meat prices have driven up the popularity of low-cost protein substitutes: Fifty tofu companies were established in the United States during the late 1970s by non-Oriental entrepreneurs.

Homeowners are deciding to remodel their old houses rather than face the double challenge of a more expensive home and sky-high interest rates. People are saying, "Let's fix that room or that furnace," William R. Green, an executive with Alcoa Building Products, told the *Philadelphia Inquirer*. The do-it-yourself market has blossomed into a $40-billion-a-year business, with annual growth rates of between 15 and 30 percent in recent years.

But for some adventurous do-it-yourselfers, remodeling is too tame; they are building their own homes. Home-building schools from New England to California will teach you how for about $500. Using local materials keeps costs down and couples often work together, although 35 percent of the students are single women.

Another new way consumers are helping themselves is by keeping and fixing up old cars, an apparent reversal of the throwaway ethic.

The *Los Angeles Times* quotes a representative from the

Automotive Service Council as saying members of his group notice that more and more consumers are willing to invest $2,000 to recondition old cars. It is a self-help response to the exorbitant cost of new cars.

Somewhere between the shift from institutional help to self-help comes the question "Can I really do it on my own?" For some people, there is a crisis of confidence, a fear that one is not yet up to the challenge of self-help, perhaps a desire to cling to the comfort of depending on others. Others are very assertive about taking care of things themselves.

Whether we like it or not, self-help fits the political and economic mood of the country. It will be around for a long time. Many of the institutions that helped in the past can no longer balance their budgets; the outstanding example is the United States government.

The macroeconomics of the industrial-welfare state is yielding to the microeconomics of the information self-help society.

The new atmosphere of self-help favors diversity, openness, even eccentricity. Let's face it: Gleaning food, midwivery, acupuncture, educating your child at home, and luxury survival homes are not exactly mainstream ideas—at least, they did not used to be. But with people relying on themselves outside the conforming structures of institutions, individualism will flourish.

7

From Representative Democracy to Participatory Democracy

The ethic of participation is spreading bottom up across America and radically altering the way we think people in institutions should be governed. Citizens, workers, and consumers are demanding and getting a greater voice in government, business, and the marketplace.

People whose lives are affected by a decision must be part of the process of arriving at that decision.

The guiding principle of this participatory democracy is that people must be part of the process of arriving at decisions that affect their lives. Whether or not we agree with the notion or abide by it, participatory democracy has seeped into the core of our value system. Its greatest impact will be in government and corporations.

Participatory democracy is revolutionizing local politics in America and is bubbling upward to change the course of national government as well. The 1970s marked the beginning of the participatory era in politics with an unprecedented growth in the use of referenda and initiatives. These contests can sometimes produce an enthusiastic voter turnout, of 70, 80, even 90, percent, because initiative and referenda ballots satisfy the need for "direct democracy," which is the heart and soul of participatory democracy.

But its influence extends beyond political issues. The participatory ethic will restructure all American institutions that serve and employ people. First and foremost, that means corporations.

All of the present impetus toward making corporations more open and more accountable, the consumer movement, the push for more outside directors, the new shareholder activism, and the trend toward greater employee rights and worker participation originate in the new ethic of participatory democracy.

The Death of Representative Democracy and the Two-Party System

Politically, we are currently in the process of a massive shift from a representative to a participatory democracy. In a representative democracy, of course, we do not vote on issues directly; we elect someone to do the voting for us.

We created a representative system two hundred years ago when it was the practical way to organize a democracy. Direct citizen participation was simply not feasible, so we elected people to go off to the state capitals, represent us, vote, and then come back and tell us what happened. The representative who did a good job was reelected. The one who did not was turned out. For two hundred years, it worked quite well.

But along came the communication revolution and with it an extremely well-educated electorate. Today, with instantaneously shared information, we know as much about what's going on as our representatives and we know it just as quickly.

The fact is we have outlived the historical usefulness of representative democracy and we all sense intuitively that it is obsolete. Furthermore, we have grown more confident of our own ability to make decisions about how institutions, including government and corporations, should operate.

We continue to elect representatives for two key reasons: (1) That is the way we've always done it, and (2) it is politically expedient. We don't want to vote on *every* issue, only the ones that really make a difference in our lives.

Essentially, we are telling our elected officials, "Okay, we've elected you to represent us, but if anything comes up that impacts on our lives, you've got to check back with us."

This demise of representative democracy also signals the end of the traditional party system.

Today the national political parties are in name only; on Capitol Hill there are 535 political parties.

What the national political parties do offer is structure. As John Herbers of the *New York Times* puts it, "the two-party system itself is little more than a hollow shell existing almost solely to provide the framework for nominating candidates."

We are becoming a nation of independents. People are expressing their distrust of political parties by refusing to identify with them. In 1964, 75 percent of us identified with one party or another. By 1976 the percentage had dropped to 67 percent, with some researchers putting it lower—at 63 percent. By 1980 the figure had edged up to 69 percent. But the days of strong party loyalty are over forever: More new voters are entering the system as independents than ever before, while older, card-carrying Republicans and Democrats actually vote as independents. Ticket splitting, voting for candidates from different parties, is the rule rather than the exception now. In 1980, 60 percent of the voters split the ticket, more than in either 1972 or 1976. Within a very short time, declaring oneself a strictly loyal Democrat or Republican will be openly considered a sign of narrow-mindedness and limited intelligence.

The political left and right are dead; all the action is being generated by a radical center.

The two-party system died because people gave up on it. Writes Herbers, "What has happened is that many people have given up trying to achieve goals through contests between Republicans and Democrats."

One activist housewife in Chicago summarized the sentiment on the local front: "They're all alike, Republicans and Democrats. We take them as they come up."

Said a Melrose, Massachusetts, housing engineer in 1980, "Every politician is the same, regardless of whether he's in Boston or Washington. That's why a lot of us may choose not to vote this November." As a result, people are focusing efforts on the local level. There, one sees not apathy but intense political activity.

Leadership involves finding a parade and getting in front of it; what is happening in America is that those parades are getting smaller and smaller—and there are many more of them.

There has been a gradual but pronounced shift of power out of the hands of elected officials to direct ballot voting through local initiatives and referenda where people, not officials, decide by a majority vote a certain course of action.

Politicians matter less and less. So there is a declining interest in national political elections. It is a natural consequence of the shift from a representative to a participatory democracy.

Political commentators and the media, of course, see this as anything but natural. We are constantly upbraided for apathy and for taking democracy for granted. And by now we all feel even guilty about it.

We should not. Low voter turnout does not automatically signal trouble in democracy. It may mean that people are more or less content whichever way an issue is settled, because it does not really impact on their lives.

In any event, exceptionally high turnout is not necessarily the wonderful thing the commentators would have us believe it is. Worldwide, the highest turnouts occur in totalitarian states. For example, only one voter failed to turn out in Albania's 1978 general election; North Korea counts on a full 100-percent turnout; and in Romania and East Germany the vote hovers at around 99 percent.

Political analysts used to associate low turnout with apathy or ignorance. But as the electorate becomes better educated, more informed, and more assertive, that rationalization is becoming increasingly difficult to substantiate. Analysts are finally beginning to understand that voters are making a conscious decision *not* to participate.

Democratic Congressman George Danielson from California says (ironically, I hope): "We have leadership—there's just no followership."

Of course that means there is no genuine leadership because *followers* create leaders.

What the people are saying is that they do not put much stock in either political office or the people filling it. By not voting they may be expressing the belief that politicians either cannot or will not do what the voters want done.

We have pulled the essence of political power out of the hands of our elected representatives and reinvested it into two main areas: (1) the direct ballot vote of initiatives and referenda and (2) grassroots political activity. In both cases citizens, not politicians, decide on a course of action and live with it.

In sum, that is what it means to have shifted from a representative to a participatory democracy.

New Political Parties

What about the cluster of new smaller political parties that has sprung up in the wake of the demise of the traditional two-party system: the Libertarian party, the Citizen's party, the Right to Life party, the Campaign for Economic Democracy (CED)?

These new parties are already making their mark on local politics:

- In New York State, the Right to Life party obtained more votes in 1979 than the old Liberal party; in Erie County, ninety candidates for local office sought the party's endorsement in 1979.
- Tom Hayden's CED group has elected candidates in many different parts of California: Santa Monica, Bakersfield, Chico, Berkeley, and Northern California's Yolo and Butte Counties. The group promotes rent control, solar energy, ending of corporate ties to South Africa, and occupational health concerns.
- Alaska has two Libertarian state legislators, one of whom promoted an initiative to reduce state personal income tax to 1 percent, which passed in 1980.

Despite growth at the local level, new political parties face obstacles at the national level from the old, well-entrenched two-party system.

Federal and state fair-campaign practice laws, and the public financing of the presidential campaign, virtually assure the two major parties a near monopoly of the political marketplace. Independent and minor party candidates cannot even appear on some state ballots and are usually prohibited from televised debates.

But even if those obstacles were to dissolve, new parties are unlikely to make their mark on the national scene. Such a development would be out of tune with the trend to decentralization. The political parties of the future will be highly localized. They will make their mark at the state and local level—where the real action is.

Initiatives and Referenda

Initiatives and referenda are the tools for the new democracy. These devices furnish direct access to political decision making, which is what informed, educated citizens want.

It is no wonder, then, that the popularity of initiatives exploded during the 1970s, when we voted on 175 state-level initiatives, twice as many as in the 1960s. There were ten state initiatives in 1970 and forty in 1978. And there were hundreds of other local initiatives.

Yet there are signs the initiative trend is just beginning. The initiative is now legal in 23 states and in 100 cities, but proinitiative groups are active in at least ten other states. The initiative process enjoys wide backing from virtually every political philosophy, from the Conservative party to Ralph Nader's Public Interest Research Group. A group called Initiative America is waging a battle to create a national initiative process.

The difference between initiatives and referenda is that initiatives appear on the ballot through direct citizen action, while referenda are a means for citizens to approve of legislative action.

The first state initiative in the United States was held in Oregon in 1904; one reason the referendum trend has taken hold recently is that people are demanding more accountability. The rise of the initiative, along with the referendum and the recall (which permits voters to recall an elected official and is legal in twelve states), represents an uncompromising demand on the part of the voters for accountability from government. These new devices, the key instrumentalities in the new participatory democracy, enable the people to leapfrog traditional representative processes and mold the political system with their own hands.

There are four important points to remember about initiatives:

- Initiative votes now resolve questions that we never before submitted to the political process.
- The most famous initiative of all, Proposition 13, was greatly misunderstood. It was the process rather than the subject that was important.
- The concept of a national initiative is out of tune with the stronger trend toward decentralization and therefore will probably be rejected.
- The initiative trend has its pluses and minuses, like almost anything else. Initiatives open the door to mischief ("mob rule" is how the fear is sometimes expressed). Yet, initiatives and referenda, in the final analysis, represent a much needed safeguard in a democracy.

Initiatives: New Questions in the Political Process

Historically, the initiative has been used most frequently for political and governmental reform, according to political scientist Austin Ranney, the author of an American Enterprise Institute study on initiatives and referenda. State-passed initiatives were the driving force behind repealing the poll tax, woman suffrage, direct election of U.S. senators, and other important political changes.

But what is most interesting about the present initiative boom is the range of nontraditional issues that has popped up on initiative ballots—energy, the environment, health, values, foreign policy, and many more.

Some two years before Jerry Brown's medfly battle, California's Mendocino County became the first in the nation to pass an initiative banning herbicide spraying from airplanes. Davis, California, voters passed an initiative to withdraw city funds from banks doing business with South Africa. Washington State voters repealed a sales tax on gasoline with an initiative.

In 1980 California and Dade County, Florida, voters considered a measure to require nonsmoking sections in business and public buildings. Several local jurisdictions have voted on the use of public funds for abortion.

In 1979 more than 300 initiatives appeared across the country. Voters in Washington, Ohio, and Maine voted on returnable bottles and disposable cans. A Washington State initiative for a nickel deposit on beer and soft-drink bottles was lost decisively with 57 percent voting against it. Ohio voters similarly rejected a dime deposit by a whopping 72 percent. But Maine kept a law banning nonreturnable bottles and cans.

In San Francisco, voters rejected an initiative to limit downtown buildings to twenty stories. And Long Beach voted on the color of its street lights. There is no end to the kind of questions we can put on the ballot. We never voted on these issues before, but we will vote on a great range of new ideas in the future.

In North Dakota, Missouri, and Michigan, votes cast recently for certain initiatives exceeded the total number of votes for governor. The famous Proposition 13 in California got some 100,000 more votes than all the votes cast for governor.

The most controversial and critical issue appearing on the initiative ballot is nuclear power, which has grown up with the 1970s initiative boom.

By 1976, when both trends were gaining steam, twenty states had antinuclear public action under way. Nuclear moratoria appeared on the ballot in Colorado, Arizona, Washington, Oregon, Maine, Michigan, Missouri, and Oklahoma.

Few of the initial attempts to ban nuclear power succeeded. But the most visible failure was California's Proposition 15, where voters decided in favor of building a nuclear power plant.

Yet, the failure of Proposition 15 to ban the plant had a paradoxical effect on the nuclear course of events in California. Although voters refused to block the plant, state legislators reacted by passing what at the time were the three toughest nuclear regulatory provisions in the country. The failure of Proposition 15 backfired in another way. California business interests, which outspent Proposition 15 proponents three to one, became intensely involved in 15 because there was so much at stake. Yet, in so doing, pronuclear businesses unwittingly helped to legitimatize the idea that nuclear questions should be resolved by vote. Eventually, the results of that change hammered still another nail into the nuclear coffin. The main reason nuclear failed, however, was that it was too expensive to build.

Since Proposition 15, voters in a number of states have tackled nuclear issues at the polls. During 1980, for example, nuclear issues were on the ballot in six states. In Washington, Montana, and Oregon, initiatives passed; in South Dakota, Maine, and Missouri, they were defeated.

The most recent direction emerging in the participatory democracy megatrend is the powerful grassroots nuclear-freeze movement. In the summer of 1982 the largest peaceful rally in U.S. history was held in New York's Central Park, demonstrating against nuclear proliferation. That surely is a clear example of participatory democracy on the nuclear defense issue.

Whatever the outcome of specific contests, the trend is becoming clear: Technical decisions, such as nuclear energy, are moving out of the hands of the so-called experts and into the political arena. That is just what you would expect in a participatory democracy where the people affected by a decision must be part of the decision-making process.

For example, sixty-one energy experts convened four years ago by the National Academy of Science were unable to agree about the technical superiority of various energy options, although they seemed to favor nuclear. Writing about the effort, the scientists concluded: "The public will have to choose between energy sources based on individual values and beliefs about social ethics—not on the advice from technical experts."

Physicist Edward Teller, speaking before the Atomic Industrial Forum, echoed the sentiment about the current nuclear debate. He said, "It isn't technology, it's politics. It isn't facts, it's perception."

Proposition 13 Was Misunderstood

In 1978 California's Proposition 13, the tax-cut proposal by Howard Jarvis and Paul Gann, passed by a strong two-to-one margin and caught the country by storm. The proposal cut property taxes by 57 percent, to 1 percent of appraised value. For the state of California, its passage meant a $7-billion loss in property-tax revenue.

Even before the rest of the states had a chance to see how California would cope with a multibillion-dollar shortfall, the spirit of Proposition 13 inspired a flurry of tax-cutting actions all across the nation.

Maryland's governor announced a state hiring freeze. Delaware passed a bill limiting state spending to 98 percent of anticipated revenues. The governors of Maine and New Hampshire called for tax limitation amendments to their state constitutions. In Montana, Nevada, Oregon, and Illinois, tax-cut advocates were in various stages of getting Proposition 13–type proposals on the ballot. Even Florida and Georgia, which have relatively low taxes, witnessed tax limitation activism after Proposition 13.

Tax limitation measures were on the ballot in Michigan, Arizona, Colorado, Florida, South Dakota, and Delaware, some of which had been in preparation prior to the passage of Proposition 13. By late 1978, "lid bills" tying the state budget growth to income growth were being promoted by groups in Wisconsin, Utah, Virginia, Ohio, and New York.

But only one year later, the tax revolution was already cooling. Two years later, newspaper accounts referred to the "tax revolt that never happened."

This all leads me to believe that Proposition 13 was greatly misunderstood. The tax revolt was not the important issue. Proposition 13 was really about the voter's discovery of the awesome power of the initiative.

I am not denying that Proposition 13 was a strong public demand for property-tax relief and accountability in government spending. It was all of that. But let us examine the process itself: The California legislature stalled for more than a year on a property-tax relief measure. In the meantime, tax-revolt groups had collected the 1.5 million signatures needed to bring their initiative to the voters. The legislature finally did pass a bill to reduce taxes somewhat, but by then the Jarvis proposal was already on the ballot. By that time, the voters had leapfrogged the state legislature and were so dazzled with the power of the initiative, few cared that the statehouse had finally delivered.

The real importance of Proposition 13 was as a test case for initiative power. It dramatized for citizens all across the country that this was a perfectly legal process available in many states and localities where a popular groundswell of public sentiment could jump over the traditional channels.

For a while, it looked as though Proposition 13 would trigger a real tax revolt. But then voters in Oregon, Michigan, and Missouri rejected tax-cut measures, and spending lids failed in Nebraska, Colorado, and Oregon.

Talk of tax cuts was by no means over, but voters were becoming choosy about which measures passed and which went down in defeat.

By mid-1979, the movement for spending lids was definitely cooling down. For one thing, voters seemed to realize that most states did not have a huge financial surplus like California's to lean on. By late 1979, all existing spending lids were in the South or West. Eastern and midwestern states were rejecting similar proposals.

- Ohioans to Limit Taxation and Spending was unable to collect enough signatures to obtain a place on the ballot for a state-spending lid.
- In Maine, a proposed state-spending lid died in the legislature.
- The president of New Jersey's United Taxpayers group said the momentum provided by Proposition 13 to New Jersey tax groups was gone.

By 1980 the tax revolt was beginning to look like a movement to maintain the status quo in tax matters. State-spending lids were defeated in Iowa, South Dakota, Minnesota, Utah, Idaho, and Maryland. Augusta, Maine, voters had defeated by a two-to-one margin a tax limit that would have cut property taxes to 1978 levels and limited future increases.

Measures that would have cut property taxes to about 1 percent of full market value were defeated in Oregon, South Dakota, Arizona, Utah, and Nevada. Michigan voters rejected three different property-tax-cut proposals. Pennsylvania's legislature rejected a proposed constitutional amendment to limit state and local spending.

Massachusetts, however, voted 3 to 1 for "Proposition 2½," limiting property taxes to 2.5 percent of market value and cutting automobile excise taxes. One reason Massachusetts bucked the trend is that property taxes there were 70 percent higher than the national average, earning the state the nickname "Taxachusetts."

But the real benchmark was the defeat of Proposition 9, or "Jarvis II," the California initiative to cut state income tax more than 50 percent.

The tax revolt never materialized, but what did happen was perhaps more important. Citizens were actively determining tax policies by voting in ballot initiatives at every step of the so-called tax revolt and learning how the initiative process operated. It was not a tax revolt, perhaps, but a revolution in the way political decisions are made in the state and local governments.

The "National Initiative" Idea Will Be Rejected

The idea of a national initiative, which is being pushed by a Washington, D.C.–based group known as Initiative America, is an interesting and in many ways attractive idea. If initiatives can work this well on the state and local level, can't we create an even more populist participatory democracy with a national initiative?

That is what the founders of Initiative America thought. John Forster and Roger Telschow had worked on state initiative campaigns and were struck by how much more enthusiastic voters were about initiative battles than about the presidential campaigns, for example. What America needed, they decided, was a mechanism to empower citizens to propose laws at the national level.

Initiative America would like to see a law giving citizens eighteen months to gather the required number of valid signatures (3 percent of the voters in the previous presidential election) to put a measure on the ballot. If passed, the proposal would become law in thirty days.

Initiative America secured former Senator James Abourezk's support for a constitutional amendment, but later became discouraged about the lack of support from public-interest groups in Washington. Forster and Telschow said they thought the other groups perceived the idea of a national initiative as a threat to their interests.

Perhaps. But what is a far greater barrier to the national initiative idea is that it is simply out of tune with the larger and far more powerful trend to decentralization. A national initiative would be a highly centralized process.

Initiatives are much more appropriate to the state and city level, where citizens are deciding by popular vote issues that only they will have to live with.

Initiatives: Good News and Bad

This discussion of initiatives has stressed the positive so far, the bottom-up victories won with initiatives. What has not been pointed out at all is that the initiative can create the monster as well as the genius.

Two negative considerations come to mind at once. First, all the standard dangers inherent in any electoral process—bribery, excessive campaign contributions, fraud—will emerge with greater use of initiatives. Second, and more threatening, the initiative can conceivably endanger the civil rights of minorities. In an initiative campaign, there is the possibility that the majority will be voting on the rights of minorities.

There are some safeguards. Like any other legislation, successful initiatives are subject to judicial review; but if the rights of minorities are not already spelled out in national or state constitutions, those rights could be jeopardized.

That is the lesson gay activists in Dade County, Florida, learned in 1977.

A homosexual rights ordinance there would have routinely become the thirty-ninth such law in the country (a major trend) had it not been for Anita Bryant. Bryant's petition drive to repeal the measure won it a place on the ballot, and her two-to-one victory margin was the first in what became a minor nationwide antigay backlash.

After the Dade County repeal, Maine and Minnesota rejected gay rights bills and a California state senator launched a drive to ban homosexuals from teaching in the public schools. More repeals of local ordinances followed in Wichita, Kansas, and Eugene, Oregon.

By late 1978, antigay feeling had peaked: Seattle became the first city in the country to retain a challenged gay rights ordinance. California voters defeated Proposition 6, which would have banned gay teachers.

Numerous other provisions limiting gay civil rights were passed, however. Although it may be surprising to some, gay groups seem to welcome the challenge of public debate. For the first time, they felt people were learning that gays don't necessarily fit the stereotype.

In trying to guarantee their own civil rights, gay activist groups have gone straight to the heart of the issue by challenging the constitutionality of *any* majority voting on the basic civil rights of a minority.

It would be a travesty were the power of the initiative used to deny civil rights in a democracy. Yet, the initiative mechanism is far too valuable to abandon. In Washington, D.C., a city council proposal gets around the conflict by preventing voters from using any initiatives and referendum procedures to change human rights laws. It may become a model for other similar ordinances.

In other areas where the power of the initiative may be abused, traditional election reform is often the model for corrective practices.

For example, one of the original purposes of the initiative was to make it harder for well-monied groups to influence laws. Like the referendum, the initiative was supposed to discover the will of the people.

But as initiative use grew more frequent, it became apparent that money played a role in determining the outcome of initiative votes, just as it influenced other political contests. To the consternation of some, a 1978 Supreme Court ruling entitles corporations to spend as much money as they please to influence the outcome of initiatives.

A 1979 study by the Council on Economic Priorities, a nonprofit research firm in New York, tried to measure just how much campaign spending influences the outcome of an initiative battle. Studying sixteen initiative campaigns, the group reported that in twelve of those the side with heavy corporate backing outspent the opposition and won eight of the twelve. In the other four, all of which the corporate side lost, neither side spent a great deal or the corporate side was outspent. The study's conclusion: that the present system is unbalanced in favor of corporations.

But how to explain the 1976 Maine "bottle bill" or "Ban the can" initiative to require deposits on most beverage cans or bottles? Corporate opponents of the Maine bill outspent proponents thirty to one. But the bill passed by a three-to-one margin. In Massachusetts, labor and business interests opposed a similar bill and won—but by a meager half of 1 percent, although they spent $2 million on the campaign versus $10,000 on the other side.

I think the answer is this: When people really care about an issue, it doesn't matter how much is spent to influence their vote; they will go with their beliefs. When an issue is inconsequential to the voters, buying their vote is a snap.

Advertisers will tell you the same thing, pointing to the massive amounts of money spent on cigarette brand advertising. If cigarette ads were aimed at getting nonsmokers to take up the habit, the ads would influence very few of us. But once the initial decision to smoke is made, there is a lot of room for advertisers to influence the relatively inconsequential decision of which brand to buy. The more deeply held a position is, the harder it is to change.

Politicians think I am mad when I tell them it doesn't really matter how much is spent on issue campaigns. Advertising executives get my point immediately.

Of course, advertisers, business interests, and politicians have worked together on numerous initiative campaigns, dipping into the whole bag of market research and advertising techniques. And business is winning many initiative votes. In Colorado, business interests campaigned against ballot initiatives on nuclear safety, throwaway beverage containers, establishment of a public advocate's office in the public utility commission, and other measures. They outspent proponents by huge amounts and they won.

Although I maintain that it occurred because people really didn't care that much, it is also clear that business's wins will provoke reexamination of initiative and referenda campaign practices and bring cries for more reforms.

In Montana, for example, there is already a bill to limit individual contributions to initiative campaigns to $75. In states where initiatives are practiced, voters will probably follow Montana's lead and limit campaign contributions, just as we have traditionally done in elections for public officials. For example, federal law sets a $1,000 limit on campaign contributions to presidential candidates (but not primary elections), and some states have laws limiting campaign contributions as well. I think we will continue to let other election reforms serve as models to correct the problems in initiative and referenda campaigns.

Other reforms in the offing: Colorado voters approved a measure requiring that those who sign initiative petitions be registered voters (that is already the law in many states). Illinois required that petition signers reside in the same election jurisdiction as the petition circulator.

Montana legislators considered several other curbs on initiatives: doubling the number of signatures required to get an initiative on the ballot, requiring that all signers be witnessed by the circulator, and limiting the number of initiatives on the ballot. The last measure was defeated.

It is critical that we continue to discover and correct any abuses in the initiative process, that we devise ways to neutralize the potential for mischief making.

In the final analysis, initiatives, referenda, and recalls offer a tremendous safeguard in a democracy by enabling any aggrieved citizen or group to bypass the established representative system and submit a proposal to all citizens.

The high voter turnout (20 percent higher in states with initiatives than in states without them), which referenda and initiatives produce, already justify their existence. Yet, there is another, stronger argument in favor of the participatory approach. Citizen initiatives frequently tackle the tough sensitive issues that legislators avoid to protect their popularity. Citizens do not. After all, the electorate need not concern itself with staying in office; it must only live with the results of its own decisions.

Participatory democracy, however, is not greeted enthusiastically in every quarter. Its detractors call it too radical and argue that representative democracy is safer because we ordinary people do not know enough to make decisions about complicated public policy issues. The voters will probably fall too easily for tricky, simplistic television advertising blitzes during the final week before an election, critics argue. If democracy has problems, we should improve representative democracy, they say, specifically, by electing better officials. But the visions of mob rule have remained simply visions. Most political scientists agree that referenda and initiatives have demonstrated, if anything, that voters are inherently conservative. The fear of radicalism is simply not justified.

The stand one takes on referenda and initiatives depends on whether one is willing to trust the people. My Jeffersonian tendencies urge me to do that, provided civil and minority rights are safeguarded in the process.

Harland Cleveland has written an eloquent passage that argues as well as any for the power of participatory democracy:

> The American people have had quite a lot of practice in the past decade or two in getting ahead of their leaders. The Federal Government was the last to learn the war with Vietnam was over. President Nixon and his staff were the last to tumble to the fact that Nixon fumbled himself out of office. The tidal wave of social change these past twenty years—environmental sensitivity, the demographic transition, civil rights for all races, the enhanced status of women, recognition of rights of consumers and small investors—was not generated by the established leaders, but boiled up from the people at large. . . .

The Participatory Corporation

Participatory democracy sounds like a political concept and it basically is. Yet, the role we play as citizens is but a small part of our lives. We also belong to a variety of institutions where we are governed as well: schools, churches, clubs. But no institution is more central to daily life than the corporation, the new-age government of the twentieth century.

In corporations, most of us earn our wages, succeed or fail at finding meaningful work, secure our health care, and invest our money. In corporations, our skills and abilities are judged and most of our social ties with others are formed. In corporations, we must define something as lofty as our self-esteem and earn something as pedestrian as our daily bread. The way corporations and large nonprofit institutions are governed influences quality of life as much as governments.

So, just as we are demanding a new, participatory role in government, we ask the same of our corporations. Just as we seek a greater voice in political decisions, through initiatives and referenda, we are reformulating corporate structures to permit workers, shareholders, consumers, and community leaders a larger say in determining how corporations will be run.

175

Four key movements are reshaping the avenues for participation in corporations: consumerism, the push for more outside board members, the new shareholder activism, and the trend toward greater worker participation and employee rights.

These trends are restructuring corporations internally, while, at the same time, corporations are seeking a new role externally by participating more and more actively in the political and social world at large.

During the 1960s and 1970s businesses heard the demands of consumers, minorities, and stockholders, while battling the growing trend toward more and more government red tape.

But it was in the late 1970s that companies finally said, "Hey, wait a minute, we have a right to speak up, too." Corporations were guaranteed the right to participate in the 1978 Supreme Court decision (*First National Bank of Boston* v. *Bellotti*) that ruled that corporations were free to campaign for or against state referenda, thereby protecting the free-speech rights of corporations. Business abandoned its traditional low-profile approach and took a more and more assertive stand on all issues that influence corporate life. That attitude is entirely in tune with the times.

For the most part, business has replaced the notion of corporate social responsibility with a policy of engaging society directly by speaking out on a variety of issues.

Washington Post reporter Bradley Graham writes: "Weyerhauser in its ads doesn't sell paper, it preaches conservation. Kellogg doesn't peddle cereal, it promotes nutrition. Bethlehem Steel argues the fine points of U.S. trade policy. American Telephone and Telegraph celebrates technology. Citibank expounds on the greatness of the capitalist system. And Mobil addresses itself to just about everything."

At the same time, business people must also acknowledge that corporations are governments in themselves, and that the participants within—stockholders, consumers, workers—will continue to make their own demands.

The Consumer Movement: Voting via the Wallet

"Consumerism is the economic expression of the American Revolution."

That is the way my friend Jim Turner explains it. Jim wrote *The Chemical Feast: The Nader Report on the FDA* and is one of the leading consumer experts in the country. In the summer of 1981, he made a presentation to a group of *Trend Report* clients about the future of the consumer movement. Jim's arguments convinced me that the thrust for participatory democracy is the ideological backbone of the consumer movement.

Two of Jim's key points about the consumer movement are important to restate here. First, consumerism is not a new movement; it is deeply rooted in American history. Second, consumerism will increase during the 1980s, with the distinct possibility that it will become extremely militant late in the decade.

A few words about each point.

The basic premise of the American Revolution is that power ought to flow from the bottom up (that is, from the people up) rather than from the top down (from the King down). That is central to American values whether you are talking politics or economics. Adam Smith recognized that when he wrote in *Wealth of Nations*, "Consumption is the sole end and purpose of production."

Jim concludes: "Consumers are to economics what voters are to politics."

What is behind the idea that consumer militancy will emerge in the late 1980s? After all, haven't we been hearing *fewer* complaints from consumers of late?

Jim argues, and I think it makes a lot of sense, that, although consumers appear less militant, it is only because they have stopped asking the government for more regulations. Producers often misunderstand this as meaning that consumers are content, Jim argues. The truth is that consumers, along with everyone else, have only given up on the government's helping them. They are still frustrated, and consumerism is already re-emerging in the marketplace.

Jim points to a 1977 Lou Harris study, "Consumerism at the Crossroads," which estimates that producers have approximately ten years, perhaps less, to begin including consumers in the corporate decision-making process—or face a virulent new strain of militant consumer action.

In other words, the time is now for corporations to accept the notion of participatory democracy as a model for consumer-relations policy. Remember the key question in participatory democracy: Are the people who are being affected by a decision part of the process of arriving at that decision?

How should businesses apply the participatory notion to producer-consumer relationships? And what will its effects be? I think there are three critical points. First, the participatory principle will transform the relationship between producers and consumers. Second, many producers remain strongly resistant to the consumer movement. Third, producers have everything to gain and nothing to lose by incorporating consumers into the corporate decision-making process.

Transformation is not too strong a word for what the participatory democracy idea would do to producer-consumer relations. That is because traditionally consumers and producers meet *only* at the point of purchase, and not before. When a corporation meets regularly with an informal consumer advisory group, it is providing access to the corporate decision-making process long before the point of purchase. Not that the corporation will always go along with its consumer group's recommendation; that is not the purpose of participatory democracy. Only that the consumers will be part of the process of arriving at that decision. The key word is *process*, and the result is definitely transformation.

For some reason, perhaps fear of losing control, too many corporations that should know better are terrified of this whole idea. Although many large companies at least pay lip service to consumerism, others, some of which are my clients, are having none of it. To say they are resistant is a dangerous understatement. They do offer, however, totally rational arguments to fight off opening up the corporate decision-making process to consumers. For example: Corporations do such a good job in market research that active consumer contributions are superfluous.

It is difficult to understand this attitude. For, in reality, producers should be eager, it seems to me, to engage consumers as early in the production process as possible. I do not think it an oversimplification to state that producers can only become more successful by learning how better to satisfy consumers.

Even if corporations sincerely believe market research is successful, why deliberately close the door to more informal contact with consumers? Perhaps corporations are simply scared because they do not understand participatory democracy. It does not mean consumers will *make* corporate decisions. Remember, being part of the process doesn't mean controlling its outcome.

The Boom in Outside Directors and Activist Shareholders

The recent upsurge in shareholder activism and the substantial increase in outside directors on corporate boards are testimony to the strength of participatory democracy in corporate governance.

Only a few short years ago stockholders mindlessly approved corporate proxies, and it was considered quite natural that most corporate boards were dominated by company officers. But the late 1970s witnessed a dramatic upsurge in pressure for corporate accountability after scandals such as corporate bribery overseas.

Many corporations voluntarily increased the number of outside directors in the boardroom because it was feared that the government just might force corporations to do so. When he was chairman of the SEC, Harold Williams went so far as to advocate that all board members should be independent except the CEO and he should not be the chairman. So far the SEC has not enforced the ideal of outsider or independent-dominated boards.

But with the help of the SEC, shareholders discovered a new avenue into corporate decision making. In 1972 and again in 1976, the SEC changed proxy rules opening the door for shareholder proposals to appear on corporate proxy material. Now any shareholder—a church group, university, or individual stockholder—can propose a resolution. If corporate management refuses to entertain it, the SEC must step in to decide whether it will come up at the next annual meeting.

Again and again these shareholder resolutions are coming before corporate boards. During the first six months of 1980, 150 such resolutions on social policy were filed with sixty-seven companies, according to a study entitled "Minding the Corporate Conscience 1980" by the Council on Economic Priorities. Thirty-one of these were antinuclear initiatives and twenty-eight concerned South Africa.

The new activism marks a dramatic change in the way shareholders participate in corporate decisions. In the past, shareholders customarily "voted with their feet." If you did not like the way a corporation operated, you expressed your displeasure by selling off your stock.

Today's shareholder activists stick around and make a lot of noise instead. In some cases, noise is all they make. Very few resolutions win a majority of votes. Nevertheless, their views are aired in public, and corporations are forced to address the issues that are raised. And there is always the possibility that a shareholder proposal will gather the votes to win.

One of the most dramatic examples of the new stockholder activism was in Sweden, often a bellwether for the United States. In January 1979, 130,000 Volvo shareholders revolted, forcing the Swedish auto maker to abandon plans to sell 40 percent of its equity to the Norwegian government for $125 million.

McGraw-Hill, Inc., the U.S. publisher, faced angry stockholders at the company's annual meeting. The stockholders were protesting McGraw-Hill's refusal to entertain a merger proposal from American Express Co. Promerger shareholders lost, but it was a visible battle in shareholder activism.

Church groups led the increase in shareholder activism. But universities, unions, and foundations took up the trend during the past two or three years.

In 1979 Yale University sold some 33,000 shares in Morgan Guaranty Trust Co. because of the bank's investment policies in South Africa.

Although corporations in some cases dislike the trend toward shareholder activism, there is widespread acceptance of the notion that there be a strong presence, even a majority, of outside directors on corporate boards. Wise managements have invoked this sentiment to get independent directors from a wide variety of fields to help guide them through turbulent times.

During the 1970s there was a phenomenal increase in the number of outsider-dominated boards. In the early 1970s outsiders were a majority of less than two-thirds of the boards of the major companies of America, according to a survey conducted by Heidrick & Struggles, an executive search firm. By 1980, 87.6 percent of the major companies studied had a majority of outside directors.

Furthermore, half the companies were said to have a majority of independent outsiders on the board. Independents not only are outside management, they have neither family nor business relationship with the corporation.

In another survey of 552 firms by Korn/Ferry International, Inc., the average board consisted of four inside directors and nine outsiders. The survey also reported that a rising number of board members, nearly three out of four, think outside board members should outnumber insiders.

Workers' Rights and Worker Participation

Consumers, shareholders, and outside directors are reshaping corporations to be more open to a whole host of social, political, and economic concerns. Yet, in many ways, only one group can make the most pervasive changes, the employees of a corporation—the lifeblood of its success and those who will pay with their jobs should it fail.

Employees and the corporations that employ them are in the process of redefining the worker's role in the institution. What is emerging is a new theory of workers' rights and worker participation. It is long overdue.

In the United States, there is a fundamental mismatch between traditional American love of personal liberty and the top-down, authoritarian manner in which the American workplace has operated. Employees habitually surrender the most basic rights, to free speech and due process, for example, when at work each day.

David Ewing, an editor at *Harvard Business Review* and an outspoken advocate of employee rights, describes the predicament of the average American worker: "Once a U.S. citizen steps through the plant or office door at 9:00 A.M., he or she is nearly rightless until 5:00 P.M., Monday through Friday."

Furthermore, traditional American management has adopted an insulting top-down approach to a worker's knowledge in his or her own job. Managers in the United States have consistently denied workers the opportunity to make substantive decisions about how their jobs should be done. Only now are we beginning to see that this elitist strategy has cost America top honors in world productivity growth.

Undoubtedly that is one key reason we are reevaluating the

contradiction between our democratic political values—which are growing even more participatory—and the archaic traditions that govern us in our jobs.

The common law that governs employers and employees is still based on the master-servant relationship.

Essentially, employees have no real rights vis-à-vis their employers, and employers are free to fire an employee "for good cause, for no cause, even for cause that is morally wrong." That is the common law.

But it seems that change is on the way. Recently there has been an explosion of activity in the area of employee rights, mostly in three key areas: (1) In the courts judges and juries are for the first time reversing common law and ruling in favor of employees; (2) certain large corporations are establishing exemplary employee-rights programs; and (3) some state legislatures have passed laws related to employee rights.

American companies are taking another look at the value of worker participation, evidenced by the recent boom in Japanese-style quality circles, groups of people working together who meet regularly to discuss work-related problems and solutions, and other similar work teams, including quality-of-work-life (QWL) groups. According to the American Center for the Quality of Work Life, at least 200 American companies have quality circles. Honeywell, for example, has 350 quality circles.

As we have all heard many times, quality circles came from the United States. The Japanese, unlike American managers, liked the idea, and now almost everyone concedes that the Japanese reputation for the highest possible quality control standards has a lot to do with quality circles.

For at least the past three decades, American management consultants and behavioral scientists have been trying to push the idea here, to no avail. American managers thought the idea mushy and unmeasurable and felt certain it would have no impact on the almighty bottom line.

Meanwhile U.S. productivity gains slid, high-quality imports gained a greater and greater U.S. market share, and American companies finally had to ask themselves: "What are we doing wrong?" Only at that point was the door opened for increased worker participation. This follows the established pattern for social change.

Change occurs when there is a confluence of both changing values and economic necessity, not before.

When personal values and economic values are aligned, social change is instituted. So long as the economic impetus was absent, the new values of teamwork and recognition of the workers' contribution seemed softheaded to managers. Now worker participation seems to make sense, as do workers' rights, because it now makes sense economically.

Any number of issues can be termed "workers' rights" or "employee rights," which are synonymous. It all depends on how you define the issue. Privacy, due process (in any dismissal action), free speech, protection in whistle blowing, participation in management, flexible work contracts, equal pay for work of comparable value, an employee newspaper that is free to take on management—all these can be construed as employee rights. But the first four—privacy, due process, free speech, and whistle-blowing protection—are most readily recognized as crucial. Citizens possess the first three rights outside of work, and people generally agree that it is highly unjust to penalize a worker for speaking out against illegal or immoral behavior on the part of his or her employer.

The lack of general employee rights is increasingly out of touch with contemporary values. We have become an increasingly rights-conscious society. Union members won collective-bargaining rights in the 1930s, and minorities won protection from discrimination under the Civil Rights Act of 1964. But the lack of employee rights for nonunion, nonminority employees grows increasingly out of touch with contemporary values.

Within the last ten years, the values of the workplace have endured their most revolutionary shaking-up ever—the invasion of the baby boom. In 1970 baby boomers, those of us born between 1946 and the early 1960s, made up only 15 percent or so of the workforce. It was easy enough to neutralize the far-out notions of a few young, inexperienced rebels. But during the 1970s, the pig in the python took the whole company over—baby boomers now make up one-half of all workers.

The baby boom transforms each institution through which it passes. The pig is now devouring the python.

Daniel Yankelovich has said, "Throughout history and certainly during the last century, American individualism stopped at the workplace door. Now it is knocking the door down too, demanding entrance."

When social scientists, management consultants, and public-opinion experts speak about the "new breed of employees," the new motivational theories, the new entitlements and rights attitudes, what they are really describing are the values of the demographic cohort that exploded on college campuses in the late 1960s and 1970s. Now they have gone to work.

Managers who really want to understand the employee-rights issue should read *Great Expectations* by Landon Jones (New York: Coward, McCann & Geoghegan, 1980).

Great Expectations is a demographic and cultural history of the baby boom, its values, its experience in education, and its appearance on the job front. Ironically, the term *employee rights* is never mentioned in the book, yet the essence of the movement appears on every page. One of the book's key ideas is that the baby boom transforms each institution through which it passes, by the sheer force of its size alone. Currently the boom is transforming the workplace, and one key manifestation is the prominence of the employee-rights issue.

Today's worker is well educated, probably a white-collar information worker, and aware of his or her rights. But the worker is not usually happy on the job, according to many observers.

One important study connects worker dissatisfaction with the employee-rights issue. An Opinion Research Corporation (ORC) study summarized in the January/February 1979 issue of *Harvard Business Review* found that one reason for worker malaise is the sense that workers are treated unfairly at work. The study covered data accumulated over twenty-five years. The findings were startling:

- During the 1950s, nearly 80 percent of the *managers* thought their companies fair; now less than 50 percent gave the company good marks.
- In the 1950s some 70 percent of *clerical* workers gave their firms a "good or very good" fairness rating; during the late 1970s the figure plummeted to approximately 20 percent.
- *Hourly* workers viewed company fairness in a much steadier although very negative fashion. Approximately 30 percent

of those surveyed in the 1950s said the company was fair, compared with about 20 percent in the late 1970s.

This study signals a powerful mismatch between today's workers and the way they are treated on the job. Now workers are better educated, more self-confident about governing themselves (in politics *and* at work), and are, consequently, more likely to demand fair treatment. Yet, at the same time, they feel they are being treated *less* fairly than in the 1950s. It is unfortunate, but that is how the workplace has been perceived until very recently.

Employee privacy is routinely violated with polygraph tests, which many groups have tried to outlaw; workers who speak out about illegal or dangerous practices have been abruptly discharged; most have no defense against a capricious dismissal by an unfair supervisor; and any dissent from company policy is considered something of a crime in most companies.

That is the bad news. What is encouraging is that change is on the way—in the courts, at the state level, and in many large, forward-thinking corporations.

"The trickle of suits by non-union employees fired from their jobs is turning into a flood," reported the *National Law Journal* in July 1979.

In August 1979, *Business Week* said, "The recent burst of employee litigiousness is a national phenomenon."

Employees may not have any rights, but they are acting as though they do. And the courts are beginning to see it their way.

Courts in fourteen states—California, Connecticut, Idaho, Illinois, Massachusetts, Michigan, New Jersey, New York, Pennsylvania, New Hampshire, Indiana, Oregon, Washington, and West Virginia—have sided with fired employees when their termination is "abusive or against public policy."

Social change through case law is a slow approach, to be sure. On the other hand, change that bubbles up from the grassroots has staying power, and in any event, attempts to pass employee-rights laws have fared miserably at the national level so far.

A national Employee Bill of Rights was first proposed in 1976 as part of a more wide-ranging attempt at corporate reform introduced by Ralph Nader's Corporate Accountability Group. It included a national code on corporate governance and employee-rights provisions in the areas of free speech and privacy. The most recent version of this legislation is the Corporate Democracy Act, introduced by eight House members during the Ninety-sixth Congress. The employee-rights section would grant rights of due process—requiring employers to show they have fired an employee for just cause—as well as free speech, protection in whistle-blowing cases, and privacy. There were no hearings held on the bill, and it will almost certainly be reintroduced again and again. But most observers believe it has almost no chance for passage.

There is action at the state level, however. California, Oregon, Maine, Michigan, Pennsylvania, Connecticut, Wisconsin, and Ohio have passed laws giving private employees the right to examine employment records and other confidentiality rights. Washington, D.C., and Utah grant state employees the same rights.

Polygraph tests are banned in Alaska, California, Connecticut, the District of Columbia, Hawaii, Idaho, Maine, Maryland, Massachusetts, Michigan, Minnesota, Montana, New Jersey, New York, Oregon, Pennsylvania, Rhode Island, Washington, and Virginia.

Michigan has passed a law protecting whistle blowers.

The state of Connecticut passed the country's first workers'-right-to-know law. Now manufacturers of suspected carcinogens must identify ingredients and other information to workers who come in contact with the substances. They are also required to distribute updated lists of new substances in usage. New York has also passed a similar law.

State by state, a decentralized approach to employee rights is being hammered out in the statehouse and the courthouse. But on an even more grassroots level, the question of employee rights is being decided one company at a time. A handful of major corporations have even gone far beyond the most liberal law or court decision, voluntarily establishing employee-rights codes that can serve as models for others.

IBM has been the acknowledged leader in privacy policy. Partly because of the potential for abuse in the computer field, IBM took an aggressive innovative stance in privacy. Personnel files can contain only essential information; evaluations must be weeded out after three years; the company does not ask about convictions or mental problems dating back more than five years; and employees are entitled to see most of their personnel files.

At Cummins Engine Co., another leader in privacy, employees receive an annual printout of their personnel files and are encouraged to correct any mistake.

In spring 1978, the president of Atlantic Richfield Co. sent a letter to its 50,000 employees, urging them to report to the government any instance of chemicals being used that might be threatening.

Several other large companies are well known for a strong policy on employee privacy; among them are Aetna Life and Casualty, American Telephone & Telegraph, Control Data Corporation, CPC International, DuPont, Prudential Insurance, and several others.

In many respects, the quintessential employee right is the right to due process. It assures an employee that he or she cannot be fired without just cause.

Polaroid Corporation's 14,500 employees have what is probably the nation's best example of due-process rights for non-union workers. Employee representatives sit on committees that represent employees with complaints in a hearing before management. Researchers claim that many management decisions are overturned in the process. But if the employee is not satisfied, he or she is free to submit the case to an outside arbitrator.

Many employees and employee-rights advocates feel the guarantee of outside arbitration is the only way workers' rights can really be ensured.

University of Pennsylvania Law School Professor Clyde Summers has made the provocative proposal that all employees, unionized or not, be granted the right to outside arbitration.

Whatever path is followed, employee rights will not be brought about in any macro, top-down way, but like so many other restructurings in America—and like the trend toward participatory democracy itself—employee rights (as well as consumerism, shareholder activism, and the trend toward outsider- and independent-dominated boards) will transform corporate America company by company, community by community, and state by state.

The key idea behind participatory democracy can be useful in our personal lives as well. In our personal relationships, it is

187

helpful to keep in mind the question I stated at the beginning of this chapter: Are the people whose lives are affected by a decision part of the process of arriving at the decision? That question applies to your marriage, family, friendships, work life, and community organizations. People must feel that they have "ownership" in a decision if they are to support it with any enthusiasm.

In the 1950s, the organization man may have come home after work and announced to the family that they were all moving to Wichita next Tuesday. But not today. People—husbands, wives, and children—have to be consulted about life-changing decisions. Or vacations. Or career changes, or Mom going back to school.

The other side of the coin is that if you can develop the skills of facilitating people's involvement in decision-making processes, you can become a very effective leader in your community and in your work.

The new leader is a facilitator, not an order giver.

8

From Hierarchies to Networking

For centuries, the pyramid structure was the way we organized and managed ourselves. From the Roman army to the Catholic Church to the organization charts of General Motors and IBM, power and communication have flowed in an orderly manner from the pyramid's top, down to its base; from the high priest, the general, the CEO perched at the very tip, down through the wider ranks of lieutenants and department managers clustered in the middle, to the workers, foot soldiers, and true believers at the bottom.

The pyramid structure has been praised and blamed, but its detractors have never come up with a better or more successful framework for organizations, although many have tried.

Other enlightened management alternatives such as Theory Y (Douglas McGregor's term for the humanistic approach to motivation on the job) were widely discussed in the 1950s and 1960s. Many of these—essentially sound management practices—were adopted by the Japanese and came back to haunt American managers during the 1970s in the form of Japan's impressive productivity gains.

But in the United States, the new management styles flourished mostly in business literature. Very few made it to the office or to the shop floor. And even the new methods we tried were still based on the hierarchical structure. Management theorists attempted to soften the rigid power flow within the pyramid's vertical structure, but no one seriously considered scrapping the structure altogether.

Smashing the Pyramid

Meanwhile, during the 1960s and 1970s a world swirling with change forced its way to the workplace door and suddenly burst through:

- The U.S. industrial economy, tailor-made for hierarchical structures, fell into deep trouble. Rising up in its place was the new information economy where hierarchies were badly out of tune. In an information economy, rigid hierarchical structures slow down the information flow—just when greater speed and more flexibility is critically needed.
- Similarly, society's centralized institutions whose very existence relied upon hierarchies were crumbling everywhere. And in their place, smaller, decentralized units were springing up, linking informally with one another, and therefore relying far less on formal structures.
- As we grew to recognize our new place in a world economy, we came face to face with our Japanese competitors, only to learn that the management structure that made them the world's leading industrial power was anything but pyramidal in nature; instead, Japanese workers, clustered into small, decentralized work groups, made work decisions themselves, and the people on top received their word as something resembling gospel.
- As we introduced more technology into society, the cold, impersonal nature of the bureaucratic hierarchy annoyed people more and more. What we really wanted was more personal interaction, more high-touch ballast in response to the further intrusion of technology into an already impersonal hierarchy.
- Finally, younger, more educated and rights-conscious workers began filling up the workplace. Raised to take seriously

the ideology of democracy (even in a representative democracy one has the right to vote), the whole notion of hierarchy and pyramids was to them foreign, unnatural.

The combined impact of these trends was powerful and decisive.

Hierarchies remain; our belief in their efficacy does not.

In effect, our belief in the ideal of the pyramid structure, which we had talked about redesigning and improving, came tumbling down, the victim of its own outdated, top-down power structure.

Looking around at the world, it was clear to many that the problems of the day—a sagging economy, political unrest, and a litany of intractable social problems—were not solvable in a world organized according to the hierarchical principle.

What was there to do? The answer to that question describes the way the new networking model evolved.

The failure of hierarchies to solve society's problems forced people to talk to one another—and that was the beginning of networks.

In a sense, we clustered together among the ruins of the tumbled-down pyramid to discuss what to do. We began talking to each other outside the hierarchical structure, although much of our previous communication had been channeled inside. That was the birth of the networking structure.

As friends, as individuals, as members of small groups or large organizations, we exchanged resources, contacts, and information with the speed of a telephone call or a jet airplane ride, with the high touch of our own voices set against the din of a world swarming with too much data and too little knowledge. Networking was a powerful tool for social actions. Those who would change the world began doing it locally, in clusters of like-minded people with a single ideological purpose.

The women's movement, for example, emerged in classic network fashion. In all parts of the country, women clustered together in small groups—usually friends or friends of friends—to reinforce their new self-concepts and thereby alter society's traditional view of women. The environmental and antiwar movements of the 1960s and 1970s had networking starts as well.

In other cases, networking is simply a vehicle for connecting people with one another, as in ride sharing and van pooling, sometimes for economic interest. California ride-sharing programs such as Los Angeles's Commuter Computer and Sausalito's Commuter Connection can save millions of dollars and millions of gallons of gasoline.

Networking is usually the first stage of a community self-help group such as those discussed in Chapter 6. The Tucson Cooperative Warehouse, for example, had a typical networking start: The leaders of three separate food groups merged their assets—a truck, a good credit rating, and an excellent bookkeeper. Baltimore's St. Ambrose Housing Aid Center began when a priest and a real estate agent started studying local housing conditions.

Now the new networking model we have all used with extraordinary success is replacing the hierarchical form we have grown to associate with frustration, impersonality, inertia, and failure.

What Is a Network?

Simply stated, networks are people talking to each other, sharing ideas, information, and resources. The point is often made that networking is a verb, not a noun. The important part is not the network, the finished product, but the process of getting there—the communication that creates the linkages between people and clusters of people.

Networking, notes Marilyn Ferguson, who has written extensively about the subject in *The Aquarian Conspiracy*, is done by "conferences, phone calls, air travel, books, phantom organizations, papers, pamphleteering, photocopying, lectures, workshops, parties, grapevines, mutual friends, summit meetings, coalitions, tapes, newsletters."

Networks exist to foster self-help, to exchange information, to change society, to improve productivity and work life, and to share resources. They are structured to transmit information in a way that is quicker, more high touch, and more energy-efficient than any other process we know.

"Networks are appropriate sociology—the human equivalent of appropriate technology—providing a form of communication and interaction which is suitable for the energy-scarce, information-rich future of the 1980's and beyond," write Jessica Lipnack and Jeffrey Stamps in *New Age*.

In an article entitled "Networking," Lipnack and Stamps, who wrote a book on the subject, list a variety of interesting examples of the networking phenomenon:

- In Newton, Massachusetts, there is a local information network, called WARM LINES, that provides a service as mundane and critical as providing parents with the names of available babysitters.
- In Denver, Colorado, you can join the Denver Open Network and gain access to a computerized file of 500 other people with a variety of different interests: That's how one inventor found an investor to finance his new self-contained water system.
- The National Women's Health Network in Washington, D.C., began in typical networking fashion with a long-distance phone call between two friends concerned about improving women's health care. Since 1974 it has evolved into a national network of more than 500 health groups. This women's health network provides information, for instance, to women bringing health-related lawsuits on cases involving DES and unnecessary operations.
- Rangeley, Maine, is the home of TRANET, Transnational Network for Appropriate Alternative Technologies, which grew out of the 1976 U.N.-sponsored HABITAT Forum. TRANET's purpose is to link people, projects, and resources in the appropriate technology community. The network has 500 members worldwide, publishes a quarterly newspaper (which exchanges 180 other publications), maintains files on some 1,500 appropriate technology projects and 10,000 individuals, has an extensive library, and is able to arrange many successful linkages.

Thousands of similar networks exist, as well as the hundreds of thousands, probably millions, more, to which all of us belong—the informal networks among friends, colleagues, discussion groups, community organizations—that never grow into the organization stage.

One indication of the popularity of the networking concept is the many and varied groups that put the word *network* in their names:

- the Consumer Education Resource Network, a resource and service network for consumer education
- the National Network, Inc., which operates services for runaway youths and their families
- the California Food Network, a grocery marketing system in San Francisco
- the Chicago Rehabilitation Network, which links neighborhood groups involved in housing rehabilitation.

These are examples of networks that have grown into stable, ongoing organizations. Some networks remain fluid and open; others dissolve, their members resurfacing elsewhere to create new networks.

Knowledge Networking

One of networking's great attractions is that it is an easy way to get information. Much easier, for example, than going to a library or university or, God forbid, the government. Washington Researchers, a Washington, D.C., firm specializing in obtaining government information for corporate clients, estimates that it takes seven phone calls to get the information you want from a government agency. Experienced networkers claim they can reach anyone in the world with only six interactions. It has been my experience, however, that I can reach anyone in the United States with only two—three at the very most—exchanges.

Although sharing information and contacts is their main purpose, networks can go beyond the mere transfer of data to the creation and exchange of knowledge. As each person in a network takes in new information, he or she synthesizes it and comes up with other, new ideas. Networks share these newly forged thoughts and ideas.

Describing this process in the magazine *Future Life,* Willard Van de Bogart writes: "Each new thought is being integrated into the next thought, producing a new cumulative awareness of human nature and the universe we live in. These new mental models are being shared within the newly developed networks throughout the world."

Recently I experienced a striking personal example of knowledge networking. Some close friends in my own network are the Foresight Group, three Swedish business consultants who have sponsored my speeches in Sweden. In late 1981, The Naisbitt Group, the Foresight Group, and our spouses met to discuss future projects. The Foresight Group gave the rest of us a presentation on their latest project, the School for Intrapreneurs (*intrapreneurs* are entrepreneurs working within organizations, and the concept is discussed more fully later in this chapter).

They used a chart that I frequently use in speeches, but their new interpretation brought an additional layer of knowledge to material I thought I knew quite well.

Specifically, the chart graphs the progress of the United States from an agricultural to an industrial to an information society by indicating how many people work in agricultural, industrial, or information occupations.

What my friends pointed out is that the transition times between societies are the times when entrepreneurship blooms. The late agricultural and early industrial era was the time of the great captains of industry (or robber barons, depending on how you look at it). Now, at the beginning of the information era, new businesses are being created at a rate six times faster than in 1950.

For me sitting in the audience, the effect was feeling my own ideas come back at me after being improved and refined by the people in my own network. That is the kind of knowledge networking Willard Van de Bogart is talking about, and it is happening within networks all over the country.

There is even a network on networking, notes Van de Bogart: the Consciousness Synthesis Clearing House in Redondo Beach, California, which is "evolving a general understanding of the networking process and the development of an over-arching perspective from which to view this vital phenomenon."

Network Structure

Networks offer what bureaucracies can never deliver—the horizontal link.

Networks cut across the society to provide a genuine cross-disciplinary approach to people and issues. Whereas bureaucracies look like conventional organization charts, boxes arranged in some hierarchical order with the leader on top, networks are quite different. Perhaps the best image of their structure comes from the late University of Miami anthropologist Virginia Hine.

Hine, who studied networks extensively (she called them segmented polycephalous networks), described them as "a badly knotted fishnet with a multitude of nodes or cells of varying sizes, each linked to all others either directly or indirectly."

What needs to be added is that networks are infinitely more complex because they are three-dimensional in nature.

Networks emerge when people are trying to change society, said Hine. "No matter what the 'cause,' the goals, or beliefs, and no matter what type of movement it is—political, social, religious . . . whenever people organize themselves to change some aspect of society, a non-bureaucratic but very effective form of organizational structure seems to emerge," she writes.

In many cases, people who want to make the changes Hine talked about have tried to get assistance from established organizations and failed. At that point they try to connect with others with similar goals, and networks are born.

Networks have been compared with the colonial committees of correspondence and the British invisible college, and with Mahatma Gandhi's "grouping unities," with which he led India to independence.

Structurally, the most important thing about a network is that each individual is at its center, as Marilyn Ferguson and others have noted. Ferguson herself is the center of perhaps the most extensive network of new-age contacts and organizations. In fact, as she says in *The Aquarian Conspiracy*, much of the information for the book was gathered through her role as a human clearinghouse for new-age ideas.

Why Now?

Why have networks emerged at this particular time? And what is so special about people talking and sharing contacts? Isn't that what we have been doing since history began? Is networking so different from the Old Boy Network, the informal way professional men have helped each other for decades?

The answer is yes. The "Old Boy Network" is one thing, networking another. The Old Boy Network is a clubbish fraternal conspiracy that protects the self-interest of a limited few. It is not widespread and it was not created out of necessity. The new networking is both ubiquitous and essential.

The "Old Boy Network" is elitist; the new network is egalitarian.

Within the networking structure, information itself is the great equalizer. Networks are not egalitarian just because every member is a peer. On the contrary, because networks are diagonal and three-dimensional, they involve people from every possible level. What occurs in a network is that members treat one another as peers—because what is important is the information, the great equalizer.

There are three fundamental reasons why networks have emerged as a critical social form now: (1) the death of traditional structures, (2) the din of information overload, and (3) the past failure of hierarchies.

The strength of traditional networks such as family, church, and neighborhoods is dissipating in American society. The gap is being filled with new networks functioning, as Marilyn Ferguson puts it, as the spontaneous modern-day equivalent of the ancient tribe. Networks fulfill the high-touch need for belonging.

We are all buried in the overload of information being generated and transmitted all around us. With networks to help, we can select and acquire only the information we need as quickly as possible. Networks cut diagonally across the institutions that house information and put people in direct contact with the person or resource they seek.

The failure of hierarchies to solve human problems has forced people to begin talking with one another outside their organizations, and that is the first step to forming a network. Clusters of people have come together to communicate about, and

197

attempt to address, the concerns and problems that traditional structures have failed to address.

Designing the Corporate Version

Now even the large organizations—the last champions of hierarchical structure—are questioning whether the hierarchical structure can fulfill their organizational goals. Many are discovering that the hierarchical method that was so effective in the past is no longer workable, in large part because it lacks horizontal linkages. In the future, institutions will be organized according to a management system based on the networking model. Systems will be designed to provide both lateral and horizontal, even multidirectional and overlapping, linkages.

What is evolving now is a network *style* of management. I am not suggesting that companies will become huge corporate networks, abandoning formal controls to allow employees to spend their time talking with each other. Instead, the new management style will be inspired by and based on networking. Its values will be rooted in informality and equality; its communication style will be lateral, diagonal, and bottom up; and its structure will be cross-disciplinary.

One of the most visible examples of the way networking values have penetrated corporate structures is Intel Corporation, a leading company in the semiconductor industry.

Writes *New York Times* business reporter Steve Lohr, "Intel is organized to avoid the bureaucratic hierarchy that is characteristic of most corporations."

At Intel network management means:

- Workers may have several bosses.
- Functions such as purchasing and quality control are the responsibility of a committee or council, not a hierarchical staff reporting to an individual leader.
- There are no offices, only shoulder-high partitions separating office work space.
- Dress is very informal.
- The company itself is run by a triune of top executives, an "outside man," a long-range planner, and an inside administrator.

- Although decisions are ultimately the responsibility of top managers, all employees are expected to participate in discussions as equals.
- Even the newest employee is encouraged to challenge superiors.

Intel's Vice Chairman Robert Noyce says, "What we've tried to do is to put people together in ways so that they make contributions to a wider range of decisions and do things that would be thwarted by a structured, line organization."

Another of Intel's executive triune, Andrew Grove, says, "We can't afford to have the hierarchical barriers to an exchange of ideas and information that you have at so many corporations."

There are a number of trends pushing for the creation of a new management style based on the network. Earlier, I stressed how much the change in the information environment has promoted the need for networking. Equally important are the changes in the people environment of organizations:

- As the managerial ranks are taken over by the baby-boom managers, we will soon discover that networking is the dominant management style of the activist baby boom, whose members figure prominently in Ferguson's *Aquarian Conspiracy*. By the late 1980s, 80 percent of total management will be under forty-five.
- Using networks, the baby boomers brought us the women's movement, the antiwar movement, and the environmental movement: They don't know how to organize any other way. This is the way they organized and communicated as young adults. It is irrational to think they will quietly blend into the hierarchical structure once they reach the executive suite.
- Furthermore, there will not be room for all the well-educated but unmanageably numerous baby boomers in the executive suite. Some 40 percent of the baby-boom workers during the 1980s will be college-educated. In an article in *Technology Review*, Roy Amara argues that the number of workers vying for each managerial position will double from the present ten to twenty by 1990. What will we do with all those well-educated Indians with chieflike tendencies? In a networking structure, small groups of talented people can

govern their own work environment and produce spectacular results.

- There will be enormous pressure on the part of these younger, well-educated, rights-conscious workers to participate in management decisions. The shift from a representative to a participatory democracy translates on the job front into a disdain for the old-fashioned hierarchical structure in favor of the networking approach—more quality circles, workers' rights, and participatory management.
- With more technology in the workplace too, we will increasingly need more human interaction, and networks can provide that. The more robots, the more quality circles. The more word processors and computer terminals, the greater the need to network laterally within an organization.

The results of the slow shift to a network management style are becoming visible.

Hewlett-Packard Co. recently instituted a management system where many managers report to their own peers. Says Frederick Schroeder, director of corporate development, "A manager may be asked to report to quite a few others to share information and increase communications."

The Army's think tank for innovation and transition is organized in a circular rather than hierarchical fashion.

In some cases, the network style grows out of a desire to downplay the symbols of hierarchical management. Even if a hierarchy remains, network values predominate. Case in point: The fast-growing computer firms such as Intel and Tandem Computer Co., where informality is legendary and where executives are stripped of all "perks" from reserved parking spaces on up. It is not surprising that the most successful new high-tech firms develop the most high-touch management styles.

But even among the most successful, Tandem is remarkable. The founder of the fast-growing $100-million-a-year company, James Treybig, emphatically states that the human side of the company is the most critical factor in reaching his goal—the $1-billion mark in annual sales. Treybig frees up 100 percent of his personal time to spend on "people projects." Tandem's people-oriented management style includes Friday-afternoon beer parties, employee stock options, flexible work hours (unlike Intel, where everyone is expected to show up promptly at 8:15

A.M.), a company swimming pool that is open from 6:00 A.M. until 8:00 P.M., and sabbatical leave every four years—which all employees are *required* to take. Reviews and meetings occur spontaneously with no formal procedures.

Tandem's informal style, however, is possible only because of the firm's rigid system of computer controls. Eight separate computer systems check on production controls, cost standards, quality controls, and management reporting systems. With the computers keeping track of company performance, managers are free to concentrate on people. This has produced highly visible results: The company has no trouble attracting good people in a highly competitive area and enjoys an extraordinarily low turnover rate of 8 percent in an industry where high turnover is legendary.

Tandem is the good example of a firm where the computer is liberator. Computers will be the linchpin in the newly evolving network style of management.

Another major influence on the move to network styles of management has been the influence of the new Japanese models, especially quality circles, and Type Z organizations, which represent a hybrid of Japanese and traditional American management practices.

Quality circles are an important part of the hierarchies-to-network shift because, in the QC model, communication and decision making occur bottom up from a network of fellow workers instead of top down from a hierarchy.

According to the Japan Productivity Center, there are 6 million Japanese workers participating in more than 600,000 quality circles. A quality circle is a small group of perhaps ten workers doing similar work who meet to discuss and solve work-related problems.

Today, one American company, Honeywell, has more active circles—350 as of May 1981—than any other firm outside Japan. American managers can learn a good deal by studying Honeywell's experience. Honeywell has been experimenting with the circles since 1974.

The basic principle behind the bottom-up style of the quality circle has been expressed well by Rene McPherson, chairman of the Dana Corporation. He writes:

> Until we believe that the expert in any particular job is most often the person performing it, we shall forever limit the po-

tential of that person in terms of both his contribution to the organization and his personal development. . . . Within a 25-square-foot area, nobody knows more about how to operate a machine, maximize its output, improve its quality, optimize the material flow, and keep it operating efficiently than do the machine operators, material handlers, and maintenance people responsible for it.

McPherson's words are a good example of how much Japanese management philosophy has permeated the belief systems of American managers.

At Honeywell, quality circles are called Production Team Programs (PTPs), TEAMS, Productivity Improvement Teams, Involvement Teams, and Participative Quality Teams.

What they are not, Honeywell managers are quick to point out, is a quick fix or short-term program to increase profits. Says Jim Widtfeldt, who runs the QC program at Honeywell, "Quality circles is a philosophy of management that assumes employees can creatively contribute to solving operational problems."

"Teams are a long-term commitment to a change in management style, not a short-term program," echoes Robert Oslund, a Honeywell industrial engineer assigned to evaluate circle experimentation.

TRW Marlin Rockwell in Windsted, Connecticut, is another company that has succeeded with quality circles. The firm's absentee rate has dropped from 6 to 2 percent, production is up 35 percent, and overall turnover has been cut to only one-fifth of its former level.

In a story about the TRW experience, *New England Business* writes: "Japan's competitive situation is very similar to that of New England: a minimum of raw materials, a large population, and a high percentage of imported energy. Why then does Japan have a growth rate that is six times greater than New England's during the first quarter of this year [1979]?"

The answer, concludes the magazine, is Japan's management style. "Japan's success is due to the way they've developed their workers," says Leonard Schlessinger of Harvard Business School.

Also relevant to the network structure is the management style described in William Ouchi's Theory Z. In a Type Z company, which is a hybrid of American and Japanese management styles, network values permeate the whole company as though it were a large family, even though hierarchies persist.

A traditional American (Type A) company operates on the principles of short-term employment, individual decision making, individual responsibility, rapid evaluation and promotion, explicit, formalized control, specialized career paths, and segmented concern.

In contrast, Japanese (Type J) companies feature lifetime employment, consensual decision making, collective responsibility, slow evaluation and promotion, implicit informal control, nonspecific career path, and wholistic concerns.

Although the two are quite different, some U.S. firms (Kodak, Cummins Engine, IBM, Levi Strauss, National Cash Register, Procter and Gamble, Delta Airlines, Utah International, and 3M) have succeeded in mixing characteristics from both type companies. All are known for their low turnover, high morale, and company loyalty.

Like Japanese companies, Type Z organizations stress long-term employment, consensual decision making, slow promotion and evaluation, and wholistic concern. But the remaining characteristics blend the traits of both Japanese and American companies: implicit, informal control with explicit formalized measures and moderately specialized career paths.

What is most interesting about Type Z organizations is the way they fit into society as a whole. Ouchi believes that Type A companies were effective so long as the traditional networks of American society—family, church, neighborhood, voluntary organizations, and long-term friendships—remained strong. "In a stable society," writes Ouchi, "individuals can develop ties outside work to complement the impersonal nature of participation in a contractual organization.

"When people had relatives, neighbors, and churches, they didn't need Dr. Spock to tell them why the baby was purple and they didn't need a company that provided them with a rich network of social contacts," writes Ouchi.

But American society's traditional networks have been weakened by geographic mobility and urbanization; as a result, people have an enormous need for a sense of belonging.

Type Z organizations can provide much of the sense of belonging needed now in American society.

From Sweden comes a vision of the future corporation as a confederation or network of entrepreneurs. Employees who function as entrepreneurs are called intrapreneurs by the Foresight Group, which has created a school in Filipstad, Sweden, to teach intrapreneurship to both employees and corporate managers.

The main idea is to reverse the creative inertia in many large corporations by developing the inside entrepreneur. The Foresight Group believes there are a lot of good ideas within organizations for new businesses. The company that can learn how to get people to *actualize* those ideas will have tapped a real gold mine.

Both parties profit: The intrapreneur gets the company's good name, contacts, resources, and money, while the company keeps a creative person who may otherwise leave to start a new business and gains the potential to develop a profitable new in-house business.

We will restructure our businesses into smaller and smaller units, more entrepreneurial units, more participatory units.

Life Within the Network Model

The vertical to horizontal power shift that networks bring about will be enormously liberating for individuals. Hierarchies promote moving up and getting ahead, producing stress, tension, and anxiety. Networking empowers the individual, and people in networks tend to nurture one another.

In the network environment, rewards come by empowering others, not by climbing over them.

If you work in a hierarchy, you may not *want* to climb to its top. At a time when decentralist and networking values are becoming more accepted and when businesses must do the hard work of reconceptualizing what business they are really in while facing unprecedented foreign competition, it is not the ideal time to be a traditional-type leader, either political or corporate.

Even in a hierarchy, there is an informal network within the formal structure. Find it. For some people, it is worth the effort to locate and work only in a network-style environment. Outside of work, this is the time to start your own network or join one and get connected with like-minded people.

Today we live in a world of overlapping networks, not just a constellation of networks but a galaxy of networking constellations.

9

From North to South

The beginning of a new decade is an ideal time to write a book about trends. Once every ten years, the U.S. Census Bureau brings into sharp focus the complex panorama of American life. And for a short while, we know a lot about ourselves. Authors who previously relied on expert "guesstimates" and anecdotal material have access to reams of hard statistical data.

It doesn't last, however. By mid-decade the picture is blurred again. Floundering as before, we are ignorant of what is really happening in this multilayered continent of a country, where for every trend there is often an equally compelling countertrend.

But for a short time (a year, maybe two), time and statistics seem to stand still and the Census Bureau offers us a dazzling inventory of the American people and their business and economic activity.

The year 1980 was no exception. The release of the census data brought forth an inundation of news stories filled with statistical fruits: The biggest change, of course, was that for the first time in American history the South and West had more people than the North and East. And it is not news to any American reader that the census of 1980 uncovered a massive shift not just in population but in wealth and economic activity from North to South.

Yet, despite the issue's familiarity, I include it here because the restructuring of America from North to South is so basic that to omit it from a discussion of the ten most important megatrends would leave a gaping hole in the total picture and would also distort the nine remaining trends. That is because the North–South shift is organically rooted in three of the other megatrends: (1) the change from an industrial to an information society; (2) the move from a national to a global economy; and (3) the reorganization from a centralized to a decentralized society. Each trend relates to the other.

But even granting that the megatrends are linked, what more is there to say about the North–South shift? We have all read numerous newspaper and magazine stories about the former auto worker still jobless in Detroit, the oil-field worker earning more than $1,000 per week in a Rocky Mountain boom town, the hundreds of thousands of jobs lost in the North, the thick help-wanted sections of newspapers and the jobs that go begging in the South.

What is there to add? Only that, despite all media attention, we do not yet fully understand the significance of the restructuring from North to South. And in many ways it still has not been stressed enough.

The simple facts are that in 1980, for the first time in the history of the United States, more Americans were living in the South and West, 118 million, than in the East and North, only 108 million.

The 1970s' demographic changes will be felt politically beginning in 1982. Seventeen house seats have shifted out of the North and East into the South and West. Eleven states gained seats and ten lost. New York was on the short end, with five seats gone. Pennsylvania, Ohio, and Illinois lost two each. Florida gained four, Texas three, and California two. Massachusetts, Michigan, New Jersey, Indiana, Missouri, and South Dakota lost one each, while Arizona, Colorado, New Mexico, Oregon, Tennessee, Utah, Nevada, and Washington picked up one apiece.

What is perhaps more important than the political or demographic changes is the economic growth that supported and encouraged the population shift. Most new jobs, two out of three, were created in the Sunbelt or western states between 1968 and

1978. The U.S. Labor Department calculates that the country gained 18.4 million new jobs, but that the Northeast and Midwest gained only 6.1 million to the South and West's 12.3 million.

At the same time the North *lost* hundreds of thousands of jobs as we shifted out of the industrial era. Because so much of the North's economy was based on manufacturing, the region was extremely hard hit. Writes John Herbers of the *New York Times:* "The urban landscape across the Northern tier of states from Massachusetts to Minnesota is marred by vacant factories, warehouses and great open spaces where such buildings once stood, visual testimony to a great migration whose impact on the nation is becoming increasingly clear."

One after another, factories closed and people migrated out of the North's industrial cities:

- Akron, the center of the nation's rubber industry, lost 16,000 manufacturing jobs and 40,000 inhabitants during the 1970s.
- Dayton lost 40,000 manufacturing jobs in the 1970s.
- Philadelphia lost a total of 140,000 jobs and 160,000 residents during the 1970s.
- Pittsburgh lost 23,000 manufacturing jobs in the 1970s.

Urban symbols of the industrial North—Buffalo, Cleveland, and St. Louis—lost nearly one-quarter of their population during the 1970s.

But while economic declines, factory closings, and job losses ravaged through the North and East, the South and West were experiencing an unprecedented boom cycle.

The South's thriving economy was the subject of almost as many news stories as the North's decline—U-Haul dealers in northern Indiana complain they cannot meet the southbound demand, while a Dearborn, Michigan, newsstand sells as many as 3,000 Sunbelt newspapers per week.

In spite of the media attention, the North–South shift is riddled with misunderstandings, oversimplification, and mythology.

North–South: The Five Key Points

The five most important things to remember about the North–South shift are:

- The North–South shift is really a shift to the West, the Southwest, and Florida.
- The North–South shift is really two stories: one about the North's decline and another about the Southwest and West's boom. The stories have no cause-and-effect relationships.
- The North–South shift is stronger than first thought, and it is irreversible in our lifetime.
- The Sunbelt explosion is really the story of three emerging megastates: California, Florida—both bellwether states—and Texas. It is also the story of the ten cities of great opportunity, all in the South and West.
- Finally, the North–South shift is presenting a crisis in infrastructure, which will eventually force both North and South to reexamine its economic goals and purposes.

North–South: Really a Shift to the Southwest—and Florida

Which regions produced the ten states where population grew most in the 1970s? Ask a well-informed group of friends that question and it is a good bet that many will correctly answer that none of the boom states was in the Northeast or Midwest.

Most likely, they will confidently predict that about half, maybe more, of the fastest-growing states were in the South. Not so.

Only one of these states, Florida, is in the South. The remaining nine are in the West. Nevada headed the list with a 64-percent population growth rate (rounded to the nearest 1 percent). Following Nevada are Arizona (+53), Florida (+43), Wyoming (+42), Utah (+38), Alaska (+32), Idaho (+34), Colorado (+31), New Mexico (+28), and Texas (+27). (You can argue that Texas is a southern state, but it is also very western in feel and geography. At the very least, it must be called southwestern.) The next two states on the fast-track list are in the West too: Hawaii and Oregon.

The fast-growing states share one similar characteristic: a romantic frontierlike quality. Their image is almost a flashback to the days of the Old West. Americans are migrating westward toward the land of opportunity where government regulation is frowned upon and where entrepreneurship is prized.

So is money-making. These same romantic Old West states top the list of places where income is expected to grow most. Again, Nevada leads with a projected 5.3 percent, while Utah, Alaska, Wyoming, Colorado, Arizona, and Florida will grow about 4.5 percent. The national average is only about 3.3 percent.

One symbol of the megashift in American money-making is that Alaska replaced Connecticut in the Northeast as the state with the highest per capita income. The Southwest is the region where income grew most during the decade, 167 percent compared with a national average of 143. Income growth in the Southeast was only a little higher, 150 percent: The Southeast (excluding Florida) is part of the Sunbelt, all right, but except for Florida, it is not enjoying the full benefit of the Sunbelt boom.

The regional differences between the West and South become more vivid when you examine the most valuable resource—educated, knowledge-rich inhabitants.

Which region offers the best-educated people? Most of us would probably guess the Northeast, despite the recent out-migration of workers. Wrong again. The West has the highest percentage of college (20 percent) and high school (75 percent) graduates.

The South, on the other hand, has the lowest percentage of educated people: 63 percent graduated from high school and 15 percent from college. They probably cannot supply enough knowledge and people power to keep up the 150-percent income growth rate of the past decade.

Percentages are deceiving, of course, and the West certainly does not have the highest number of educated people. Nevertheless, it is important to note that the limited population of the West is generally well educated, doubtless a draw for the dozens of companies that have opened new facilities there.

More and more, the sunrise industries of the new information age are opening up facilities in the Rocky Mountain states of the Old West:

- Hewlett-Packard's new plant now employs 2,800 people in Boise, Idaho, a town once associated strictly with industrial concerns such as Boise-Cascade and Morrison Knudson.

- Colorado Springs, Colorado, has become a mini-high-tech center, having attracted Hewlett-Packard, as well as Texas Instruments, TRW, and Honeywell.
- Intel, the maverick microchip company, will open plants in Salt Lake City and Albuquerque.
- Tucson, Arizona, has attracted both an IBM and a National Semiconductor factory.

Politically, the country, too, seems to be moving westward, along with its high-tech information companies.

Look at our recent presidents. Jimmy Carter was the first elected from the Southeast and he was defeated by a westerner, Ronald Reagan. But the last four elected presidents have come from somewhere in the Sunbelt: Johnson was from Texas, Nixon from California.

North–South: Two Separate Stories

The shift from North to South is really two different stories: the decline and stagnation of mature industries in the Northeast on the one hand, and the growth and development of new industries in the Southwest on the other. The Sunbelt boom did not occur at the expense of the North. We are dealing with two entirely different trends. Nevertheless, many of us have accepted the myth of the large-scale migration to the South.

Analysts who chased after the hard numbers discovered that the Sunbelt boom did not occur because companies closed up shop in the North and reopened in the South—only about 3 percent of the South's growth can be accounted for that way. Admittedly, what did happen was that when companies sought an attractive location for an expanded facility, the Southwest or West was most often selected. Later, if a recession forced a plant shutdown, the facility in the North was invariably closed because it was older.

Similarly, international competitors such as Japan, which entered the industrial age later than the United States, gained a technological advantage after a while because of that late entry, since the newcomers must buy the most up-to-date equipment. Hence, Japan's steel industry boasts the latest electric furnace technology, while in the United States, steel companies still rely on the antiquated open-hearth furnace. Industrial newcomers, whether in the South or in a developing country, eventually gain a technological edge over their more mature competitors. That was a key factor in the Sunbelt boom.

The Sunbelt migration myth is based on some historical reality, however. During the 1940s and 1950s, textile companies did move out of New England and to North and South Carolina. This much-cited shift turns out to be the *only* example.

The decline of the North has more to do with the shift from an industrial to an information society than it has to do with any movement of North-based companies to the Sunbelt. As America shifted out of an industrial society, it was clear that the industrial Northeast would suffer most.

Another reason behind the North's decline is the shift from a national to a global economy. As other countries began to take on many of the old industrial tasks, our domestic industries, especially autos and steel, faced increasingly stiff competition.

The Northeast was particularly sensitive to the global economy shift because, as the birthplace of the industrial revolution in this country, its factories were the oldest and its industries matured first. The threat of less expensive, foreign labor is an old story in the Northeast. Yankee shoemakers came face to face with the budding global economy when, in the 1950s and 1960s, they were deluged with inexpensive, and later more expensive, Italian shoes.

In this decade a bigger chunk of America's economy—the core auto and steel industries—was scarred by stiff foreign competition. And the affected geographic area has spread from the Northeast to North Central states—with Ohio, Michigan, and Pennsylvania hardest hit.

The stress on the manufacturing sector is especially intense: Auto workers, for example, must battle three megatrends at once—foreign competition (the shift from a national to a global economy), automation (the shift from an industrial to an information society), and finally the movement from North to South.

The rise of the South and West, however, grows out of entirely different trends, not the least of which is the national search for energy. Energy and energy equipment are the backbone of the Texas boom; the search for energy is fueling the new-age boom towns in the Rockies, just as the search for gold created their nineteenth-century counterparts. "We've had it all happen before," says Colorado Governor Richard Lamm. Colorado's mountain counties had more people in 1900 than in 1970. Denver, like Houston in the South and Calgary in the North, has become a center in the search for energy. Denver boasts some 900 energy companies, and half the town's downtown office space is said to be leased by energy-related companies. The attractiveness of mild winters in the South was, of course, a key energy consideration, and many of the Southwest's booming businesses are energy-related.

But another important driving force behind the South's development is the nationwide megatrend toward decentralization, as discussed in Chapter 5. Decentralization applies to businesses as well as to people.

Until the 1970s, industry was so concentrated in the Northeast and Midwest that American business virtually ignored the South and West as industrial areas. The present North–South shift is really a spreading out, a thinning out of industry from the overpopulated Northeast to the wide-open space of the Southwest and West.

It makes sense. The group of western states that is growing fastest in income and population represents the most thinly settled region in the nation. The Rocky Mountain states, with 25 percent of the U.S. land mass, have only 4.3 percent of the U.S. population. In these states there are approximately twelve people per square mile, compared with an average of sixty-two people per square mile nationwide. But in New Jersey, in the heartland of the industrial Northeast, there are nearly 1,000 people.

For a city dweller in the overcrowded Northeast, decentralization is not necessarily a bad thing. There are some indications that the quality of life in the Northeast is improving with the outflow of people.

Says Norman Krumholtz of Cleveland's Center for Neighborhood Development: "A ten-mile trip to downtown Cleveland from almost any direction takes about twenty minutes at rush hour now, quite a bit less than it did when the city had 200,000 more residents."

Jay Bordie, Baltimore's Commissioner of Housing and Community Development, believes the quality of life has improved in Baltimore, too. "There's less noise in public buildings, crime is down, and the parks and playgrounds are less crowded," he claims.

Contrast these descriptions with the complaints from fast-growing Nevada: "With growth we're getting pollution, housing prices are skyrocketing, traffic in Carson City is horrendous at rush hour, the city is running out of water, building permits are limited, and we've got sewer problems," says Bob Hill, the State Planning Coordinator in Nevada.

In short, the shift from North to South is really an amalgamation of at least three other megashifts that fit together organically. There is one additional shift involved—the movement from an either/or to a multiple-option society. Just because most of us lived in the Northeast before, it does not follow that we will now all move to the South. Not by a long shot. We enjoy stressing our geographical differences. And many people in New England and the Midwest wouldn't trade their crisp autumn and blustery winters for all the sun in the Sunbelt and a top-paying job to boot—to the distress of many economic policy analysts and state job counselors. For those who loved their region the only answer was to endure the massive industrial dislocation by finding another job in their hometown or taking early retirement.

The North–South Shift Is Irreversible in Our Lifetime

The shift in population and economic strength from North to South is only the beginning. The restructuring of America from North to South is gaining increased momentum now as we begin to experience the consequences of the initial mass migration of jobs, people, and economic activity.

Personal income, living standards, education levels, housing, investment, the flow of pension funds—all these indicators were shaken up during the North–South shift of the 1970s. These are secondary indicators (the primary being population and job creation), which measure the ripple effect of the basic shifts. The end result is a more solidified shift from North to South. These secondary effects increase the momentum of the initial shift, strengthening and intensifying it.

For this reason, I would argue that despite all the media attention, the North–South shift still has not been stressed enough. Perhaps the point is that we have not yet acknowledged that we are dealing not merely with a statistical abstraction but an economic reality. Because of the ripple effect, it is a reality that cannot easily be turned around. More likely, what we have is a trend that is virtually irreversible in our lifetimes.

An examination of some of these secondary indicators makes the case:

- *Living Standard.* Metropolitan residents of the Northeast have the lowest standard of living in the country, according to the Conference Board. The national average indexed at 100 is actually the living standard of the Los Angeles area. But Boston's index is 86.9 and New York City's is 86.7. The highest living standards are found in Dallas (121), Houston (117.3), and Washington, D.C. (128.8), where high federal salaries drive averages up.

- *Income.* Per capita income increased most in the Southwest (167 percent during the past decade) and least in the Middle Atlantic (129 percent) and New England states (134 percent).

- *Housing.* The ripple effect is quite pronounced here. Housing starts in the Northeast were a robust 22 percent of the nation's total in 1966. In 1981, the figures had fallen off sharply to 8.8 percent, according to the National Association of Home Builders. Meanwhile the South claims *nearly half* the country's housing starts, 47.7 percent (1981 projections), up from 40.8 percent in 1978.

- *Investment.* Again, this indicator foretells a powerful restructuring at work. Investment in capital equipment increased 23 percent in the Northeast and Midwest, compared with 74 percent in the South and West. The figures were computed by the Northeast-Midwest Institute, whose director volunteered: "We knew it was bad, but we didn't know it was that bad." Investment in commercial and industrial buildings fared even worse: declining 14 percent (in the Northeast and Midwest) while increasing by one-third elsewhere.

- *Pensions.* Pension benefits are flowing into the Sunbelt. The Census Bureau estimates that some 1.5 million Americans sixty-five and older moved to the South or West during the 1970s. The government also calculates that the South and West reaped a net gain of between five and seven billion dollars a year in pension benefit disbursements during the 1970s.

- *Education and Age Levels.* As previously noted, the West has the highest percentage of educated people. Next is the Northeast. Perhaps that region's advantage in human resources is the trump card that encourages New England's high-tech renaissance. But now the question is: Will the Northeast be able to hold on to its educated workers?

"The lessening of job opportunities in the Northeast has come at the worst possible time," says Donald Starsinc, chief of the state and national estimate branch in the population division of the Bureau of the Census.

"Young adults are very mobile and they're going to be looking for jobs elsewhere. What's left behind are the poor and elderly," he concludes. The facts bear this out.

The median age in the Northeast is 31.8, nearly two years higher than the national average of 30. "In about ten years, colleges in the Northeast will have a hard time finding students," says Peter Francese, publisher of *American Demographics*.

The Midwest is experiencing a powerful brain drain that may well spread to the Northeast. Only 19 percent of the 1980–81 Michigan State University graduates took local jobs, compared with more than half in 1973. At Northwestern's Kellogg School of Management, more than 25 percent of the graduates move South within three years, according to the school's accounting-department chairman. Eight years ago, only a few relocated to the Sunbelt.

Whether or not it spreads eastward, the brain drain out of the North is one of the strongest indicators that the North–South shift will grow more pronounced throughout the 1980s.

The Megastates: Florida, Texas, and California

As long as statisticians and economists measure growth rates, there will always be the danger of mistaking increasing growth rates for actual increases.

For example, when sparsely populated Nevada grows at an astronomical 64 percent, we often fail to note that the huge increase amounted to a net gain of only 310,000 people. Illinois added about the same amount of people (308,000) and registered a paltry 3-percent increase in population, which impressed no one.

But the picture grows even more distorted with *economic*

Megatrends

growth rates. These tell us that Nevada is in the midst of a big boom cycle while New York is strictly in the doldrums. Or is it? Nevada's state income is projected to grow by $8 billion in the next twenty years, but quiet old sagging New York State will grow by $55 billion over the same time period.

In fact six of the ten *slowest-growing* states are listed among the ten states that will grow the most in actual income: New York, Illinois, Ohio, Michigan, Pennsylvania, and New Jersey.

An article by Rick Janisch in the *Washington Post* provocatively titled "Quelling the Myth of the Frostbelt's Industrial Decline" explored this point:

> When economists measure growth, they normally look at the rate of growth. The problem is that an economically tiny state may grow at a rapid rate with little actual gain in income. . . . Because a state starts out small it only needs to grow a little to increase its rate of growth sharply. . . . A large developed state may grow a great deal in absolute terms but still show a sluggish growth rate on paper.

It is a valid argument. More important, it is a reminder that, although there has been a powerful shift from North to South, many of the markets of the North will remain busy and vital. Admittedly, much of the recent growth in the South and West is a Nevada-type boom: sky-high growth rates that do not translate into enormous increases in actual growth.

But there is a big exception. Actually, there are three: the megastates of Florida, California, and Texas. These three states begin with sizable population and income, and increase with large growth rates as well. In fact, the three Sunbelt giants are almost entirely responsible for the Sunbelt mystique.

For economic growth, give me Texas, California, and Florida and you can have the other forty-seven.

Much of the nation's population growth in the 1970s, about 65 percent, was in the Sunbelt. But most of that, more than 40 percent of the nation's population growth, occurred in only three states: California, Texas, and Florida. They gained 9.25 million people. And the Census Bureau fully expects the big three to remain the big population gainers for the remainder of the 1980s. During the brief period between the 1980 census and

July 1981, the Census Bureau estimates that 90 percent of the population growth occurred in the South and West.

California and Texas are the nation's first and third largest states, with populations of approximately 23.7 and 14.2 million respectively. Florida is seventh with a population of 9.7 million. Florida's population increased 43 percent, Texas's 27 percent, and California's 18.5 percent.

These three states were the big winners in congressional seats after the 1980 census, with Florida gaining four, Texas three, and California two.

The biggest population increase of any metropolitan area, 1.5 million people, was in the Los Angeles vicinity. And Florida housed the metropolitan center with the largest population rate increase, Fort Myers–Coral Gables, which grew by 95 percent during the 1970s. Another Florida community, Tampa–St. Petersburg, increased by 44 percent, the third fastest growing.

But the megastates did not grow by luck alone. From 1972 to 1977, capital investments in manufacturing increased nearly 300 percent in Texas and 110 percent in California. Texas has replaced Michigan as the number-one state in new capital investments in manufacturing, investing $5.3 billion to Michigan's $3.7 billion in 1977.

The megastates share a number of interesting characteristics. All three are on the cutting edge of the whole immigration question, both legal and illegal; more than half of all Hispanic-Americans live in either Texas or California. "California has become the Ellis Island of the 1980s," said one population researcher. During 1980 legal migration to California was between 150,000 and 200,000, part of a total population increase of 450,000. Moreover, thousands more entered the state illegally. During the 1970s California's Anglo population declined from 89 to 76 percent as a host of Asian and Hispanic neighborhoods popped up, especially around Los Angeles. "Little Saigon" is near Westminster and Olympic boulevards. There is a Korean area in downtown Los Angeles. In Monterey Park, a suburb of Los Angeles, one-third the population is Chinese, while in nearby Carson, California, there are 10,000 Samoans.

All three megastates are highly international in their orientation. Miami, for example, is the gateway to the Caribbean and to all of South America and is quickly becoming one of the world's major international banking centers. By 1980 Miami boasted some 43 international bank branches, with 20 more scheduled to open shortly. Miami is also headquarters for the Latin American and Caribbean operations of more than 100 U.S. corporations. By the end of the 1980s, their numbers will increase enormously, with perhaps 500 companies with Latin American headquarters in Miami.

California, meanwhile, is the major gateway between the world's two fastest-growing areas: the Asia-Pacific Basin and the American West. The state is therefore taking a huge chunk of the transpacific trade.

"What happens in the Philippines, Japan, and Korea has a greater impact on us and is of more immediate interest to us than most events in Massachusetts," says California Senator S. I. Hayakawa.

Like the other two megastates, California is behaving increasingly like a nation, an economic dynamo independent of the United States. Last year California alone created 212,000 new jobs, 27 percent of the U.S. total. Its agricultural trade contributed over $4 billion in exports, a rise of 43 percent. Over $1 billion of this total was cotton, with China as a major buyer and fabricator of clothing for reexport to U.S. markets.

California is looking to the future with an emphasis on agricultural performance and microelectronics. With an information economy securely based in Silicon Valley, California is pressing to dominate the world market in this new technology. Governor Brown, for his part, wants his state to compete more effectively with Japan. A trend-setting series of programs have been announced to meet this objective in ways that surpass anything launched nationally. A notable feature of these initiatives is their similarity with Japanese models.

Another recent initiative is the Commission on Industrial Innovation, which identifies and promotes programs necessary to establish California as a continued leader in high technology. Members of the commission include corporate, academic, labor, and state government leaders.

Brown has also announced a major effort to spur innovation in the university system through a new focus on agricultural and microelectronics research. Similar efforts are being launched in Florida. These highly developed state programs create growing integration with the global economy and add a dimension to the

Washington-based debate on protectionism that cannot be ignored.

Texas enjoys a special relationship with Middle Eastern countries, especially Saudi Arabia: In fact, it's said to be the only place where Saudi businessmen feel really at home. The long-shared border with Mexico, of course, helps give Texas an international flavor.

What is happening now is that a new Sunbelt axis is replacing the old axis of the East.

The old economic, financial axis between New York and Chicago is being replaced by a new Los Angeles–and–Houston axis.

Writes William Stevens in the *New York Times*, "This time the connective tissue (between Houston and Los Angeles) consists not of rails, wheat, and heavy industry, but of petro-chemicals, oil, space age technology and the wanderlust of expatriates from the North seeking new horizons and opportunities."

The Houston–Los Angeles power axis is political as well as economic. Texas and California produced four of the seven front-runners in the 1980 presidential election. Only one was from the Northeast.

The Future: Confronting the Challenge of Infrastructure

The massive North–South migration has played havoc with the physical and social infrastructure that supports economic activity. That is one aspect of the North–South shift the nation has only started to address.

Governors Jay Rockefeller and Richard Lamm describe the problem in a *New York Times* op-ed piece:

> The public sector is hurt: people leave school systems, sewer systems, streets, hospitals, and other public infrastructures already in place in the northeast, and move to high-growth areas that are already strained by ballooning growth and that must duplicate the public infrastructures of schools, transportation, sewage and hospitals at a great expense, while the snow belt loses the tax base to preserve its infrastructure.

For the abandoned cities of the Northeast, it seems as though the long litany of infrastructural woes is endless:

- New York City has reduced its police force by 21 percent, its fire fighters by 7 percent, and its sanitation workers by 16 percent since 1975. But New York's subway and transit system is in the worst shape of all: Already running a $170-million deficit, the Metropolitan Transit Authority figures it needs $14 billion for repairs over the next ten years. New York City itself needs $30 to $40 billion over the next ten years for long-delayed repairs to capital facilities.
- The Chicago Transit Authority is just barely making its payroll each week. Meanwhile, the city's school system must come up with a bussing plan—extremely difficult in such a segregated city—and the $25 million needed to implement it.
- The city of Detroit is virtually bankrupt, having already cut services substantially. The city has laid off some 1,000 police officers and must cut the city workforce by some 1,200 workers. "We are fresh out of miracles," says Mayor Coleman Young. "We are at the edge of an abyss."

Meanwhile, Houston has trouble transporting its residents, repairing its streets, providing adequate water, working traffic lights or sewers, collecting the garbage, or keeping the flood waters (caused by excessive development) away from people's doorways.

"The things that make Houston great," says Barry Kaplan, an urban historian at the University of Houston, "are the same things that cause the problems. [Houston is] one of the last bastions of the type of economics practiced before the New Deal."

Ten Cities of Great Opportunity

Following are brief profiles of what I consider the ten new cities of great opportunity.

All of the ten new cities of great opportunity are in the Southwest and West.

Albuquerque

Albuquerque, the nation's forty-ninth largest city, grew 34.5 percent in the 1970s to a 1980 population of 328,837, and expects to maintain a steady growth of between 2.7 and 3 percent annually for the next decade. Central to this growth has been the influx of many new-age information and high-tech industries. During the last two years alone, Intel, Signetics, Honeywell, and Sperry Flight Systems have opened new facilities in Albuquerque. These new facilities, and expansions of existing industries, have added over 13,000 new jobs to the area in two years.

Albuquerque has been bucking the trend toward higher taxes by consistently lowering taxes in recent years. Higher state taxes are unlikely, too, because of New Mexico's $600-million surplus, mostly due to energy-severance taxes. In 1983, the surplus should reach $1 billion—and continue growing rapidly.

Unlike many Sunbelt cities, Albuquerque has no water problems whatsoever. The city has enough water to support three times its present population. But Albuquerque does have a crime problem: The forty-ninth largest city ranks twenty-third in major crime. Part of the problem is the city's youthfulness: Albuquerque is the nation's second youngest city, with an average age of 24.7

In the future, Albuquerque is looking to get into the energy business. "We have energy resources: We'd like to encourage oil and gas companies to locate here," says industrial development specialist Bruce Criel.

Austin

Austin, Texas, once considered the San Francisco of the Southwest because of its laid-back alternative lifestyle, has become a boom city almost overnight. From 1970 to 1980, Austin's population ballooned by 36 percent—faster than Houston, Dallas, San Antonio, or El Paso. Austin's economy, once based almost solely on the University of Texas, has attracted the blue-chip companies of the new information age. IBM, Texas Instruments, Tracor Inc., Motorola, and Data General Corp. have turned Austin into a miniature Silicon Valley. Austin boasts an unemployment rate of only 3 percent. Says Austin's mayor, Carole McClellan, "Whether we like it or not, we're going to grow."

But public reaction is not completely positive. Austin may be one of the first Sunbelt towns to question its growth. And that may help ensure Austin's quality of life in the future. Bumper stickers now proclaim: "Keep Austin Austin" and "Austin: Not a Little Dallas." In February 1980 citizens signaled their resentment by defeating bond issues to finance such growth projects as water and sewer extensions to developing areas, while giving the go-ahead to park expansions. Notes Mayor McClellan, who campaigned as an advocate of controlled growth, "the issue is how well are we going to grow."

Denver

Denver, the once sleepy cowtown nestled in the eastern slope of the Rockies, is now rivaling Houston as the "energy capital of the U.S.A." Already, Denver is clearly the central staging area of the mountain states. Gone are the days symbolized by the "unsinkable" Molly Brown's Brown Palace Hotel. But gone too are the days when you could park downtown all day for seventy-five cents and feel properly dressed wearing jeans, boots, and a work shirt.

The Denver of today is filled with high-rise office buildings, parking rates that rival New York City's, and three-piece suits. The driving force behind this change is energy, mostly oil and coal: Energy-related loans are now the United Bank of Denver's largest single loan portfolio—$1.2 billion. There are more independent oil companies in Denver than any other city, including Houston. Noted one businessman who moved from Houston to Denver in 1980: "The deals being made here remind me of Houston twenty years ago."

Denver's energy companies include Exxon, Texaco, Mobil, and Atlantic Richfield. More than 1,200 other Denver companies provide energy-related services and equipment. In the last five years alone, downtown office space has more than doubled. Twenty-seven major office buildings were under construction in 1979 and twenty-four were begun in 1980. The Denver Chamber of Commerce counts 200,000 new jobs created between 1976 and 1981. Unemployment is extremely low, averaging around 3 or 4 percent.

Denver's population is exploding too. Although the city

proper lost people in the 1970s, Denver's metropolitan area doubled in population during the last twenty years. One hundred immigrants arrive daily. In fact, the Denver suburb of Aurora is the fastest-growing city in the country, up 111.1 percent in the last decade. Unlike many other boom towns, Denver's influx has included many professionals. For example, there are now over 4,000 geologists in the area.

Says J. Thomas Reagan, a petroleum engineer who is vice president of the United Bank of Denver, "Denver is either the headquarters, regional office, or district office for all of the companies planning projects in the area."

Phoenix

People in Phoenix will tell you that the city enjoys more than 300 days of sunshine a year. All that sun and a pro-business attitude have attracted numerous high-tech, information-age industries in the last few years, including Hughes, GTE, Intel, Honeywell, Digital, and Motorola.

Unemployment in the Phoenix area averages just over 5 percent. Phoenix is the regional and corporate headquarters for many companies operating in the Southwest and the center of the Southwest's distribution system.

Phoenix owes much of its phenomenal growth to the fact that it has no inventory tax, no corporate-franchise tax, and relatively low personal and corporate taxes. But Phoenix still has a lot of room to grow: It is estimated that 35 to 40 percent of its area is presently underdeveloped.

Since 1950 Phoenix has grown from just 17 square miles to 330 square miles. Its population, 790,000 in 1980, increased 30 percent during the last decade. The metropolitan area is home to more than 1.5 million, and the chamber of commerce expects it will exceed 2.3 million by the end of the 1980s.

Salt Lake City

Salt Lake City itself lost population during the 1970s, but the greater metropolitan area, the Wasatch Front of the Rocky Mountains (a five-county area along the western slope), grew 37.9 percent during the last decade.

First settled by Brigham Young and well known as the center of the Mormon Church, Salt Lake has attracted numerous high-tech industries in recent years, including Rockwell International, Sperry Univac, and Litton. The chamber of commerce estimates that in the next ten years over 178,000 new jobs will be created. American Express is planning a central data processing facility in Salt Lake, which alone will generate 13,000 new jobs.

Salt Lake has a lot of things going for it: The average age is under twenty-five; crime is way below the national average. Education averages 12.8 years of schooling.

Salt Lake promises to be a central staging area for energy development on the western slope of the Rockies, complementing Denver to the East. There has already been a major price war among the commercial airlines for the Salt Lake–Denver air traffic.

San Antonio

In 1980 San Antonio became the tenth largest city in the country, and its leaders see a vigorous future ahead. "We have a chance to become the brightest spot in the Sunbelt," says City Councilman John Steen. Employment is growing 3 to 4 percent annually. While most job growth was generated locally, San Antonio leaders expect a large inflow of new facilities from outside the region during the 1980s. "We're getting a big migration from Silicon Valley," says Bob Farrington of the chamber of commerce. In recent years, Advanced Microsystems, Control Data, Tandy, and Farinon, Inc., have opened facilities in the San Antonio area. New industries created 10,000 new jobs in 1980 and 1981, estimates the chamber.

San Antonio wants to continue attracting high-tech, "no smokestack" industries. Says Bob Farrington: "We're after high-tech industries now; in the future we're going for the medical industries."

San Antonio boasts many advantages for it—unique lifestyle with both a cosmopolitan and Spanish flavor, and a low cost of living. The city's biggest problem is how to balance growth, development, and prosperity, and still maintain a unique quality of life.

San Diego

Richly immersed in a Spanish past, San Diego is now celebrated as the host city for aerospace and high-tech companies such as Signal, Wickes Corporation, Aerotech General, Oak Industries, and TRW.

San Diego, one of the nation's fastest-growing cities, became the eighth largest U.S. city in 1980. The city is expected to increase by approximately 42,000 people a year throughout the 1980s, according to the San Diego Chamber of Commerce. To keep pace with this growth, almost $1 billion is being invested in projects, including an $86-million transit system (the first all-trolley urban system to be built in this country in more than thirty years), new office and commercial buildings, a hotel, a shopping mall, a 2,000-unit middle-to-upper-income seaside housing complex, and a convention center.

Job growth is a steady 4 percent a year. New jobs in San Diego increased by 300,000 during the 1970s, according to the San Diego Chamber of Commerce. Employment is expected to exceed 1 million by 1990.

San Jose

San Jose is located in the Santa Clara Valley, but is better known as the center of the Silicon Valley, which boasts the richest concentration of high-technology industries in the world. In 1980 Santa Clara County high-tech companies manufactured 29.8 percent of the total U.S. shipment of semiconductors and related devices, 11.6 percent of U.S. electronic computing equipment, and 26.1 percent of U.S. guided missile and space vehicle production. Santa Clara is "a land where technologists ride the wavecrest of the future," wrote Peter J. Brennan in *Scientific American*. In recent years such companies as Apple, Atari, Intel, and National Semiconductor have opened shop in the San Jose area, joining IBM, Hewlett-Packard, and Lockheed. Approximately 210,000 Santa Clara residents out of an employed labor force of 683,000 were employed in high-tech firms in 1980. Area unemployment averages about 5 percent.

But Santa Clara County offers an attractive high-touch counterbalance to its high-tech industries: The thirty-two wineries in the valley produced more wine than was shipped to the United States from France, Germany, Italy, and Spain combined.

San Jose's population has grown dramatically in the last decade. San Jose is the nation's seventeenth largest city, with a 1980 population of 625,763, up a remarkable 36.1 percent since 1970. The metropolitan area, Santa Clara County, is home to over 1.3 million people. The San Jose Planning Department projects that Santa Clara's 1990 population will reach 1.5 million.

Despite the city's rapid growth, *New West* ranks San Jose second in terms of quality of life among cities of 300,000 or more in the eleven western states. The Midwest Research Institute classed the San Jose metro area fourth in the nation for quality of life.

Tampa

Tampa and surrounding Hillsborough County has traditionally been a business center. But the Tampa Bay area of today is growing by leaps and bounds. It has grown over 30 percent in the last decade to a 1980 population of 640,300. And the City Planning Commission projects the population will reach 781,700 by 1990. This population boom has been coupled with an equally impressive employment boom. According to local developers, "Tampa is a magnet for both in-state and out-of-state business seeking to take advantage of the state's massive population growth." Total nonagricultural employment increased a startling 56.7 percent from 1970 to 1980, far outstripping the accompanying growth in population. And 60 percent of this new job growth has been in new and existing high-tech industries.

In 1981 alone, some twenty-seven new industries and major expansions created an additional 2,000 jobs with an added capital investment of over $80 million. Companies locating in or about the Tampa area in 1981 included Carleton Controls, Coldwell Banker, Delta Airlines, Deluxe Check Printers, Dolphin Airlines, Dunlop & Associates, ITT Technical Institute, Telecredit Inc., and Tri Tronics Inc. They join such companies as Honeywell, IBM, and GTE. Unemployment in the area in 1980 was only 5.8 percent, far below the national average.

The Tampa–St. Petersburg area is the third fastest-growing area in the country. But, notes the Tampa Chamber of Commerce: "We don't like growth for growth's sake; we only welcome high-quality growth. If an industry can't be clean, it can't be here."

Tucson

Once considered a sleepy retirement town, Tucson's population increased 26.1 percent during the 1970s. The Tucson Chamber of Commerce expects population will double by the year 2000. And Tucson is planning for that day. High-tech industry has helped spur the growth and is expected to remain the area's most important industry.

In 1979 National Semiconductor located a major facility in Tucson, and in 1980 IBM opened a plant that employs over 6,000 people. Hughes Tool has a major plant in the area. In addition, Learjet, which has its headquarters in Wichita, Kansas, conducts all marketing, service, and finishing operations out of Tucson.

Tucson's image as a retirement community is undeserved. The average age is 28.2, a full two years younger than the national average and three years younger than the average in the Northeast.

For the skilled and the mobile, and especially the young, these cities represent the promise of continued growth and prosperity. But what are the prospects if you are unemployed in the North? What it boils down to is the need to change or adapt. Moving to the Southwest is an option that many have taken. But if you don't want to move, you must adapt. That means acquiring skills in a sunrise industry operating in your area. Life choices are no longer either/or. Manhattan will continue to be an important information-switching station for the world, while the four boroughs around it continue in rich decline.

Lowell, Massachusetts, the birthplace of the industrial revolution in America, has lost its industrial base, but it is today the world headquarters for Wang Laboratories, one of the great leaders in the new information society.

10

From Either/Or to Multiple Option

Personal choices for Americans remained rather narrow and limited from the postwar period through much of the 1960s. Many of us lived the simple lives portrayed in such television series as *Leave it to Beaver* and *Father Knows Best*: Father went to work, mother kept house and raised 2.4 children. There were few decisions to make; it was an either/or world:

- Either we got married or we did not (and of course, we almost always did).
- Either we worked nine to five (or other regular full-time hours) or we didn't work, period.
- Ford or Chevy.
- Chocolate or vanilla.

Admittedly, we sometimes got a third choice: NBC, CBS, or ABC. *Look, Life,* or the *Post*. Strawberry ice cream. But it was still either/or, a society of mass markets and mass market advertising, where homogenized tastes were easily satisfied with few product choices.

Not anymore. The social upheavals of the late 1960s, and the quieter changes of the 1970s, which spread 1960s values throughout much of traditional society, paved the way for the 1980s—a decade of unprecedented diversity. In a relatively short time, the unified mass society has fractionalized into many diverse groups of people with a wide array of differing tastes and values, what advertisers call a market-segmented, market-decentralized society.

Remember when bathtubs were white, telephones were black, and checks green?

In today's Baskin-Robbins society, everything comes in at least 31 flavors.

There are 752 different models of cars and trucks sold in the United States—and that's not counting the choice of colors they come in. If you want a subcompact, you can choose from 126 different types. In Manhattan, there is a store called Just Bulbs, which stocks 2,500 types of light bulbs—and nothing else. Its most exotic bulb comes from Finland and emits light that resembles sunshine. Today, there are more than 200 brands (styles, as the industry calls them) of cigarettes on the U.S. market.

This is the analog for what is going on in society. Advertisers are forced to direct products to perhaps a million clusters of people who are themselves far more individualistic and who have a wide range of choices in today's world. The multiple-option society is a new ballgame, and advertisers know they must win consumers market by market, an approach some are calling "guerrilla warfare."

The either/or choices in the basic areas of family and work have exploded into a multitude of highly individual arrangements and lifestyles. But the basic idea of a multiple-option society has spilled over into other important areas of our lives: religion, the arts, music, food, entertainment, and finally in the extent to which cultural, ethnic, and racial diversity are now celebrated in America.

Family: A New Definition

Most of us raised or were raised in a typical nuclear American family: Father was breadwinner, mother took care of house and children, usually two. But today, there is no such thing as a typical family. And only a distinct minority (7 percent) of America's population fits the traditional family profile.

Instead, the diversity in American households of the 1980s has become a Rubik's cube of complexity. And like Rubik's cube, the chances of getting it back to its original state are practically nil.

Today's family can be a single parent (male or female) with one or more children, a two-career couple with no children, a female breadwinner with child and househusband, or a blended family that consists of a previously married couple and a combination of children from those two previous marriages. Although conservative profamily groups vehemently object, the term *family* is being expanded to include important relationships between people not related by blood or marriage, but by voluntary association: unmarried couples, close friends or roommates with long-standing relationships, group houses where people living together have grown into a community.

But what is even more basic is the way the family, or at least the household, consists of only one individual.

The basic building block of the society is shifting from the family to the individual.

More than ever before people live alone—a remarkable one in four is a single-person household, compared with one in ten in 1955. These individuals are the young who have not yet married, the elderly, and the newly divorced. And they are so numerous that the basic building block of society is now the individual rather than the family. Divorce, and the women's movement, of course, facilitated many of the changes in American family life. During the 1960s and 1970s, there was increasing acceptance of divorce and of nontraditional families.

These new family models will be with us for a long time, and American families will grow even more diverse. That is the conclusion of a report by demographers at the Joint Center for Urban Studies of MIT and Harvard, entitled, "The Nation's Families 1960–1990." Among its findings for the year 1990:

- Husband-wife households with only one working spouse will account for only 14 percent of all households, as compared with 43 percent in 1960.

- Wives will contribute about 40 percent of family income, compared to about 25 percent now.
- At least thirteen separate types of households will eclipse the conventional family, including such categories as "female head, widowed, with children" and "male head, previously married, with children."
- More than a third of the couples first married in the 1970s will have divorced; more than a third of the children born in the 1970s will have spent part of their childhood living with a single parent (and the emotional and financial consequences of this trend will be commensurately large).

Two-career families are, of course, having an impact on corporate recruiting, employee morale, and productivity. A 1980 survey sponsored by the Exxon Corporation, "Corporation and Two-Career Families: Directions for the Future," found that:

- Two-career-family employees are more resistant to relocation, especially if their employers are unlikely to assist a spouse to find employment in a new area.
- Companies that do help usually only offer informal contacts with other companies or job counseling.
- Corporate perceptions about who takes care of children have changed, and childcare options are beginning to increase. Eighty-three percent of the corporate respondents believed more men feel the need to share parenting responsibilities, but only 9 percent of the corporations offer paternity leave.
- A substantial minority (45 percent) believed that the difficulties of two-career families have not affected business operations.

Women: The Option Explosion

More than ever before, for women, it is not either/or. Women are exploring and acting upon a wide variety of options to the traditional female roles. They are joining the labor force, going back to college, entering professional schools, and working in blue-collar jobs in record numbers. At the same time, women who have been working for perhaps a decade, some with established professional careers, are deciding to have a child later in life, after thirty, even after thirty-five or forty.

Increasingly, women over thirty are becoming mothers for the first time. Overall the U.S. birthrate has not risen, but it has gone up among women in their thirties. The mean age of new mothers at Chicago's middle-class Northwestern Memorial Hospital is now thirty-three.

Kathy Weingarten, a clinical psychologist at Wellesley College and the author of a three-year study of midlife first-time mothers, says, "when we began our study in 1976, the 'late-timing' parent was a thirty-year-old. By the time we finished our interviews in 1979, the boundaries had shifted dramatically, and we had focused on the range in age of thirty-seven to forty-four."

The national trend toward later motherhood is dramatic. From 1975 to 1978, there was a 37-percent rate of increase in the number of women from age thirty to thirty-four who had their first child, according to the National Center for Health Statistics. For women aged thirty-five to thirty-nine the increase was 22 percent. "It used to be that when a woman decided not to have a baby at age thirty-five, that was it," according to Weingarten. "Now women at age forty-two are still asking themselves the question."

More women are working, and many more are going to college. Today there are more women in college and graduate school than men. Many of the new college women are over thirty-five. And they are not all getting education degrees either.

Women are studying law, medicine, and business. By 1990 the number of women earning business B.A.'s will be *eight times* that of the 1960s.

The proportion of women law students grew from a mere 6.9 percent as late as 1969 to 31.4 just a decade later, according to the Law School Admission Council. In the very best law schools, first-year classes are 50 percent or more female.

And women are starting new businesses at a phenomenal rate. Between 1972 and 1979, the number of self-employed women increased 43 percent, five times the rate of increase for men. There are more than 3 million women business owners and sole proprietorships now in the United States.

As women continue to exercise personal options, choices for men will increase as well. Some men will have the freedom to become full-time fathers, students, part-time workers, or to share a job with their partner. But one thing is clear: The traditional nuclear family (which has always depended on the wife subordinating too many of her individual interests to those of her husband and children) seems unlikely to return any time soon.

Work: Not All Nine to Five

It used to be that we (males, anyhow) got a job at the office or factory after graduation and worked regular full-time hours until retirement at sixty-five. There were men's jobs and the few women who worked held women's jobs. Now, of course, women make up nearly 40 percent of the workforce. And the employment world is a buffet of multiple options: part-time, flex-time, working at home, working partly at home and partly at the office, job sharing. We still have a long way to go, but jobs have grown substantially less gender-bound.

A measure of the growth in part-time employment is the temporary-service industry. That $2.5-billion industry has grown at an annual rate of about 20 percent in the last few years. At that rate the industry's business doubles every 3.5 years. The biggest growth area by far is in word processing, where the availability of temporary workers cannot keep up with the demand. It is interesting to note that all temporary-service firms that employ white-collar information workers are prospering, while Manpower, Inc. (the largest of the temporary-service agencies, but one heavily loaded with blue-collar temps), is just holding its own as it tries to move wholly into the white-collar side.

Traditionally, there has always been a sharp distinction between "men's and women's jobs." Now these gender-bound occupations are yielding to multiple option. Women are moving into blue-collar jobs that used to be exclusively male.

From 1970 to 1977, the number of women in blue-collar jobs doubled. By 1978, women held almost 20 percent of the nation's 29 million blue-collar jobs.

According to the most recent U.S. Bureau of Labor Statistics, there are:

131,000 women bus drivers
 50,000 women punch-press operators

41,000 women animal caretakers
26,000 women butchers
14,000 women printing-press operators
10,600 women brick masons
 5,700 women auto mechanics

The dramatic symbol of men in previously female-exclusive jobs is the voice of the male telephone operator, nonexistent a decade ago. The number of male nurses and male secretaries is increasing impressively too.

This decline of gender-bound jobs is important to the comparable-worth issue, the demand that women should receive comparable pay for work of comparable value. The important question for business throughout the 1980s is: Why should a maintenance worker be paid more than a secretary? The answer, historically, has been because women have always been secretaries and men have always been maintenance workers, and men have always decided (with a little help from the marketplace) who gets paid more. Traditionally we have justified higher pay for men because they supported the family. But that is a responsibility many men now share with their working wives. Consequently, the value of traditional women's work will undoubtedly be challenged. In January and February 1982 some 1,200 (nearly all women) nurses went on strike against four San Jose hospitals. The issue was comparable worth. The nurses want to be paid as much as pharmacists. The nurses consider nursing and pharmacy comparable professions. In San Jose a pharmacist's salary begins at $31,000; nurses start at $22,700.

Carpenters make more than nurses because women have always been nurses and men have always been carpenters—and men decide.

We are entering a period during which we will be reevaluating the contributions of jobs and skills to the larger tasks, a difficult thing to do, but something that business should have done a long time ago to get a better sense of who is contributing what to an enterprise.

The Arts: A Multiple-Option Muse

If there is one thing that characterizes the arts today—all of the arts—it is multiple option. There are no dominant schools, no either/ors. We are between eras everywhere, and it will be some time before we settle down to a clearly definable period in any of the arts. In the meantime, thousands of schools and artists bloom and no new leaders emerge.

There are today more artists creating more works of art than ever before in our history.

Art critic Hilton Kramer puts it this way: "The single factor that most completely dominates the art scene at the present moment is the sheer number of objects and events that crowd into it. Any attempt to acquire a sense of the quality or vitality of art in the 1980s must therefore be seen in relation to the immensity and variety of the activity itself. We have literally known nothing like it in the past."

This explosion of activity and the exciting diversity of contemporary art is important to notice because it tells us the multiple-option society is only now beginning because the visual arts are always the cultural bellwether.

About this phenomenon the French artist Jean Dubuffet has said, "Literature is 100 years behind painting. Just compare a painting today with a painting by Raphael, and then compare a page of Sartre with a page of Diderot, and you will see what I mean. The forms of painting have changed completely, whereas those of literature have hardly evolved at all. And, in art, action follows form."

Multiple option is the byword in architecture, too. The architectural term *postmodernism* tells us practically nothing in descriptive terms, yet it makes sense because the only thing that is sure about contemporary architecture is that it follows what was descriptively called modernism.

The architecture of the early 1980s is, in the words of architecture critic Ada Louise Huxtable, "an atmosphere of ferment and change."

There is only one unifying element amid all the diversity, says Huxtable, "the desire to pursue all possibilities for a richer and more varied kind of architecture. The sense of exploration and experiment, using all of history and technology as source material, is the leading spirit of the new work. . . . It is an active and exhilarating time, and we are about to see a great deal more of this stimulating, disturbing, provocative and promising building. This is a very different kind of modern architecture than we have learned to love or hate."

In classical music there are virtually no schools of any kind; hundreds of composers are going in their own directions, listening to their own muses. On the performance side there is an impressive decentralization in music as first-rate performing companies and music schools crop up all across the nation. In dance today, there is a new rich pluralism and eclecticism, with a great number of styles being developed.

To discover the multiple options in pop music, move your FM radio dial around a bit: In a matter of seconds you can choose:

- album-oriented rock
- easy-listening pop
- big-band jazz
- progressive jazz
- rhythm and blues
- oldies but goodies
- country rock
- rock country
- progressive rock
- disco
- punk rock

(Where is Cole Porter when we need him?)

Religion: A National Revival

The United States is today undergoing a revival in religious belief and church attendance. But except for the Southern Baptists, none of the major old-line denominations is benefiting; they all continue in a two-decade decline.

The new interest in religion is multiple option: No one religious group claims a significant portion of the growth. Rather, increases are occurring across the board in bottom-up, made-in-America churches, representing a checkered variety of beliefs and preferences.

A very important point is that the strictest and most demanding denominations, especially the Southern Baptists, are growing fastest, while the liberal churches continue to lose members.

This should not be surprising. During turbulent times many people need structure—not ambiguity—in their lives. They need something to hang on to, not something to debate. The demand for structure will increase, supplied not by the old, established denominations—Catholics, Episcopalians, Methodists, Presbyterians, and Lutherans—but by the Southern Baptists, the Mormons, the Seventh-Day Adventists, and by the great array of the new, native-grown fundamentalist faiths, by the charismatic Christian movement and the youthful Jesus movement. There are thousands of independent Christian churches and communities in the United States today. The Reverend Jerry Falwell's Thomas Road Baptist Church in Lynchburg, Virginia, and the Reverend Robert Schuller's Chrystal Cathedral in Garden Grove, California, are well-known independent churches. Their congregations are among the largest in the nation, but thousands and thousands of others, many with fewer than 100 members, have sprung up across the country. Since the 1960s there has also been the widespread interest in Eastern religions, and such groups as the Hare Krishnas are gaining a growing number of followers.

One measure of the extraordinary growth of America's religious revival is that evangelical publishers now account for a third of the total domestic commercial book sales.

The phenomenon of the electronic churches has been widely reported. There are today more than 1,300 radio stations and dozens of television stations devoting all or most of their time to religion.

The revival of religion in America will continue, I think, for as long as we remain in a transitional era because of the need for structure during times of great change. The nation experienced a similar increase in religious pluralism during the Great Religious Awakening of America's mid-1700s, a period when we were transforming from an agricultural to an industrial society.

Specialty Food: Designer Fruits and Vegetables

"Once upon a time ... mustard came in two flavors—French and Gulden's," writes Marian Burros, the *New York Times* food editor. "There was only one kind of bagel and two kinds of vinegar—white and red."

Today you can find Creole-style mustard, peanut mustard, black-olive mustard, mustards with anchovies, hickory-smoke flavor, green peppercorn, garlic, Russian-style, mustards in combination with honey, and, among others, "all-natural," salt-free Arizona champagne mustard.

There is now tarragon vinegar, along with raspberry white-wine vinegar, blueberry vinegar, peppercorn red-wine vinegar, Oriental rice vinegar, and strawberry, black currant, and cherry vinegar, among others. The biggest seller in specialty vinegar, according to Burros, is Italian balsamic.

There are now a dozen varieties of dried mushrooms.

Nothing, however, can equal the varieties of honeys and teas on the shelves of specialty food shops, says Burros. "There are honeys from almost every country, flavored by almost every variety of tree, bush and flower. And just when it seems there is no other variety of tea to market, someone finds one: tea flavored with 'natural bourbon vanilla,' bing cherries and butterscotch; herb teas made in cubes, much like bouillon; decaffeinated teas; sangria tea flavored with dried berries, natural orange and lemon flavor."

Today coffee beans are being mixed with flavorings, including amaretto, dried orange peel, cinnamon sticks, toasted almonds, and chocolate. You can now have any of these coffees in the morning with your chocolate bagel.

Ethnic foods now account for one-third of the 1,768 frozen foods introduced in the last five years. This is a big jump from the 13 percent during the previous ten years.

Yogurt has gained widespread acceptance, and its flavors have been multiplying. Another ethnic food, tofu (soybean curd), has started to hit the general consumer market. Tofu has been in the United States a long time as an ingredient in Oriental dishes. Now it appears in supermarkets and restaurants in all areas of the country. By mid-1981 sales were running at an annual rate of more than $50 million—about the level of yogurt sales ten years ago. In another decade tofu sales are expected to reach $500 million annually, the volume of yogurt sales today.

Once almost all Americans ate white bread, but in recent years sales have dropped, as people turned to alternatives. White bread now has dropped to only 65 percent of the market, and the decline (at about 5 percent per year) is accelerating. In 1981 white-bread sales in some parts of the country were running 10 percent behind 1980.

According to the Market Research Corporation of America, which does a census on what families eat, ethnic-foods consumption has increased 47 percent since 1972.

Exotic produce has moved from specialty stores to supermarkets, where we can now buy kiwis and kumquats, bean and alfalfa sprouts, bok choy, rutabagas, garbanzo beans, and many other varieties. Pedi Brothers, a produce wholesaler just outside of Chicago, now sells 2,800 kinds of fruits and vegetables.

New exotic produce is being developed all the time: designer fruits and vegetables, new in taste and color, and at top prices.

Among the recent arrivals are yellow papayas from Hawaii; pear-apples, an Oriental fruit being grown in California that looks like an apple and tastes like a pear; very long-stemmed strawberries; seedless cucumbers; spaghetti squash; and white eggplants from Texas.

Stay tuned.

Cable Television: Something for Everyone

Cable television is an analog for the multiple-option society. Across the nation ABC, CBS, and NBC are being supplemented by almost 5,000 cable systems.

A cable system is like a supermarket. It buys programs and services from many sources, which are then put on the system's channels. For a monthly fee, individual subscribers order the programs and services that suit them. The cable systems deliver all local television programming, television programming from nearby cities, and programming from distant networks whose signals are sent by satellite. Extra fees are charged for some programs (including movies) brought in by satellite. The early cable supermarkets had only a dozen channels on which to display their goods, but new systems boast more than 100 channels. By the end of the 1980s cable television will offer as many as 200 different channels of entertainment and services.

That's a lot of options.

Cable television will be like the special-interest magazines: You will be able to tune in *Runner's World* or *Beehive Management*.

Even now there are at least fifty different networks the cable systems can buy from. Among them are the Spanish network, several children's networks, the art network, the health network, the black networks, the all-weather network, the Christian Brothers Network and other church-affiliated networks, a number of all-sports networks, and the all-news networks. Almost every day some new source of programming is announced.

In the spring of 1982 the United States Chamber of Commerce started the American Business Network, or Biznet, for those who want to keep closer tabs on business-related political, legislative, and regulatory development.

Thirteen nuns in Our Lady of Angels Monastery in Birmingham, Alabama, launched the Eternal Word Network in the fall of 1981, broadcasting for four hours each day by satellite to 300,000 cable subscribers. By 1984 the Sisters hope to be broadcasting twenty-four hours a day.

Cable television is beginning to do a lot more than supplement the networks. For the first time, during one month in the summer of 1981, films shown by Home Box Office (the big national pay-TV movie network) during prime time drew more viewers than ABC, CBS, or NBC. The networks' share of the total national television audience started on a downward slide in 1977. It is now below 90 percent and will continue to decline until by the end of the 1980s it could be as low as 50 percent of audience share, as we move increasingly from broadcasting to narrowcasting.

Ethnic Diversity: Abandoning the Melting Pot

In this multiple-option era, Americans have learned to accept, even celebrate, ethnic diversity. We have given up the myth of the melting pot at last and everyone is free to be exactly what they are. Since there is so much diversity everyplace else in American culture, ethnics are not so much noticed as *different* as they are in tune with the country's general mood and values.

We have moved from the myth of the melting pot to a celebration of cultural diversity.

It is a far cry from the way Americans handled ethnicity in the past. We seemed to put new immigrants through a metaphorical blender until they came out homogenized Americans, with little remaining of their former heritage.

It was taken for granted, for example, that newcomers would be packed off to language school to learn English almost immediately. Although many Americans resent the way Spanish-speaking Americans continue speaking their native tongue within self-sufficient Spanish-speaking communities—and never learn English—the fact that they are able to do so is a mark of the high level of cultural diversity already existing in this country. It also reflects the enormous increase in the numbers of Spanish-speaking Americans: Two decades ago it would have been impossible. Today, the United States has the fourth largest Spanish-speaking population in the world.

In recent history, we have not encouraged immigration, either. Between 1952 and 1965, immigration policy, in the words of *Newsweek* magazine, "treated the American national character like a prized recipe, to be preserved in perpetuity in its exact ethnic composition." During the 1970s, however, an average of half a million immigrants entered the United States legally each year, adding a new dimension to the term "ethnic diversity." The recent publication of the 1,076-page *Harvard Encyclopedia of American Ethnic Groups* listed information about some 100 ethnic groups living in this country, from Acadians to Zoroastrians. This massive reference book, which was five years in the making, reports there are now fifty groups with sizable populations in the nation.

One key factor behind the increasing acceptance of ethnic diversity has been the rapid growth of two minorities in particular: Spanish-speaking Americans, who now officially number approximately 15 million (millions more are here illegally) or about 6.4 percent of the population; and Asian-Americans, about 3.5 million or about 1.5 percent of the U.S. population.

With three sizable minorities now in the nation—the largest being blacks, with 26 million or about one-tenth of the U.S. population—the either/or world where Americans were either black or white is over forever. That was a world structured to encourage uniformity rather than diversity. Blacks, as the only recognized ethnic group, encountered racial and ethnic prejudice; whites, who were themselves ethnically diverse, tried to emulate (subconsciously perhaps) the Wasp ideal.

With more racial and ethnic groups now (think of Asian Orientals and Latins, who are black, white, and brown), uniformity is impossible, and white Americans are identifying with their own ethnic roots to join the new game of diversity.

Even the major ethnic groups are diverse. Latins are Mexican, Puerto Rican, Cuban, Guatemalan, San Salvadoran, Colombian, and from a variety of Central and South American countries. Asians are Chinese, Filipino, Japanese, Korean, Vietnamese, as well as Laotian, Indonesian, and Samoan.

Although their numbers appear small nationally, they are clustered in groups that magnify their numbers considerably. The new wave of ethnic Americans is having an enormous impact on local communities:

- In Aurora, Illinois, a Chicago suburb, there are 14,500 Latins, about 18 percent of the population. Much of Aurora's main street has a strong Latin flavor.
- Selma, Alabama, is home to 120 Hmong tribesmen from Laos.
- Two thousand Tai Dam, a Southeast Asian tribe, have settled in Iowa.

Wherever they live in America, the newcomers are changing the landscape locally and leaving a strong imprint that varies from one community to another, as diverse as the ethnic groups themselves. Writes *Newsweek* magazine:

They are changing the American landscape, proliferating into unexpected niches, each following an irresistible ethnic call. Korean greengrocers have sprouted all over New York City, nestling bins of knobby and unexplained roots next to red Delicious apples, while Greeks have all but taken over the coffee shops, conquering the quick lunch business under their ubiquitous symbol: the drink container with a picture of

245

a discus thrower. In New Orleans, Vietnamese immigrants have converted their housing-project lawns into vegetable gardens, irrigating them with the same long-handled canvas buckets they once dipped into the Mekong. The amplified call of the muezzin echoes through the south end of Dearborn, Michigan, five times a day, calling the faithful to prayer at their mosque. Just as Americans have finally digested the basics of soccer, cricket has emerged as the avant-garde immigrant sport, played by exuberant Samoans on the fields of Carson, California, and earnest Jamaicans and Trinidadians in Brooklyn's Prospect Park.

But none of the new groups individually can begin to match the numbers and the potential influence of Spanish-speaking Americans.

By 1990 some experts believe black and white Spanish-speaking Americans will be the nation's largest ethnic group. The Mexican population of Los Angeles, for example, is second only to Mexico City, and Miami is two-thirds Cuban. It is my opinion that the present debate about bilingual education will eventually have to be settled in favor of Spanish speakers and that we will be transformed into a bilingual country before the end of the century.

This will occur because of two major reasons. The sheer numbers alone will continue to increase in proportion to other ethnic groups because there will be more immigration and because the birthrate of Latinos is twice that of whites and 60 percent higher than that of black Americans.

But the more important force is economic—American business is going after the Spanish-speaking consumer in his or her own language and all of us will begin to learn some Spanish in the course of that process, whether we are writing advertising copy, hearing a Spanish ad on television or radio, or noticing bilingual instructions on a pay telephone or bus transfer.

An April 1981 issue of *Advertising Age,* which was devoted to Hispanic marketing, cited one of the most important studies available to advertisers about the Hispanic market. The study, entitled "U.S. Hispanics—A Market Profile," was conducted for the National Association of Spanish Broadcasters by Strategy Associates of Miami. It concluded that Mexican-Americans had a median income of $13,439; Puerto Ricans, $8,787; and Cubans and other Spanish, a high of $15,342. In comparison, the nation's median income is $19,116. The cities of greatest Spanish influence in America are Los Angeles, New York, Miami, Chicago, and San Antonio; the states are California, with 4.5 million Spanish speakers, Texas, with 3 million, New Mexico, with 476,000, Arizona, with 441,000, and Colorado, with 340,000.

Once advertisers seriously aim for the Spanish-speaking market, we will all get a much stronger sense of Latin culture, language, and music—and that will enrich American society and increase our options still further.

Ralph Tyler, the well-known U.S. educator, used to say that you can tell you are being educated if your options are increasing, and that the reverse is happening if they are decreasing. Similarly, a society can tell it is growing if the options for its citizens are increasing. It is extraordinary for a society as mature as the United States to be growing—at least by this measure—so vigorously. One has only to think about the Soviet bloc countries in these terms to see how stagnant they are by comparison.

Much of the multiple-option nature of the United States is addressed to our own individuality; we have greater and greater opportunities for self-expression—in education, religion, the arts, in our work, as well as in the marketplace.

On the producer side in all these areas, it means there can be a market for just about anything, as we get more and more accustomed to new flavors being introduced every day.

Conclusion

We are living in the *time of the parenthesis,* the time between eras. It is as though we have bracketed off the present from both the past and the future, for we are neither here nor there. We have not quite left behind the either/or America of the past—centralized, industrialized, and economically self-contained. With one foot in the old world where we lived mostly in the Northeast, relied on institutional help, built hierarchies, and elected representatives, we approached problems with an eye toward the high-tech, short-term solutions.

But we have not embraced the future either. We have done the human thing: We are clinging to the known past in fear of the unknown future. This book outlines one interpretation of that future in order to make it more real, more knowable. Those who are willing to handle the ambiguity of this in-between period and to anticipate the new era will be a quantum leap ahead of those who hold on to the past. The time of the parenthesis is a time of change and questioning.

As we move from an industrial to an information society, we will use our brainpower to create instead of our physical power, and the technology of the day will extend and enhance our mental ability. As we take advantage of the opportunity for job growth and investment in all the sunrise industries, we must not lose sight of the need to balance the human element in the face of all that technology.

Yet, the most formidable challenge will be to train people to work in the information society. Jobs will become available, but who will possess the high-tech skills to fill them? Not today's graduates who cannot manage simple arithmetic or write basic English. And certainly not the unskilled, unemployed dropouts who cannot even find work in the old sunset industries.

Farmer, laborer, clerk. The next transition may well be to technician. But that is a major jump in skill level.

As Third World countries take over many industrial tasks, the United States must be prepared to take the lead in the innovative new tasks of the future—or face the prospect of being a Great Britain, whose steel and automobile companies are merely disguised widespread-employment programs. All the while, as we tread water, unwilling to choose the winning businesses of the future and unable to let go of the losers, Japan and the "new Japans" of the Third World are free to eclipse our lead in electronics, biotechnology, and the other sunrise sectors.

But do we have the courage to abandon our traditional industries, industries that other countries can now do better. Do we have the innovative ability to venture forward into the future?

One good sign is that some American businesses appear to have discovered the advantages of the long-term approach and the appropriate reward systems, have developed the capacity to change the direction of a business as the world changes, and have recognized the opportunities inherent in being the world's leading provider of information, knowledge, and expertise.

Even while we think globally, the place to make a difference politically is at the local rather than the national level. Whether the issue is energy, politics, community self-help, entrepreneurship, the consumer movement, or wholistic health, the new creed is one of self-reliance and local initiative. In this new era of geographic diversity and decentralization, the conformity of mass society is a thing of the past. The divestiture of AT&T's local companies and the shift of responsibility from Washington back to the States could not have taken place twenty years ago. These prominent decentralist actions represent the culmination of a long process that has been evolving since the 1960s.

The political notion of governance is being completely redefined. Today's well-educated, well-informed citizen is capable and desirous of participating in political decisions to a greater extent than the present representative system permits. Hence the growth in referenda, initiatives, and recalls during the 1970s. Despite occasional outcries to the contrary, we do not want strong leadership in national affairs because we are basically self-governing. And we are gradually extending the ideal of democracy into corporations, where we are demanding a greater voice as consumers, shareholders, outside directors, and (most importantly) employees.

This newly evolving world will require its own structures. We are beginning to abandon the hierarchies that worked well in the centralized, industrial era. In their place, we are substituting the network model of organization and communication, which has its roots in the natural, egalitarian, and spontaneous formation of groups among like-minded people. Networks restructure the power and communication flow within an organization from vertical to horizontal. One network form, the quality control circle, will help revitalize worker participation and productivity in American business. A network management style is already in place in several young, successful computer firms. And the computer itself will be what actually smashes the hierarchical pyramid: With the computer to keep track of people and business information, it is no longer necessary for organizations to be organized into hierarchies. No one knows this better than the new-age computer companies.

The computer will smash the pyramid: We created the hierarchical, pyramidal, managerial system because we needed it to keep track of people and things people did; with the computer to keep track, we can restructure our institutions horizontally.

Amid all the other restructurings, America is engaged in a massive migration from the Northeast and Midwest to the Southwest (and to Florida). That population shift came about in large part as a response to three megashifts discussed in this book: (1) People are moving away from the thickly settled Northeast, where industrial society flourished earlier in this century, but where dying industries are leaving behind abandoned factories and jobless people; (2) the foreign competition we experience, especially in automobile and steel, as part of an interdependent world economy is forcing many of the old industries to close; and (3) the decentralization of business and the search for new energy sources are enabling people to find a job in an area where they would like to live (large numbers of young people, for example, have moved to the Rocky Mountain states).

Each of the ten cities of opportunity has recently attracted one or more new facilities in the new information industries. The North–South shift is irreversible in our lifetime. What is unclear is how the country will adjust to the changes. These are the questions for which local and regional planners must find innovative solutions. Are there ways to adaptively reuse the valuable infrastructure being left behind in the North? Ways to meet the growing demand for instant infrastructure in the Southwest? The burden falls most heavily on the cities where change is greatest, such as Detroit and Houston.

Although the North–South shift sounds like an either/or choice, it is not. Even geography can be multiple option because we have diversified into a society where almost anything is possible. The wide range of choices in work arrangements, the new definitions of family, the enormous diversity in the arts, the dazzling array of newly promoted specialty foods, are only some of the reflections of a society that is exploding with diversity. One measure is the way we have responded to the new wave of immigrants in recent years: We have finally abandoned the myth of the melting pot and learned to celebrate ethnic diversity. The new languages, ethnic food and restaurants, and the additional layer of foreign cultures all around us seem to fit the multiple-option mood. This new openness enriches us all.

Such is the time of the parenthesis, its challenges, its possibilities, and its questions.

Although the time between eras is uncertain, it is a great and yeasty time, filled with opportunity. If we can learn to make uncertainty our friend, we can achieve much more than in stable eras.

In stable eras, everything has a name and everything knows its place, and we can leverage very little.

But in the time of the parenthesis we have extraordinary leverage and influence—individually, professionally, and institutionally—if we can only get a clear sense, a clear conception, a clear vision, of the road ahead.

My God, what a fantastic time to be alive!

Notes

This book draws mostly from the *Trend Report* and from The Naisbitt Group data base. Other sources are listed below.

Megatrends are regularly updated through *John Naisbitt's Trend Letter,* published by The Naisbitt Group, 1211 Connecticut Avenue, N.W., Washington, D.C. 20036.

Introduction
3   For a thorough treatment of content analysis and an excellent bibliography on the subject, see "Content Analysis and the Study of Sociopolitical Change," by Morris Janowitz in *Journal of Communication,* vol. 26, no. 4, 1976.

ONE   Industrial Society → Information Society
13   Daniel Bell has written extensively on the information society. Among the pieces I have found most useful are "Techne and Themis" from *The Winding Passage,* Abt Books, 1980; "Welcome to the Post Industrial Society" in the February 1976 issue of *Physics Today;* "Thinking Ahead," which appeared in *Harvard Business Review,* the May–June 1979 issue; and "Notes on the Post Industrial Society (I & II)" in *The Public Interest,* Spring 1967.

16   Peter Drucker is quoted in a speech by N. B. Hannay, Vice President, Research and Patents, Bell Laboratories, at Northwestern University, March 5, 1980. I have been particularly influenced by Drucker's *Managing in Turbulent Times*, New York: Harper & Row, 1980.

17   The Dennison study is cited in "The Service Sector of the U.S. Economy," by Eli Ginsberg and George Vojta, *Scientific American*, March 1981.

17   A summary of Birch's study entitled "Who Creates Jobs?" appeared in the Fall 1981 issue of *The Public Interest*. Birch's findings are discussed more fully in Chapter 9.

18   The figures on the membership of the World Future Society and future-oriented periodicals appear in an unpublished manuscript by Gavin Clabaugh, who served as researcher on this manuscript.

20– Marc Porat's study, *Information Economy: Definition and Measure-*
21   *ment*, was published by the U.S. Department of Commerce/Office of Telecommunications in May 1977, OT Special Publication 77–12 (1).

21   See "Info City," *New York* magazine, February 9, 1981.

24   Statistics on the information explosion appear in Daniel Bell's "Techne and Themis," *The Winding Passage*, p. 54.

25   Figures on the numbers of computers appear in "Next a computer on every desk," the *New York Times*, August 23, 1981.

26   *Goodbye Gutenberg*, subtitled *The Newspaper Revolution of the 1980's*, was published in 1980 by Oxford University Press. It is by far the best book I have seen on the subject.

29   Fears about the impact of microprocessor communications appear in an article by Harley Shaiken in *Technology Review*, January 1981.

30   Colin Norman writes in *Futurist*, February 1981.

30   The *New Scientist* estimate appears in "The Social Impact of Microprocessors," October 12, 1978.

30   The *Newsweek* estimate appears in the June 30, 1980, issue.

30 The *In These Times* article is "Microshock in the Information Society," January 21–27, 1981.

30 The Lund study is discussed in an article by him in *Technology Review*, January 1981.

31 The Education Department/National Science Foundation study's conclusions are reported in "U.S. Report Fears Most Americans Will Become Scientific Illiterates," the *New York Times*, October 23, 1981.

31 The Carnegie Council Study is reported in the *Washington Post*, November 28, 1979. Estimates of illiterates appear in a Ford Foundation report, "Adult Illiteracy in the United States," the *Washington Post*, September 9, 1979.

33 The estimate of jobs involving computers by 1985 appeared in *Newsweek*, March 9, 1981.

33 The math teachers' quote appears in "New Literacy for the Computer Age," *Technology Review*, May–June 1981.

34 The *Wall Street Journal* article on executives and computers appeared January 28, 1981.

35 The estimate that one-third of the personal computers shipped up until 1980 ended up in business appeared in *Business Week*, December 1, 1981, p. 91.

35–36 An article about working at home by computer appears in *Business Week*, January 26, 1981.

37 Steve Jobs is quoted in *Business Week*, December 1, 1980.

TWO   Forced Technology → High Tech/High Touch
48 I have written about high tech/high touch in *Metropolitan Home*, November 1981.

49 Harley Shaiken estimated the robot numbers in "A Robot Is After Your Job," the *New York Times*, September 3, 1981.

52 The article by John Hess appeared in *Geo*, March 1981.

THREE   National Economy → World Economy
60 On the U.S. productivity edge: *The Economist*, January 24, 1981.

61– The "new Japans" are discussed in "Make Way for the New Ja-
62 pans," *Fortune,* August 10, 1981.

63– The idea that the auto market has reached saturation in the
64 United States and Europe appears in *The Economist,* January 3,
1981.

64– Information on mergers and purchases of auto companies is
65 gleaned from news reports in the *New York Times:* December 19,
1980; January 11, 1981; and May 27, 1981; *The Wall Street Journal,* April 27, 1981; and *The Economist,* July 11, 1981.

65 On automobile components: the *New York Times,* May 26, 1981,
and January 9, 1980; and *Transnational Perspective,* January
1981.

68 A discussion of Germany's and Britain's structural adjustment
policies appears in a review of *Structural Economic Policies of West
Germany and the United Kingdom,* in *New Scientist,* January 15,
1981.

70 The Commerce Department study was carried out by the Office
of Foreign Investment and cited in the February 1981 issue of
World Papers.

70 The Conference Board Study was reported in *The Wall Street
Journal*'s Business Bulletin, February 2, 1981.

71 The number of foreign banks in the United States appears in
World Papers, February 1981, and in *The Economist,* August 30,
1980.

71 Figures on Chase and Citibank's income are in a *New York Times*
article, "Brazil Reigns in Its Economy," December 8, 1980.

75 Barbara Ward's article, "Another Chance for the North," in *Foreign Affairs,* Winter 1980–1981.

FOUR Short Term → Long Term
79 The example of American Standard appeared in an article by
Thomas C. Hayes, the *New York Times,* January 11, 1981.

81 Reginald Jones's statements appeared in *U.S. News & World Report,* June 15, 1981.

81 Julian Scheer's comments are from "The Trouble with Business,
Says Business, Is Business," the *Washington Post,* May 10,1981.

81   William Agee's quote appeared in "Playing It Safe and Losing Out," the *Washington Post*, January 17, 1982.

81   Lester Thurow is quoted in "Where Management Fails," *Newsweek*, December 7, 1981.

82   The interview with Lewis Young of *Business Week* is from *The Ward Howell Roundtable*, February 1981.

82   Michael Schulhof's comments are from "Scientists in Business," the *New York Times*, February 1, 1981.

83   Kenneth Mason in "Key Executives 'Chuck It' for Career Changes," the *Washington Post*, August 3, 1981.

83   David Vogel writing in "America's Management Crisis," *New Republic*, February 7, 1981. Vogel cites the poll on technology and the poor technology training of American and British executives.

84   Reginald Jones from *U.S. News & World Report*, June 15, 1981.

84   The *Business Week* comments appeared in "How Companies Can Lengthen Their Sights," July 30, 1980.

84   Edwin Murk is quoted by Jane Bryant Quinn, *Newsweek*, February 13, 1981.

84   Thomas V. Jones is quoted in *Business Week*, "How Companies Can Lengthen Their Sights," June 30, 1980.

84   The Heidrick Struggles Survey is reported in "Playing It Safe and Losing Out," the *Washington Post*, January 17, 1982.

85   Theodore Levitt's comments are from "Marketing Myopia," *Harvard Business Review*, September/October 1975.

86   Walter Wriston's comments were made in a speech to the Securities Industry Association in New York City on January 21, 1981.

86   Alfred Chandler's comments appeared in *The Wall Street Journal*, February 15, 1981.

88   Information on Singer is from "Singer Moving into Aerospace," the *Miami Herald*, November 18, 1981.

88   Background on Schlumberger, Inc., appeared in the *New York Times*, September 15, 1981.

89   Background on Sears is from "The New Sears," *Business Week,*
November 16, 1981.

89   Done T. McKone is quoted in "Turning Around Libby-Owens,"
Business Week, August 10, 1981.

FIVE   Centralization → Decentralization
Most of the information and examples in this chapter comes
from the *Trend Report.*
   However, some good background on federalism appears in
several articles by John Herbers in the *New York Times:* August
10, 1980; January 21, 1981; March 27, 1981; September 27,
1981; in an op-ed *New York Times* piece, May 3, 1981, by Dick
Thornburgh, the Republican governor of Pennsylvania; and in
a column by David Broder in the *Washington Post,* August 24,
1980.

103   Adlai Stevenson is quoted in the *New York Times,* December 16,
1980.

123   On regional values: *The Wall Street Journal,* February 3, 1981.

126–   The Herbers articles on geographic decentralization that I
28   found so useful appeared March 23, 1980; March 24, 1980;
June 8, 1980; August 3, 1980; and April 24, 1984.

128   On rural crime: *U.S. News & World Report,* May 26, 1980.

SIX   Institutional Help → Self-Help
134–   Improved health habits are discussed in "Americans Shift Their
35   Habits, Surgeon General Finds" in the *Washington Post,* December 6, 1980; and in "Wine Outsells Spirits," in the *New York
Times,* June 14, 1981.

135   Examples of business-backed fitness programs are from the
Trend Report and from "Working Out at Work, or How Corporations Intend to Trim the Fat," in *Next,* March–April 1981.

136   The notion that 75 percent of the people care for themselves
without seeing a doctor comes from Dr. Tom Ferguson, an expert on medical self-care.

136   On home health care: "Health Care at Home: A Booking Market" by Bonnie Nance Frazier, *U.S. News & World Report,* February 9, 1981; and "Do-It-Yourself Medical Tests Are
Abounding," by Tabitha M. Powledge, the *New York Times,*
March 16, 1980.

136   Dr. Ferguson is quoted in *U.S. News & World Report,* February 9, 1981.

137   Governor Brown is quoted in *Trends & Forecasts* by Jean Carper and John Naisbitt, January 27, 1981.

137   American Wholistic Health Association membership figures appear in "Wholistic Health Gains," the *Washington Post,* November 19, 1981.

138   *Anatomy of an Illness as Perceived by the Patient,* by Norman Cousins, W.W. Norton & Co., in 1979.

138–   A number of examples of self-help organizations in this chapter
53   appeared in *People Power: What Communities Are Doing to Counter Inflation,* published by the U.S. Office of Consumer Affairs. There is no publication date, but it appears to have gone to print in 1980, the final year of the Carter administration. This book is a treasure trove of self-help information, profiling numerous innovative programs across the country. The programs mentioned in this chapter are listed below with the page where they appear in *People Power.*

The Helping Hand Health Center, p. 334.
Dr. Milton Seifert's "Patient Advisory Council," p. 356.
The Wholistic Health Center of Hinsdale, p. 303.
Childbearing Center, p. 308.
The Kentucky Mountain Housing Development Corp., p. 100.
Renew, Inc., p. 108.
Jubilee Housing Inc., p. 116.
Brothers Redevelopment, Inc., p. 124.
Jeff-Vander-Lou, Inc., p. 152.
Boston Urban Gardners, p. 51.
Greenmarket, p. 35.
Tucson Co-operative Warehouse, p. 33.
St. Mary's Food Bank, p. 40.
Tri-County Community Council Food Bank, p. 42.

Because of the networklike nature of these organizations, however, it is possible that one or two may no longer be in existence.

140   Figures on graduate midwives: the *New York Times,* January 24, 1981.

141   Increases in home births: "Homebirth, an alternative," *New Age,* December 1980.

142   The Gallup Poll on education appears each fall in *Phi Delta Kappan.* The survey referred to was in the September 1979 issue.

143– On private schools: *The Libertarian Review,* March 1981.
44

144   Estimate of 1 million home-educated students: "What Happens When Parents Turn Teachers," the *New York Times* annual winter survey, January 10, 1982.

144   "Growing Without Schooling," 729 Boylston Street, Boston, Massachusetts 02116.

145   An article on Dr. Rich's methods appears in the *New York Times* April 8, 1980. Other information on her methods appears in the *Trend Report.*

145– Recently there have been several excellent articles on entrepre-
49   neurships. This section draws from them all. "Small Business: Job Role Highlighted" by Steve Lohr, the *New York Times,* January 18, 1980; "Small Business Is Working Its Way out of Federal Neglect," by the same author in the *New York Times,* February 24, 1980; "In Praise of Small Business," the *New York Times Magazine,* by Arthur Levitt, Jr., December 6, 1981; "Venture Capitalists Ride Again," in *The Economist,* October 11, 1980; "Small Companies: America's Hope for the 80's," *Inc.,* April 1981 (extremely useful).

147   George Gilder on alternative indexes from "The Entrepreneurian Future," an adaptation of a chapter from *Wealth and Poverty,* appearing in *The American Spectator,* December 1980.

149   The *Wall Street Journal* article on executive shifts to small business, March 13, 1981.

149   Jerry Rubin's op-ed piece appeared in the *New York Times,* July 30, 1980.

150   "Lots of helping hands," by Alan Gartner and Frank Riessman, appears in the *New York Times,* February 19, 1980.

150– Drucker is quoted in *U.S. News & World Report,* December 21,
51   1981.

SEVEN Representative Democracy → Participatory Democracy

> An excellent article for general background of the death of the two-party system appears in the *New York Times Magazine* on December 9, 1979, "The Party's Over for the Political Parties," by John Herbers. The Herbers quote and the quote from the Chicago woman are from that article.

161 Most of the many examples cited in this chapter appeared in the *Trend Report.*

161 Figures on party identification appear in the following: "Studies Find Future in Political Parties," Adam Clymer, the *New York Times,* April 20, 1981; and in *The Gallup Opinion Index,* "The Election: A Shift to the Right? The Gallup Poll Post Mortem," December 1980, Report No. 183, p. 29.

162 Voter turnout in totalitarian states: "Non-voting, a Sign of Decay or Health," *The Wall Street Journal,* October 15, 1980.

162 Representative Danielson is quoted in *The Wall Street Journal,* December 14, 1979.

164 The most comprehensive article on initiatives and referenda is "Power to the People," by Michael Nelson, in *Saturday Review,* November 24, 1979.

165 The full name of the AEI study is *Referendums: A Comparative Study of Practice and Theory,* edited by David Butler and Austin Ranney.

175 Harland Cleveland's remarks are from a speech delivered to the National Association of Schools of Public Affairs, October 21, 1980, in San Antonio, Texas.

176 The *Washington Post* article "The Corporate Voice" by Bradley Graham appeared March 25, 1979.

176 *The Chemical Feast* was published by Viking Press in 1970.

179 The Council on Economic Priorities Study appears in the *New York Times,* August 19, 1979.

180 The Heidrick & Struggles study is reported in "Outsider-Dominated Boards Spurred by Calls for Independence," *The Wall Street Journal,* October 3, 1980; the Korn Ferry study in "Board Outsiders Win Favor," the *New York Times,* March 31, 1980.

182   Professor Clyde Summers in his January-February 1980 article in *Harvard Business Review* cites the common law on employer/employee relationships—H.G. Wood, Master and Servant # 134, 1877.

182   For numbers of quality control circles, see *Business Week,* "The New Industrial Relations," May 11, 1981; and "A Partnership to Build the New Workplace," June 30, 1980.

185   The *Business Week* article "Coping with Employee Lawsuits" appeared August 27, 1979.

185   The list of fourteen states where courts have ruled in favor of employees was compiled by Professor Alan Westin, a recognized authority on employee rights.

186–87   Employee rights: Davis Ewing, "A Bill of Rights," *Across the Board,* March 1981.

187   Professor Summers's article appears in the January–February 1980 issue of *Harvard Business Review.*

EIGHT   Hierarchies → Networking

189   Douglas McGregor's *The Human Side of Enterprise* was published in 1960 by McGraw-Hill.

192   Marilyn Ferguson's *Aquarian Conspiracy* was published by J.P. Tarcher in 1980.

193   Lipnack and Stamps, "Networking," in *New Age,* June 1980. Their book, *Networking,* was published by Doubleday in 1982.

195   Willard Van de Bogart's "Information Networks," *Future Life,* December 1981. The reference to the Consciousness Synthesis Clearinghouse also appears here.

196   See Virginia Hine's "The Basic Paradigm of a Future Socio-cultural System," *World Issues,* April–May, 1977.

198   Intel's management style is discussed in "Overhauling America's Business Management" by Steve Lohr in the *New York Times Magazine,* January 4, 1981.

199–200   For background on baby-boom managers and the way their style will evolve into networking, see "Management in the 1980's" by

Roy Amara in *Technology Review*, April 1981, and Charles Post, "Post War 'Baby Boom' Managers Take Charge," in *Iron Age*, August 18, 1980.

200   Hewlett-Packard's management style is discussed in *Business Week*, June 30, 1980.

200–   "What Makes Tandem Run" appears in *Business Week*, July 14,
201   1980.

201   The number of QC circles at Honeywell is reported in *Business Week*, "The New Industrial Relations," May 11, 1981.

202   Rene McPherson is quoted in "Notable and Quotable," *The Wall Street Journal*, May 2, 1980.

202   An article on Honeywell's quality control circles appears in *Training/HRD*, August 1980.

202   The *New England Business* article appeared August 16, 1979.

203   William Ouchi's *Theory Z* was published by Addison-Wesley in 1981.

NINE   North → South
208–   There were probably thousands of articles summarizing the
209   1980 census. Two that stand out are "Who's Gaining, Losing in Population Race," *U.S. News & World Report*, February 16, 1981; and "U.S. Census Bureau Releases 1980 Count," by Robert Reinhold, in the *New York Times*, December 17, 1980.

209   Summary of Labor Department study appeared in "West, South Got Most Jobs," the *Washington Post*, April 11, 1980.

209   This particular Herbers piece appeared September 20, 1980.

209   Reports of job losses by city appeared in the *New York Times*, January 9, 1980; August 4, 1980; September 20, 1980; and *U.S. News & World Report*, January 12, 1981.

211   Figures on the percentages of graduates by region appeared in an article by Sam Allis, "Where the Most Educated Americans Live," in *The Wall Street Journal*, November 4, 1980.

211–   Moves of high-tech firms to the Rocky Mountain states are re-
12   ported in "Rocky Mountain High," *Time*, December 15, 1980.

212   The figure that only 3 percent of the South's growth is attributed to plant migration from the North appears in "The Sunbelt—Shape of Things to Come," *Industrial Distribution,* January 1981. In addition, David Birch concluded that between 1969 and 1976 only about 2 percent of all private-sector annual-employment changes in the United States was the result of physical relocation. Birch's figure has been quoted extensively by academic writers.

213   Governor Lamm's quote and the comment on population in Colorado's mountain counties appear in an article by John Herbers in the *New York Times,* August 31, 1980.

214   Energy Companies in Denver: the *New York Times,* August 5, 1980.

214   Mr. Krumholtz and Mr. Brodie are quoted in "Born Again," *The Wall Street Journal,* May 19, 1981; Mr. Hill in the *New York Times,* January 25, 1981.

216–17   Sources of the secondary indicators are listed below:

    Living Standards and Income: "U.S. Study Confirms Growth in the Sunbelt," the *New York Times,* May 3, 1971; and "South Leads, Northeast Lags in New Living Standard Measure," *The Wall Street Journal,* November 25, 1980.
    Housing: "Northeast May Lose Ground in Housing," *The Wall Street Journal,* February 18, 1981.
    Investment: "Energy to Foster Boom in West, Sun Belt Investment Will Slow," *The Wall Street Journal,* October 28, 1980. An article by John Herbers in the *New York Times,* September 20, 1980.
    Pensions: "Pension Funds Flow to Sunbelt Spurs Shift of Investment Capital," the *New York Times,* May 20, 1980.
    Education and age levels: "More Stress in Economy Is Predicted for Northeast," the *New York Times,* June 7, 1981.

217   Brain drain information appears in "Now a Brain Drain from the Frost Belt," *U.S. News & World Report,* September 21, 1981.

218   "Quelling the Myth of the Frostbelt's Industrial Decline," by Rick Janish, appeared in the *Washington Post,* January 4, 1981.

219   Investment figures appeared in "Pension Funds Flow to Sunbelt Spurs Shift of Investment Capital," the *New York Times,* May 20, 1980.

219 Article on California's new ethnic cities appears in the *New York Times,* August 21, 1981.

220 Article on banking in Miami, "Miami Drawing World Banks," appeared in the *New York Times,* December 10, 1980.

220 Senator Hayakawa is quoted in "Angry West," *Newsweek,* September 19, 1979.

220 California's economy reported in "The People's Republic of California," *The Asia Mail,* June 1980.

221 The William Stevens article appeared in the *New York Times,* February 29, 1980.

221 The governors' remarks appear in "Balanced U.S. Growth," the *New York Times,* March 7, 1971.

222 The infrastructure problems of New York, Chicago, and Detroit are reported in *Newsweek,* May 4, 1981.

222–29 The city profiles are based primarily on interviews with local officials and locally published materials.

TEN Either/Or → Multiple Option
232 List of car and truck models appears in the *Washington Post,* "How '82 Cars Rate in the Mileage Department" (a publication of the EPA list), September 13, 1981.

233–34 The Harvard study on families is discussed in detail in *Behavior Today,* June 9, 1980.

234 The Exxon study on two-career families was released at a news conference held June 25, 1981, in New York City.

235 Two good articles about the trend toward later motherhood are: "More Older Women Are Becoming Mothers, Study Shows," by Glenn Collins in the *New York Times,* September 29, 1980; and "At Long Last Motherhood," *Newsweek,* March 16, 1981.

236 Growth of temporary service industry: "Hiring Shifts to Part-Timers," the *New York Times,* December 14, 1981.

236–37 Gender-bound jobs: *National Forum: The Phi Kappa Phi Journal,* Fall 1981.

241   Marian Burros on multiple-option food: "Specialty Food Explosion: Where Will It End," the *New York Times*, October 26, 1981.

241   Ethnic frozen foods: "Ethnic Foods Accounted," *The Wall Street Journal*, December 3, 1981. Tofu Sales: *Advertising Age*, August 24, 1981.

242   White-bread consumption: *The Wall Street Journal*, August 20, 1981.

242   Pedi Brothers reported in: "Exotic Produce Arrives Along with Top Prices," the *New York Times*, September 17, 1980.

244   *Newsweek* article, "The New Immigrants," July 7, 1980.

244   *The Harvard Encyclopedia of American Ethnic Groups* was published in 1980 by Harvard University Press.

245   Ethnic communities in Illinois, Alabama, and Iowa are reported in the *New York Times*, June 28, 1981, and in *Newsweek*, July 7, 1980.

245–
46   The *Newsweek* article is "The New Immigrants," July 7, 1980.

246   "U.S. Hispanics—A Market Profile" appeared in *Advertising Age*, April 6, 1981.

Conclusion

249   The phrase "the time of the parenthesis" I first heard from Jean Houston.

Index

no-tech managers, 83
  reasons for short-term
    orientation, 80–82
  reconceptualizing, 86–96
    by banking, 90–92
    companies' efforts toward,
      86–90
    as constant, long-term process,
      94–96
    nonbusiness examples, 92–94
  signs of change, 84
Look, 99
Los Angeles, California, 111, 154,
    216, 219, 221
  Commuter Computer, 192
  self-help in education in, 143–44,
    145
  Spanish-speaking population of,
    246, 247
Los Angeles Times, 46, 156–57
Louisville, Kentucky, 141
Lowell, Massachusetts, 229
LTV, 81
Luddites, 29
Luehrmann, Arthur, 34
Lund, Robert, 30–31
Lutherans, 240

McClellan, Carole, 223, 224
McDonald's, 98
McGraw-Hill, Inc., 180
McGregor, Douglas, 189
Machinists union, 100
McKone, Don T., 89
McLean, Virginia, 140
McLuhan, Marshall, 12–13, 56
McPherson, Rene, 201–202
Madison, Wisconsin, 113
Magazines, 99–100, 123
Mahoney, William, 105
Maine, 120, 144, 186
  initiatives in, 166, 167, 168, 169,
    171, 172
Managers, 20, 31
  networking by, *see* Networks,
    informal, trend toward
  short-term results and, 80–84
  see also Employee rights

Manpower, Inc., 236
Manufacturing, 127, 209, 213, 219
  foreign investment in U.S., 70
  U.S. share of world, 55, 56, 61,
    62, 63
  see also Information society, shift
    to; *specific industries*
Manufacturing Data Systems, Inc.,
    88
Manufacturing jobs, shift from, *see*
    Information society, shift to
Marathon Oil, 87
Marcus Garvey Preschool and
    Elementary School, 143
Maritime Research Information
    Service (MRIS), 25
Marketing:
  electronic, 46
  law of the situation and, 84–86
  reconceptualizing process and,
    86–90
Market Research Corporation of
    America, 242
Marriage, 41
  see also Family, diversity in
    American
Marshall Electronics, 136
Marx, Karl, 17
Maryland, 51, 111–12, 168, 169,
    186
Mason, Kenneth, 83
Massachusetts, 112, 169, 173, 185,
    186, 208
Massachusetts Institute of
    Technology, 14, 17, 31
  Center for Policy Alternatives, 30
  Program on Neighborhood and
    Regional Change, 146
Maternity Center Association, 142
Matheson, Scott, 107
Meany, George, 93
Medical establishment, 132, 133,
    134, 136, 138
Medical Self-Care, 136
Medical technology, 41–42, 74, 139,
    226
Melcher, John, 121
Mendocino County, California, 165